OVERCOMING VIOLENCE

Johnston McMaster

Overcoming Violence

DISMANTLING AN IRISH HISTORY AND THEOLOGY:
AN ALTERNATIVE VISION

the columba press

First published in 2012 by
the columba press
55A Spruce Avenue, Stillorgan Industrial Park,
Blackrock, Co Dublin

Cover by Bill Bolger
Origination by The Columba Press
Printed by the MPG Books Group

ISBN 978 1 85607 754 5

Contents

INTRODUCTION

Twentieth century Irish history has been dominated, not only by change, but by brutal and sectarian violence. The twentieth century pervasive culture of violence was rooted in earlier centuries of violence. If modern Irish history began in 1600, then the culture of violence, so much part of the last century, has been in the making for some time. The century of plantation, Catholic rising, Cromwell's revenge and the Williamite wars, was an age of atrocity. It was also a century of religious wars characterised by an active and violent god. The patterns of sectarianism, with many of their origins in the seventeenth century, were deeply religious. The destructive pattern of theology and violence became a strand of Irish history and culture. It was a highly visible strand in the decade that changed Ireland from 1912-1922. God and guns were inseparable and the religious dimension to violence and killing, as well as the respective slogans, were pervasive when yet another phase of sectarian violence and bloodletting erupted in 1969. True, by the time this most recent phase of sectarian violence had ended (though a few on both sides have still not got the democratic message of the people of Ireland, nor realised the futility and destructive, including the self-destructive power of violence), Ireland has become more secular, though that may be better described as a declericalised Ireland. Nevertheless, sectarianism has not gone away in its political and religious forms, with its 'live' potential for violence and exclusion.

After the revolution of 1912-1922, there was something of a collective rush to ignore or deny the brutal violence that had been an integral part of that decade. Collective amnesia set in, and a decade of centenaries now looms with the temptation to ignore, even airbrush, that decade of religiously inspired and justified violence. During the decade of centenaries, 2012-2022, the 50th anniversary of the civil rights campaign will also be marked. In itself the campaign was constitutional and non-violent, but was tragically overtaken by the dominant culture of vi-

olence, paramilitary and state. The centuries old culture of violence had not been dealt with, its ideology and theology deconstructed and demythologised.

Again the temptation is real to draw a line under the most recent violence. Acknowledging the past, especially the violence
of the past, is proving exceptionally difficult. Blame games are
an avoidance tactic, not least because there is no innocence. Self
or group justification is also a refusal to acknowledge the sectarian brutality of the immediate past. Neither of these goes to the
heart of the violence, the gun in politics and the use of brutal
violence to deal with historical, political cultural and religious
differences. Ireland has had a history and theology of violence,
the latter dimension never really analysed or acknowledged by
the churches, which until the last years of the twentieth century,
have had a privileged role and status in Irish society. We still do
have to ask the critical and uncomfortable question as to why
one of the most religious societies in Europe, has been and remained one of the most violent.

Until we undermine the mythology and theology that has
underpinned our culture of violence, we may not take the gun
out of Irish politics, and may never realise the moral imperative;
never again. We need to take violence out of the psyche, personal
and collective, tackle the theological roots of sectarianism and
the culture of violence. To do that we need critical analysis of the
bad theology, Protestant and Catholic, which has been around
for centuries, and a deconstruction of the myth of redemptive
violence. The latter deludes itself that violence pays, achieves,
defends, that might is right and peace comes through milit -
arised victory. We also need to struggle and wrestle with an
alternative value system, a new action-based ethic of non-violence, justice, peace and compassion.

This book is an attempt to do this and will begin with an
analysis of the historical roots of Irish violence, before critically
examining the theological and biblical basis that have nurtured,
justified and sustained violence. Faith does have a counter testimony, its own devastating critique of violence and a violent
god. The last two chapters will begin to re-vision a different
culture in Ireland and how we can nurture, not just faith com-

munities, but human communities of resistance to sectarian violence, all forms of violence, and nurture communities of compassion.

In Ireland we have the opportunity to dismantle a centuries old culture and build a new one of active non-violence and compassion, at the heart of which there is also social and restorative justice and peace.

Johnston McMaster
Irish School of Ecumenics
May 2011

Johnston McMaster is a lecturer at the Irish School of Ecumenics, and is Co-ordinator of the Education for Reconciliation Programme.

CHAPTER ONE

The Roots of Sectarian Violence

If the ancient Irish myths reflect times past, then violence has been part of the Irish landscape since the known beginnings of organised society. That Ireland has had a long standing culture of violence is beyond dispute. To blame it on external, colonising forces is only part of the story. But which external forces? Should we blame it on the Vikings and scapegoat all the Doyles who currently live in Ireland? Or the French Normans or the English Tudors? Will all the Fitzgeralds feel appropriately guilty? Or is the culture of violence really the fault of all those Celts who immigrated to Ireland or invaded Ireland way back in the dim mists of BCE? Which gene pool is not external to Ireland? So blaming the culture of violence on foreigners is really a cop-out since we are all foreigners who once upon a time came here, displacing or eliminating the previous occupants. Or when the phase of violence settled down we assimilated and used violence to defend ourselves against the next foreign arrivals.

Blaming it on external forces is only part of the story and maybe even a vague part. The truth is we have woven our own patch of violence into the historical quilt and the violent dynamic has been as much internal as external. In ignorance, prejudice and fear we have turned it on each other, all the more brutal because it was internal, and every violent conflict has left a legacy for the coming generation. The burden of Irish history is violence and young lives in particular have been sacrificed on the altar of our violent god, crafted and shaped in our tribal, ideological image. The god of Irish history is a dangerous fiction of our own making, re-made in each successive generation. In 1912 and1916 Ulster unionists and Irish nationalists made up their god for another battle, this time in a nationalistic image, invoked in Covenant and Proclamation, and later in Constitution to give legitimacy to violence and the violent founding of states.

But where did this culture of violence come from? Leaving aside a psychological explanation and the role of fear, tracing historical roots is even more complex. Identifying original violence may be impossible. All that the Hebrew Bible can offer is the powerful myth of Cain and it is certainly not historical. Powerfully true as all myths can be, but not historical fact. The political roots of the violence that engulfed Northern Ireland in 1969 may be closer in historical terms. The century that shaped and defined the north-eastern part of Ireland was the 17th century. Modern Irish history began here with a century of religious wars, not only in Ireland, but also in Europe. The battles fought on Irish soil at the end of the century were European before they were Irish, but they left a violent legacy in Ireland, and we need to remember 1690 for that reason and not as a sectarian Protestant victory for all time. The whole of the 17th century established patterns of sectarian conflict and violence that remain. The Plantation of Ulster had its roots in the nine years war at the end of the 16th century.

The Nine Years' War

The war was an Ulster crisis even though the crucial battle and defeat for the key player, Hugh O'Neill, Earl of Tyrone, took place at Kinsale in West Cork. The war began in 1594 when the Enniskillen fortress was besieged. An English army attempting to bring in food supplies was cut off with loss of life. 'Thus was established a problem of warfare in which under-strength English garrisons in the southern approaches to Ulster were taken and re-taken, and armies sent in assistance became vulnerable to attack.'[1] Hugh O'Neill joined the fray in June 1595 when he ambushed an army led by Marshall Bagenal en route from Newry to relieve a Monaghan fort. The battle of Clontibret 'heralded the birth of a formidable new Gaelic Irish army, well trained and equipped.'[2] O'Neill had pretensions to govern Ulster and when this was blocked he joined the rebellion. Totally committed to arms and violence he was proclaimed a traitor in 1595. By 1601 O'Neill had 4,000 horse and foot and he had the most 'advanced weapons – muskets, calivers and pikes – to supplement the traditional axes, javelins and bows.'[3]

Hugh O'Neill was undoubtedly power hungry and a person

1 Lennon, Colm, *Sixteenth Century Ireland: The Incomplete Conquest* (Dublin: Gill and Macmillan, 1994), p.292
2 Ibid, p 293
3 Ibid, p 293

of considerable wealth. His income in Ulster in 1593 was £80,000 per year. Ireland had been invaded by the Tudors and O'Neill's fight was with Queen Elizabeth I. The latter was empire building and so too was O'Neill. He was committed to the Spanish regime and was also seeking recognition from Elizabeth as Earl and O'Neill. He was not beyond playing both sides. A major victory for O'Neill occurred in 1598 at the Yellow Ford on the Blackwater in Co Armagh. O'Neill's combined forces met those of Marshall Henry Bagenal with devastating effect. It was a debacle for the English with 830 killed and 400 wounded, and 300 deserting to O'Neill.[4] In March 1599 the Earl of Essex arrived in Ireland with an army of 17,300 determined to defeat O'Neill. A series of battles followed and in September the Earl was ordered north by the Queen with 4,000 soldiers to confront O'Neill. Both men met at Carrickmacross on 7 September 1599 and during a half-hour meeting O'Neill explained his claims to Ulster. The result was a very shaky truce which led to Essex's downfall. Without permission from the Queen, Essex left for London to try and explain his poor negotiations. In 1601 he was executed as a traitor.

O'Neill was encouraged to increase his war efforts and his expansionism. He pushed beyond Ulster and was in the midlands and south by early 1600. O'Neill had a religious motivation to his war efforts and that was to restore Catholicism as well as pushing for full economic and political privileges for Irish people. He wanted Spanish support and this also meant papal support. O'Neill had to show his religious and political legitimacy and did this by sending a Waterford priest, Peter Lombard, to make the case to Pope Clement VIII. The Pope was uncertain about supporting Spanish involvement in Ireland, though he did grant an indulgence to those taking up the Irish cause.

Mountjoy became Lord Deputy in 1600 and was more than ready to use his large army. Mountjoy was given to attrition, establishing provocative garrisons and campaigning in winter as well as winning over disaffected followers of O'Neill's forces.[5]

---

4 Ibid, p 296
5 Ibid, p 299

At the beginning of 1601, King Philip III of Spain decided to ratchet up the Anglo-Spanish war. On 21 September 1601, some 3,400 Spaniards landed at Kinsale. Mountjoy with 7,000 soldiers besieged Kinsale with the intention of defeating the Spanish before O'Neill arrived. O'Neill did arrive in December after a march from Tyrone through the midlands. Mountjoy's army was caught in the middle. At dawn on Christmas eve, 1601, the Spanish and O'Neill attacked Mountjoy. It was a disaster for O'Neill, his own army not properly formed and the Spanish staying put in Kinsale. Losses were heavy, the Spanish surrendered and O'Neill led his defeated and battered forces on the long trek back to Tyrone. It was the beginning of the end.

Hugh O'Neill surrendered to Mountjoy on 30 March 1603, at Mellifont. Three days earlier Mountjoy had received news of Elizabeth's death but did not inform O'Neill. The latter, without this knowledge, submitted to the dead Queen, renouncing all dependence upon foreign rulers, the title of the O'Neill and overlordship rights over the chiefs of Ulster … [6] O'Neill might have negotiated a different peace agreement had he known of Elizabeth's death. As it was he was given a royal pardon and held on to most of his lands. Within Tyrone he had power and overall he was back to where he was at the beginning of the war in 1595. O'Neill had gained nothing in a nine years' war. An independent Catholic Ireland had not been achieved.

For the English it was an expensive victory. Their expenditure amounted to £2 million while for O'Neill it was a military expenditure of £500 per day. The English army lost thousands of soldiers, not counting the civilians who also died from slaughter and injury, starvation and disease.

It was a heavy price to pay for 'complete control of Ireland' and O'Neill's overthrow, in effect, defeated the Gaelic aspiration of ending English rule in Ireland.[7] The positions of O'Neill, Tyrconnel and Maguire of Fermanagh were so fragile that they left Rathmullen in Donegal in 1607 for Spain. Their flight from Ireland became known as the flight of the earls and with it the

6 Ibid., p 301

7 Kinealy, Christine, *A New History of Ireland* (Stroud: Sutton Publishing Company, 2004) p 80

independence of Gaelic Ulster came to an end. O'Neill ended up in Rome supported by a papal pension until he died in 1616.

It was an ignominious end for the Gaelic earls, especially O'Neill. The lust for power and violence had achieved nothing. The Tudor colonisers could claim victory in the nine years' war, but at huge financial cost. Above all, thousands of lives were lost, especially as in all war and violence, the lives of the non-combatants, the innocent sufferers. The demise of the last bastion of Gaelic independence in Ulster opened up new opportunities for the Crown, now held by James VI of Scotland and James I of England. He never visited Ireland but he left an enduring and violent legacy.

2 The Plantation of Ulster

The Tudors had conquered Ireland but it was an incomplete conquest. Ulster, the last bastion of Gaelic culture and independence remained a troublesome place. Not for the first or last time had Ulster said no! The problem was how to govern and control this fractious province. James I had to ensure domination and control and this led 'to the single most disruptive event in northern Irish history: the Plantation of Ulster.'[8]

Elizabeth had attempted earlier plantations in Ireland, a large scale one in Munster which resulted in Protestant Bandon where even the pigs were Protestant! There were other smaller ones but the schemes were not successful. James had to make sure that his Plantation policy for Ulster really worked. Until the nine years' war, Ulster had been a stronghold of Gaelic and Catholic Ireland. Plantation would ensure that the defeated Gaelic world would not rise again.

The King drew up his Articles of Plantation in 1609. The Plantation was on a scale greater than anything attempted before. It was a policy of formal colonisation and involved the counties of Armagh, Cavan, Coleraine, which was renamed Londonderry, Donegal, Fermanagh and Tyrone. Antrim and Down were planted privately by the Hamiltons and Montgomerys at the turn of the century.

The purpose of the official Plantation was to control the trouble-

---

8 Lundy, Derek, *Men that God Made Mad: A Journey Through Truth, Myth and Terror in Northern Ireland* (London: Jonathan Cape, 2006), p 56

some part of Ireland and to replace the false religion of Catholicism with the true faith of Protestantism. Though the first planters arrived in 1610, it took a number of years to really implement. Lands were confiscated and offered to planters for low rents in lots up to 2,000 acres. It was intended originally to reward those who had given military service in Ireland, but eventually was open to a wider constituency.

The governing conditions of the settlement were that as far as possible the land should be subject to Protestant tenants, that defences should be built for their protection and that the settlers should not mix with the natives. The best quality land was granted to either English or Scottish undertakers. They had primary responsibility for the defence of the settlements.[9]

Those who had been employed by the Crown in Ireland were also given land and could sublet to the native Irish, though the latter's rent was higher than that of English or Scottish sub-tenants. Some land was given to the native Irish but at a higher rent than to others. The Crown reached agreement with merchants from London and they were responsible for the area west of the River Bann. In 1613 Derry became the City of Londonderry and Co Coleraine was renamed Co Londonderry. A fractious pattern was set. A year later the building of the walls began.

The planters themselves were English, Welsh and mainly Scottish. The latter group brought with them the second model of the Protestant Reformation to Ireland. The Scots were Presbyterians, strict Calvinists, a religious ethos which was the antithesis of Irish Catholicism. The Plantation left Ulster with these quite distinct religio-ethnic groups. The native Gaels were Catholic, now alongside Anglicans and Presbyterians. Though the latter two were Protestant or children of the Reformations, they would remain antagonistic to one another until Dr Henry Cooke 'published the banns' between them at Hillsborough in 1834. The patterns of conflict were being set. The conflict was agrarian, political and religious and it would be difficult to separate out this unholy trinity. The conflictual questions were: 'Who has the land? Who holds power? How should God be

9 Kinealy, op. cit, pp 84-85

worshipped? Or, more, succinctly, plough, sword and book.'[10]
Put another way: Who controls the territory? Who dominates
society? Who has the true faith?

The settlers or planters soon set about answering the questions. The majority Protestants were Presbyterians and their
religious identity made them quite distinctive. Insecurity meant
that the sword and the Bible were never far apart with a deep
antagonism towards the Gaelic Catholics. Other differences
were pronounced. The native Gaels were pastoral farmers while
the settlers were into arable farming. The planters also brought a
different style of architecture, building stone cottages, schools,
churches and marketplaces. They created an organised society
through building neat towns like Moneymore and Drapers -
town, some complete with water supply. Land was cleared for
crops and well planned towns built, all of which developed in
the planters a cultural superiority, or a superiority of identity
which paradoxically remained largely insecure. Eventually neat
streets and well kept land would be deemed to be 'more
Protestant looking'. After all, poorer quality land was left or
rented to the Catholics. Cultural patterns were being set for
centuries to come.

The Plantation strengthened Presbyterians in Ulster and
undermined Catholicism. 'In fact, one of the most enduring
legacies of the plantation was the spread of Presbyterianism to
Ireland.'[11] That in itself was to create a pattern of tension given
that the Anglican Reformation in Ireland was anything but successful. In fact, some of the Presbyterian ministers in Ulster were
there because of a dislike of the restoration of Anglican episcop -
acy in Scotland in 1610. Not surprisingly there was a mutual dislike between Anglicans and Presbyterians in Ireland and Penal
Laws, enacted by the Anglican state and national church, were
designed to repress Presbyterians as well as Catholics. Perhaps
the greatest irony was that 'James, a Scottish King who disliked
the Presbyterian Church, was responsible for extending it to
Ireland.'[12]

The religious tensions have shaped an enduring pattern in

10 Lundy, op.cit, p 57
11 Kinealy, op.cit, p 88
12 Ibid , p 88

the north-east of Ireland. Pope Clement VIII had urged and supported war in 1600. 'All those who fought with O'Neill were
given the same spiritual status as Crusaders battling against the
Turks. Ulster was their base, for it was resolutely Catholic and
Gaelic at the time. O'Neill referred to his troops as the Catholic
army of Ulster ...'[13] The state policy of planting Ulster with
mainly Presbyterians from Scotland exacerbated the religious
tensions and placed theology at the heart of the conflict.
Plantation introduced differentials such as 'religion, ethnic status,
social class and levels of cultural civility.'[14]

The defeated were Catholic, Gaelic, looked upon as un-
civilised and were now the economically dispossessed. The
Protestant planters were culturally superior and economically
privileged. They were also insecure, as settlers often are, and felt
themselves to be permanently under threat. Theologically they
were separatist: 'Scottish Presbyterians, marked off from other
planters by their non-Englishness and by their religion.'[15] Above
all they had arrived in Ulster with their theology of covenant
closely aligned with a theology of election, chooseness, which
easily slipped into religious superiority as well as separatism.
Covenantal theology was also to prove an enduring legacy with
its conditional loyalty understood in political terms as well as
religious. Three hundred years after the first Scots Presbyterians
arrived in Ulster, the Ulster Covenant was to become the foundational document of the new Northern Ireland. In 1912 it was
the gun and the book (Bible) rather than the sword and the
book.

The Plantation of Ulster created multiple patterns of sectarian
division. Patterns of land ownership and territoriality remain.
Patterns of cultural superiority, triumphalism and domination
are still deep in mindsets. Religion remains a marker of divided
identity and loyalty, even in a more secular age. If the Plantation
was intended to control and stabilise the north-east of Ireland, it
was a failure. It may well have ensured 'that Ulster would never

13 Brewer, John D and Higgins, Gareth I, *Anti-Catholicism in Northern
Ireland, 1600-1998: The Mote and the Beam*, (London: Macmillan Press,
1998), p 20
14 Ibid, p 21
15 Ibid , p 22-23

be stabilised.'[16] The Plantation also created, albeit later in 1921, an 'ethnic frontier', which seems likely to remain into the far distant future as a contested frontier. It left the legacy of a discontented people, resentful Catholics on the one hand and insecure, fearful and distrustful Protestants on the other. Patterns of sectarian differences were set in the 17th century and were continued through mutual segregation and separation embodied in education, religion, theology, sports, and housing, all of which have been maintained with the help of militarised politics, which even faith has never successfully challenged, still less transformed.

The Catholic Rising and Cromwell's Revenge

The settler community remained in a state of insecurity. Defensive bawns betrayed an underlying fear that the displaced population would hit back at any time and reclaim what had been lost. The insecurity was exacerbated by the fact that the plantation was not as complete as intended. Scots and Gaels were often living back to back. Displacement was not as thorough as had been hoped.

> Although the Ulster plantation had been achieved with relat -
> ive ease, it had created within the whole of Ireland new divi-
> sions, resentments and factions that emerged mostly after
> James I's death in 1625. Religion was at the heart of much of
> the conflict.[17]

Protestant insecurity and Catholic resentment did not make for a peaceful Ulster. Rather it was a sectarian tinderbox with all the ingredients for a community conflict and violent outcome.

The roots were to be found in the Elizabethan conquest and confiscations. Land was lost then and again at the plantation. The displaced took to the mountains and forests forming irregular armies. 'This tradition of secret military societies, from the stories and rapparees, through the agrarian secret societies right down to the Irish Republican Army (IRA), is of immense significance in the working out of Irish history.'[18] 'Secret armies' have

---

16 Lundy, op.cit , p 58
17 Kinealy, op.cit., p 91
18 Stewart, A.T.Q., *The Shape of Irish History* (Belfast: The Blackstaff Press, 2001), p 81

been part of the Irish historical landscape since the conquests of
Elizabeth and the plantation of James.

> Sustaining themselves on song and legend, Gaelic poetry,
> and the memory of ancient wrongs and more recent dispos-
> session and exile, the native Irish longed for the day when
> they could take back their own. Above all, the unifying effect
> of the old religion ... It could at least be represented as a de-
> fence of Catholicism and the Gaelic heritage.[19]

The Presbyterian Protestants were Calvinists, covenantal
people, God's elect. Covenantal theology was a driving force in
their mentality. They came to Ulster with a history of covenants,
the first in 1557 was a theological covenant to make the
Reformed Church the established religion in Scotland. In 1638
the Scots signed a national covenant, more political, but no less
religious and in opposition to Charles I. Covenants implicated
God in politics and in the political destiny of a settler people.
God had chosen them and was on their side. 'Covenants thus
gave a sacred gloss to politics and reinforce the tendency to represent political conflicts.'[20]

In 1641 a series of plots emerged as part of a destabilising
process in Irish politics. The third plot of June or July in that
year was driven by grievances about plantation and the treatment of Catholicism. A rising was in the making and on 5
October at Glaslough, Co Monaghan, a plan was agreed to sieze
Dublin Castle. It was not only Dublin Castle that was taken.
'Using the network of Ulster families as an organising framework for the rising, each group siezed castles in its own area.'[21]
The settlers' worst fears were realised. A Catholic, Gaelic rising
was under way and soon law and order in Ulster collapsed. The
rising also spread to other parts of Ireland.

With confusion on all sides, religion became a security blan-
ket. Protestant Bibles were torn up and Protestants were refused
burial out of fear of pollution of consecrated ground. 'The mar-

19 Ibid., p 81
20 Brewer and Higgins, op. cit, p25
21 Gillespie, Raymond, *Seventeenth Century Ireland* (Dublin: Gill and
Macmillan, 2006) p142

shalling of religion to support each side's position drew on the doctrine of providence, the idea that God not only existed but was actively at work in the world supporting his chosen people.'[22] With both sides claiming divine activity and support, no doubt God gave legitimacy to killing. By 1642 the Irish rising was complicated by the English Civil War with people taking contradictory sides. The Old English in the Pale were on the side of the Irish and the settlers in Ulster were divided between King and Parliament. Sectarian killings were characteristic of the Irish rising with an estimated 4,000 Protestant settlers massacred, some by drowning in the River Bann, and their murders followed by vicious reprisals. The war soon spun out of control and 'looting, revenge and gratuitous violence came to dominate those months, much to the concern of the gentry and clergy'.[23]

In June, 1642, Irish Catholics formed the Confederation of Kilkenny, which governed the Catholic-controlled parts of the country, and supported King Charles I. Their motto was 'For God, King and Fatherland, Ireland United'. Later Charles agreed to restore Catholicism to Ireland.[24] The Confederation of Kilkenny was guided by the Catholic bishops who at this stage in history could be described as loyalists or royalists!

The effect of the rising on the settler Protestants was traumatic and lasting. '… it was a critical moment for Protestant consciousness, the coming of "a tempest long foretold".' The event burned its way deeply into the Protestant psyche and the drowning of Protestants in the River Bann was commemorated in 1991 and still features on Orange banners. Protestants were convinced that Catholics could not be trusted. They were not only brutal and violent, they were determined to wipe out the 'true faith', which God's elect must maintain and defend by force. This was the action replay of the Israelite war with the Canaanites and ensured the lasting popularity of the Hebrew Bible (Old Testament) in the settler mindset. The violent texts have remained as a real paradigm. A further pattern was estab-

---

22 Ibid, p 146
23 Ibid, p 147
24 Kinealy, op. cit, p 97

lished. More extensively:

> A pattern of behaviour is established for the future, to be re-
> activated again and again – in 1689, in 1798, in 1912 and 1920
> and after 1969. But in Northern Ireland the course of history
> had altered the pattern so that each religion fears the other. [25]

By 1642 a covenantal army, under General Munro had arrived
in Ulster from Scotland. The settlers drew some security from
the Scottish presence and with all the officers members of the
Kirk, the first presbytery of the Presbyterian Church in Ireland
was set up in Carrickfergus. Munro set about crushing the rising
with some brutality, but suffered a serious setback with defeat
to an Irish force at Benburb in 1646. It was a crushing defeat
which led Munro to wonder if it was God's judgment. Even God
could turn against the elect! Meanwhile the Pope celebrated the
Scots defeat with a *Te Deum* in Rome. But the Israelites were
meant to exterminate the Canaanites. That was the storyline and
three years later God's deliverer arrived in the form of Oliver
Cromwell.

Cromwell set about his role with a bloody vengeance, storm-
ing Drogheda in September 1649 and Wexford a month later.
The garrison at Drogheda refused to surrender and Cromwell
slaughtered them in a savage act of war. The indiscriminate
slaughter of civilians is a later invention and among those killed
in the garrison were English Royalists. The English Civil War
was impinging on Ireland. Cromwell's revenge was still brutal
and was driven by religion. Cromwell was strongly anti-
Catholic and admitted himself in the House of Commons that
no priest was left alive in Drogheda and all its Catholic churches
were burned. Cromwell rationalised his killing as God's judgement on barbarian murderers and God should have all the
glory. Cromwell was God's agent eliminating the Amalekites of
biblical infamy.

Cromwell was only in Ireland for a few months but left a bitter legacy which has burned its way deeply into the Catholic
psyche. Cromwell was determined to rid Ireland of Catholicism.

---

25 Stewart, op. cit., p 82
26 Rafferty, Oliver P., *Catholicism in Ulster 1603-1983: An Introspective
History*, (Dublin: Gill and Macmillan, 1994), p 40

He boasted that he would not interfere with anyone's conscience, but freedom of religion 'did not extend to the free practice of Catholicism.'[26]

Cromwell attacked Catholicism at the level of practice and worship. 'Worship was outlawed, priests were hunted and killed, church buildings were demolished and the laity were deprived of the sacraments.' By the time of Cromwell's death and restoration of the monarchy, 'there were three Catholic bishops left in Ireland, all based in the old Gaelic core of Ulster'.[27]

The rising was crushed and Catholicism was suppressed with the intent to destroy it. Cromwell's legacy remains and surfaced in the last years of the 20th century when his death mask was put on display in Drogheda only to be removed after a few days because of the outrage and protest of the present populace. His legacy has also remained as a role model for Ian Paisley and the slaughter in Drogheda invoked in loyalist wall murals in North Belfast as present justification for violent anti-Catholicism. At the time Catholic landowners had the choice of going to hell or Connaught, something which Cromwell never said, but was the slogan of Protestant extremists in Co Armagh at the end of the 18th century as they attempted to drive Catholics out of the county. Abusive and repressive history repeats itself.

Whether Cromwell threatened hell or Connaught is irrelevant. Land displacement did take place. Catholic landlords were in the majority before 1641 but by 1652 Protestant landlords were in the majority. Meanwhile Connaught itself was filled with refugees from Cromwell's vengeance. The 1640's were to leave an indelible mark on Irish history and relationships in Ulster. An official day of thanksgiving for deliverance from the Irish rebellion was declared. Sermons were preached each year expressing gratitude for 'that signed deliverance of us from that general intended massacre of the whole body of Protestants in Ireland'.[28] A Pope-burning ceremony took place in 1685 in Athlone. Pamphlets and histories became a form of lurid massacre literature and though exaggerated were believed

27 Brewer and Higgins, op. cit. , p 29
28. Gillespie, op cit, p 180

and shaped Protestant memory.

In the decade following, up to 100 priests went into exile, leaving from Carrickfergus and 'The 1650s' were par excellence the age of the mass rock. The Act of Settlement of August 1652 deprived Catholics of their land in three provinces.[29] The diocese of Derry was without a bishop for twenty-five years. By 1685 the settler insecurity returned with a Catholic King on the throne and Catholics being appointed to positions of power. James II was perceived as attempting to establish 'Romanism' which would mean loss of Protestant power and privilege and might even lead to a repeat of the 1641 Protestant massacres.

The Williamite Wars
When James sent a regiment to Ireland in 1689, Protestants interpreted this as an invasion by Catholics. By this stage the position of James was insecure since William and Mary had arrived in England the year before to take the English throne. In effect, James was a King without a Kingdom, except perhaps for Catholic Ireland. James had failed to regain his English throne and in December, 1688, he fled to France. Supported by the French King Louis XIV, he sailed for Ireland in 1689 and landed at Kinsale. He marched to Dublin and received a great welcome and from there headed to Derry. The Church of Ireland bishop appeared to be in support of James, but the Presbyterians refused entry to the walled towns of Enniskillen and Derry. Both towns were refugee centres with Derry bursting at the seams with up to 30,000 refugees, such was the Protestant insecurity in Ulster.

On the 29 January 1689, the Ulster Presbyterians sent William a congratulatory address and by March Enniskillen had declared its allegiance to him. The gates of Derry were closed against James and the siege began lasting for over 100 days. William was reluctant to become involved in Ireland. He was, after all, European and had his own problems in his principality of Orange in the Netherlands. William's key concern was never Irish politics but European politics. He had been heavily involved in the Dutch wars of the 1670's and had a 'profound

29. Rafferty, op cit, pp 42-43
30. Gillespie, op cit, p 291

hatred of King Louis XIV and of France'.[30]

As William hesitated because of European power politics, an English ship, the Mountjoy, arrived in the Foyle, broke the boom and relieved the walled and besieged town. The siege of Derry, perhaps more than any other event of the 17th century, has shaped Protestant identity and provided a lasting slogan for a continually beleaguered and insecure people. 'No Surrender' and the heroics of the apprentice boys in closing the gates against James, have become the defining myth of Protestant identity.

William eventually did arrive at Carrickfergus on 14 June 1690, with an army of 15,000. William marched south and encountered James at the River Boyne on 1 July 1690. William by now had 40,000 men facing a Jacobite army of 25,000. It was in fact a battle between two European armies with Dutch, Danes, English, Brandenburgers, Huguenots and Ulster Protestants – 'not quite the Orange host that lives on in Protestant imagination'.[31] The opposition included French soldiers, who were detested by the Irish. It was a short skirmish which William easily won and within a few days James had left Ireland for exile in France.

The Battle of the Boyne has been long remembered, not least each 12 July by the Orange Order. It is commemorated as a decisive defeat for Catholics and 'twelfth' commemorations not only re-enact a Protestant victory but are intended to convey the perpetual message of Catholic defeat. Marches and wall paintings of William of 'pious and immortal memory' are too simplistic. This was not a battle between Protestants and Catholics with Protestant victory. The international armies on both sides suggest something more complex. The Williamite wars were Euro - pean not Irish and Ireland itself was merely a theatre for a European conflict.

> William's intervention in Ireland should be seen in the European context rather than as a championing of Protestantism. His Irish involvement was not central to his plans; rather it was forced on him by Louis XIV's support of James II in Ireland ... Louis could not be left with Ireland as a

---

31. Stewart, op cit, p 98

jumping-off point for a possible invasion of England. William, however, was anxious to leave Ireland as soon as he could and head for the main theatre of European war. His presence in mainland Europe was made all the more urgent by the fact that Louis XIV declared war on William's United Provinces in November 1688.[32]

William had to win the Battle of the Boyne for European reasons which is why his European allies, the Hapsburgs of Vienna and the Pope, all Catholic, were opposed to the expansionist politics of Louis.

In Vienna and Rome, William's victory was celebrated with religious ceremonies. After the Boyne, Louis withdrew his soldiers and in a larger scale battle at Aughrim in 1691, with greater loss of life, Louis lost one of his generals. Demoralised by such a defeat, the Jacobite army left Aughrim for Limerick.

The local significance of the Boyne was that 'It marked the end of the long tug of war that had gone on for most of the century between Catholic and Protestant for the possession of the land'.[33] The minority Protestants of Ireland now held most of the land, a loss to Catholics which remained until the bitter land wars of the 19th century. The legacy of the Boyne returned with a vengeance and the territoriality issue remains behind the Orange insistence to walk wherever they choose, even through predominantly Catholic areas. The Boyne has become a mythologised piece of history or, perhaps better, a largely fictionalised story in Protestant memory. It was a series of battles fought in a European context on Irish soil which expresses why Catholic Vienna and the Pope supported William. This is not a cheap debunking of a great Protestant victory. It is the acknowledgement of complexity which colours every conflict then and now. To 'remember 1690' is to remember its complex European context and to more truthfully locate the politics of identity elsewhere.

The Williamite wars came to an end with the siege of Limerick in 1691. Patrick Sarsfield, the Irish commander, was prepared for a long siege but William wanted to end a highly expensive war as quickly as possible. Sarsfield got favourable

---

32. Gillepie, op cit, pp 291-2
33. Stewart, op cit, p 99

terms and surrendered with articles in the Treaty of Limerick allowing up to 11,000 combatants to leave for France. These military articles were upheld but the same could not be said of the civil articles. William was well known in his Dutch principality for tolerance between Catholics and Protestants and not surprisingly the treaty allowed for Catholics 'to enjoy such privileges in the exercise of their religion as are consistent with the laws of Ireland, or as they did enjoy in the reign of Charles II'.[34] The people of Limerick were offered security and protection and Jacobite landowners were guaranteed their possessions. William may have been tolerant but the Irish parliament had to ratify the Treaty which it did not do until 1697. However, Protestants had already interpreted these European battles as a Protestant victory in Ireland and the Treaty was meaningless. Penal laws followed from the Irish parliament against Catholic practice of religion and Catholic land ownership. The Protestant Ascendancy would reach its height in the 18th century.

But there was little love lost between Ascendancy Protestants and William. He died in 1702 and the real William was soon forgotten. The myth-making had begun and the Ascendancy set about creating William in its privileged image.

> ... his birthday on 4 November became a day for the celebration of the political status quo: an established church, Protestant parliament and monarchy. It is no accident that when Dublin Protestants wished to erect a statue of William III in College Green in the heart of the city they chose to depict him not as the victor of the Boyne, but as a Roman emperor, a symbol of classical, republican government and an embodiment of virtue.[35]

William was being re-invented, fictionalised to meet the needs of 18th century Ascendancy politics. At the end of the century he would be re-invented again in the sectarian image of the newly formed Orange Order (1795), the conqueror who would legitimise their dominance of Catholics and Protestant supremacy. Not surprisingly the Order was born in violence involving Catholic Defenders, and to maintain Protestant privilege

34. Ibid, p 99
35. Gillespie, op cit, p 298

and ascendancy as well as a Protestant monarchy and throne.

The events of the 17th century shaped the future, especially of the north-east of Ireland down to the present. The roots of sectarian violence were put down in this century of religious wars. Patterns of fear, mistrust, hatred, violence and territory were set. They were destructive patterns of violence and counter violence. By the end of the 18th century, the beginning of the 20th century and for the last third of the 20th century they repeated themselves in violent and brutal ways. Sectarian hatred in its religious and political forms has remained and, after a decade of the 21st century, has not gone away. State violence and the violence of the physical force traditions have dominated the last four centuries of Irish history. The culture of violence is deep and pervasive, is both Irish and British and has been largely shaped by a violent 17th century, driven by theology and religion.

CHAPTER TWO

A Century of Violent Politics

The Protestant Ascendancy was at its height in the 18th century. In 1704, Queen Anne, William and Mary's successor, produced an 'Act to prevent the further growth of popery'. This was economic in its intention to destroy the Catholic landowners. In the same year, Anne also produced an 'Act for registering the papish clergy'. Priests were required to renounce all Jacobite loyalties and Catholic schools were prohibited. Not only was the Protestant Ascendancy at its height, so too were the Penal Laws. The latter also applied to Presbyterians which led to large-scale Presbyterian emigration from 1708 onwards to north America, creating a Scotch-Irish identity and providing numerous American Presidents. The 18th century was relatively quiet following the sectarian violence and wars of the previous century. It was not until the end of the century that sectarian violence reappeared on a serious scale. The last decade in particular saw community violence in mid-Ulster, giving birth to the Orange Order. The United Irishmen were formed in 1791 with constitutional aims that were lost in the violence of the 1798 Rising. This too was sectarian violence, especially on the part of government forces, leading to the significant 19th century, which was to become a century of violent politics. In the first third of the century there was a massive constitutional achievement, Catholic Emancipation, achieved through the non-violent activity of Daniel O'Connell. His constitutional achievement deserves more attention than it has received. O'Connell's non-violence is a neglected alternative in a century otherwise dominated by violent politics.

The Birth of the Orange Order

Orangeism has never represented the totality of Protestant culture. It is but one strand in an often unrecognised cultural diversity. Orangeism though has played an aggressively disproport - ionate role in Ulster politics, with all but a handful of unionist MPs in the history of Northern Ireland being loyal members. Nationalists would describe the Northern Ireland state from

partition to the abolition of local government in 1972 as an
Orange state. That was how it was experienced by a nationalist
community often on the end of employment and housing dis-
crimination. For the first decade of Northern Ireland's existence,
the Catholic Church feared the power of Orangeism to destroy
its education system. Dispute over Orange marches did not
begin with Portadown in the mid-1990's, but was a reality in
Portadown and elsewhere from the mid-19th century. Dispute
over marches is as traditional as marches themselves.

The origins of the Orange Order are in the 1790s and sectarian
conflict in mid-Ulster. Rural conflict was spreading and in Co
Armagh it reached boiling point. The rural communities were
characterised by old religious animosities and inbred hatreds.
Protestant insecurity was exacerbated by Catholic Relief Acts.
This was not helped by Catholics sloganising with 'our day is
coming and then we will deal with you'. The Treaty of Limerick
in 1691 had banned Catholics from holding weapons. Protestants had weapons, especially those who had belonged to the
Volunteers. Catholics now attacked Volunteer homes and attacked militia in their efforts to arm. 'In mid-Ulster particularly,
men were on the prowl, night after night, seeking to destroy the
property of those they hated'.[1]

Mid-Ulster was already sectarian and there were political
and economic dynamics at work. Weaving was a traditional
Protestant occupation but Catholics had now entered this work-
force. Protestants perceived their industry to be at risk and
when Catholics had too little land for bleaching greens, the com-
petition for land became not only fierce but violent. Land auc-
tions were characterised by riots and a 'general breakdown in
social control' became inevitable.[2] A three-way split in religion
and politics added sectarian fuel. In Co Armagh, Anglicans,
Catholics and Presbyterians were in equal numbers, though
each was strongest in particular areas thereby creating sectarian
fault-lines. There was also a political three-way split with some
on the side of the radicalism of the United Irishmen. Others
were so subservient to their lords and masters as to be ultra-

1 Haddick-Flynn, Kevin, *Orangeism: The Making of a Tradition* (Dublin:
Wolfhound Press, 1999), p 127
2 Ibid, p 128

conservative, while yet others were in-between as Whigs, the politics of Lord Charlemont and William Brownlow of Lurgan.[3]

In this cockpit of sectarian conflict two groups in a physical force tradition emerged. The Peep O'Day Boys were Protestant and the Defenders were Catholic. The Defenders were so named because of their protection of Catholic homes from Peep O'Day dawn raids. Both organisations came into existence after a cattle fair incident in Markethill.[4] In time each could mobilise large numbers.

All of this tension, violence and at times violent outrages, were building up during the early 1790s. In 1794, in the aftermath of a large Defender funeral, mourners imbibed too much alcohol and smashed and fired Protestant homes. Protestant farmers flocked next day to Benburb in defence. The following day, an emerging leader, 'Buddra' Wilson formed an organis- ation called 'The Orange Boys'. They invoked King William as protector of the Protestant people, adopted the Masonic struct- ure and created codes and passwords with some ritual. Holding hands they 'swore on oath to protect their people, defend the Protestant constitution, and maintain a resolute loyalty to the crown'.[5] Hyssop may or may not have been introduced, but later became part of Orange ritual, evoking the Passover story from the experience of ancient Israel and giving a theological basis, ie a deliverance motif, to the newly formed Orangeism. It could be said that Co Armagh now had two groups of defend- ers, defending themselves from each other.

The following year saw the formation of the Orange Order. In a cottage in Loughgall, Dan Winter and his wife hosted a dance on Friday 12 July, 1795. It was, in effect, a Peep O'Day dance and Boys claimed that on their way home from the dance they were attacked. Gunfire ensued, members grew and the Militia stepped in. However, this was only round one. Skirmishes continued through to September when the Defenders claimed a victory. The Peep O'Day Boys were then supplied with arms by a wealthy landlord and another battle occurred at the Diamond crossroads, a few miles from Loughgall. Between 30 - 60 Defend ers were killed. Out of this hamlet battle, the Orange Order was

3 Ibid, 128
4 Ibid, p 130
5 Ibid, p 133

formed and in a Loughgall pub 'the founders of the new society drew lots for the first lodges'.[6]

They took their name from the Royal House of William, now known as the 'Great Deliverer' and they would be known as Orangemen. The actual name was the Loyal Orange Society. 'They were, as their forefathers had been, "William's Men" and accepted the constitutional settlement which William had won for them'.[7] Warrants were issued to lodges and tradition has it that in Dyan, Co Tyrone, the warrant was signed in blood. That may or may not be the case, 'but it is not fantastic, given that Orangemen of a later generation used their blood when signing the Solemn League and Covenant against Irish Home Rule in 1912'.[8]

The Orange Order was founded in violence and continued in violence.

> The Orangemen sealed their initial success with a wave of terror directed against the Catholic community in north Co Armagh in the autumn of 1795. They drove thousands of families out of the area and pushed hitherto uncommitted Catholics into the hands of the United Irishmen. The programme helped bring about a union of the Defenders and the United Irishmen in 1796.[9]

This wave of terror became known as the Armagh Outrages and the Orangemen blamed the outrages on uncontrollable Peep O'Day Boys who were not members. It was soon claimed that Catholics had fired their own homes for compensation purposes. Then, as now, blame can be shifted around, responsibility denied and the enemy scapegoated. As with many violent incidents and events, the truth of the matter is difficult to establish, but whoever exactly was responsible for the Armagh Outrages, it was part of the culture of sectarian violence with its roots in the 17th century. The roots and ethos of Orangeism does not somehow stand outside this violent culture and control. It was part of it and continued with others in the tradition.

6 Tanner, Marcus, *Ireland's Holy Wars: The Struggle for a Nation's Soul 1500-2000* (London: Yale None Bene, 2001), p 191

7 Haddick-Flynn, op cit, p 141

8 Ibid, p 143. It is a pious fiction since it is now known that only one person signed in blood

9 Tanner, op cit, p 192

Early Orangeism 'represented a cohesive combination of landlords and tenants acting jointly, and stiffened Protestant resistance to the propaganda of the United Irishmen. The Order set about the political management of the areas in which it was strong'.[10]

Orangeism did spread and soon there were military lodges and lodges in the midlands of Ireland and Limerick, Cork and Kerry. It was expressed in religious rituals and symbols, as many as the popery it opposed, and it drew on biblical imagery and texts, mostly from the Hebrew Bible. Yet its roots were in political violence and from the outset it was involved in political management in those areas of strength. Its loyalty was to the Crown and to the Protestant Act of Settlement, ie a Protestant Constitution. Political management has continued, especially in its role within unionism, including attempts in 2009 to bring divided unionism together in opposition to Sinn Féin and the fear that the latter will be returned as the largest party in the Northern Ireland Assembly. Orangeism remains a mixture of religion and politics, the politicised combination offering bad religion and bad politics.

The 1798 Rising
On 14 October, 1791, at McArt's Fort on the Cavehill above Belfast, the Society of United Irishmen was formed. It was the birth of modern Irish republicanism and was inspired by the American revolution of 1776 and the French revolution of 1789. Belfast's plantation was largely Presbyterian and the French revolution in particular had made a significant impact. Belfast was a politically radical town and not only did Presbyterians assist financially in the building of the first Catholic church in Belfast, they marched to and participated in the opening and consecration. Bastille Day was commemorated in Belfast and it was not surprising that the founders of the United Irishmen were Presbyterians. William Drennan, the son of a Presbyterian minister was its key leader in Belfast. Other ministers, such as William Steel Dickson of Portaferry, Sinclair Kilburn of Belfast and James Porter of Greyabbey were involved with the United Irish newspaper, the *Northern Whig*. Up to thirty ministers were

---

10 Haddick-Flynn, op cit., p154

implicated in the Rising of 1798, including William Sinclair of Newtownards and David Bailie of Killinchy. The United Irishmen adopted three resolutions. The first called for the people of Ireland to unite against English influence in the country's governance. The second called for a radical reform of parliament and the third asserted that such reform would not work unless Irish people of every religious persuasion were united. It was a call for unity between Catholic, Protestant and Dissenter. They also wanted Tom Paines' *Rights of Man* to be distributed to every religious tradition in Ireland. This was radical politics rooted in radical theology as Steel Dickson's *Scripture Politics* was to show. Some of the Presbyterians were also radically apocalyptic in their theology.

The movement began non-violently, seeking constitutional reform of the Irish parliament, justice and a degree of equality. Not all of the United Irish supporters were prepared for complete equality in relation to Irish Catholics. Land ownership and power made some cautious and conservative. The persuasive dynamic was still sectarianism. The founding of the Orange Order in violence in 1795 had made it clear in one of the oaths that the Order was established to defend Protestant privilege and not Protestant liberty. The mantra of civil and religious liberty has always been subservient to privilege. Sectarian animosity prevailed and in the decade of the 90s sectarian embers flared into a blaze. 'One might say that in 1795 the eighteenth century ended, and the seventeenth century began all over again.'[11] Defenders were recruited into the United Irishmen, which further alienated their Protestant co-religionists. Violence as an outcome of the 90s looked more and more likely. Not for the first or last time in Irish history sectarian violence was to overtake and in the end defeat the demand for radical parliamentary reform. By 1796 'a very formidable insurrectionary movement' was in place.[12]

There were also external factors. The arrival of a French fleet in 1797 off Bantry in West Cork alarmed the establishment, even though a severe storm destroyed the French. Ireland yet again

---

11 Stewart, A. T. Q., *The Shape of Irish History*, (Belfast: Blackstaff Press, 2001), p 126
12 Ibid, p 127

could be the back door for a French invasion of England. The Protestant establishment was fearful. Archbishop Newcome of Armagh reminded Catholics and Protestants that rebellion was forbidden and he hoped that Catholics would hear St Paul's command that slaves were to obey in all things their masters. In the north, Catholics were taking oaths of allegiance to the King and a parish priest in north Antrim publicly pledged 'to support with our lives and our fortunes the blessed constitution of this country and His Majesty's happy government'.[13] Not all Catholics were so loyal, as attacks on Protestant clergy in Limerick showed.

The Irish government responded to the 'providential' deliverance in Bantry Bay by brutally suppressing the United Irishmen. General Lake adopted a scorched earth policy in the north and made use of cruel torture to suppress the United Irishmen. He arrested Henry Joy McCracken and when appointed commander-in-chief, Lake turned his brutality on the Dublin area. 'Yet, regardless of his brutality, the United Irishmen continued to win support, and by the beginning of 1798 had almost 300,000 members'.[14] Government arrested a number of leaders in Dublin which sparked a series of risings on 26 May, 1798. Dublin was too heavily defended and the rising there was unsuccessful. Wexford and Wicklow provided a different story with the rising led in Wexford by two Catholic curates, Father John Murphy of Boulavogue and Father Michael Murphy of Ballycarnew.

It is disputed that events in Wexford descended into sectarian violence but the killing of 200 Protestant prisoners by burning in a barn in Scullabogue makes it difficult to deny the charge of sectarian violence. For many Protestants in the area the rising was experienced as sectarian and this was how it was perceived by the northern Presbyterians and helped to create the disillus - ionment they felt following defeats in Antrim and Down.

On 7 June, the rising broke out in Antrim, followed by Down a few days later. The Defenders failed to materialise leaving the insurgents 'overwhelmingly Presbyterian'.[15] Within a day the rising was routed at Antrim and though an initial victory was

13 Tanner, op cit, p 127
14 Kinealy, Christine, *A New History of Ireland* (Gloucestershire: Sutton Publishing, 2004) p 141
15 Stewart, op cit , p 129

won at Saintfield, encouraging men from the Ards peninsula to move in numbers towards mid-Down, the rising ended with bloody defeat at Ballynahinch on 13 June. The towns of Wexford and Enniscorthy were held by Wexford rebels but crushing defeat soon followed and by 21 June the last rising stronghold at Vinegar Hill, Wexford, was taken and the rising was over.

The response of government forces was brutal. Little mercy was shown, with those who surrendered at the Curragh in Kildare being slaughtered. It is estimated that 30,000 died in Wexford and surrounding counties. The total number who died in the Rising is not fully known. Figures vary between 50,000-100,000, out of a population of 5 million. This makes the estimated numbers dead in a few weeks of violent conflict;

> ... by far the largest number in any modern war or rebellion on Irish soil since the ravages of the sixteenth and seventeenth centuries, and nearly ten times those of the most recent Troubles.[16]

Mansergh's comparison is based on 30,000 dead, but if the figures are between 50,000 and 100,000, then the rising saw a loss of life even thirty times higher than the most recent Troubles in Northern Ireland. County Wexford itself lost 25 per cent of its population during the rising.[17]

Another rising occurred in 1803 led by Robert Emmet and was defeated in a few hours. Emmet was a veteran of 1798 and his execution created a romantic hero which kept alive the romantic nationalism that eclipsed any sense of political failure and defeat.

The rising of 1798 was led by people who wanted the democratisation of Ireland. 'At issue was the right of the people to participate in their own national democratic institutions'.[18] The desire for justice and democracy was brutally crushed by state violence, which was supported by northern Protestants as well as the Protestant establishment. That sectarian violence took

---

16 Mansergh, Martin, *The Legacy of History*, (Cork: Mercier Press, 2003) p 170

17 Kinealy, op cit, p 143

18 McBride, Ian, *Eighteenth Century Ireland*, (Dublin: Gill and Macmillan, 2009) p 413

over in Wexford may well have been fueled by Orange-based rumour, but it does not make sectarian violence any less. What happened in '98 cannot be separated either from the 'first outbreak of violence in County Armagh, which had such a vital impact on relationship between Protestants and Catholics throughout the island'.[18]

The rising had been a close call for those in power, including those in Westminster. By 1801 the Act of Union had created the United Kingdom with the Irish parliament abolished, radical Presbyterians eclipsed by those who saw their future as secure in a Protestant/British alliance. Presbyterianism became increasingly characterised by political and theological conservatism and the 19th century was to continue in violence, except for one huge constitutional achievement.

Catholic Emancipation

Violent sectarian conflict continued into the 19th century. This was especially obvious in the north with Catholics massacred at Struel Wells, near Downpatrick in 1802. The first sectarian riots to occur in Belfast happened in 1813. In Derry, the December Orange demonstrations were accompanied by violence and in Ederney, Co Fermanagh, several Catholics were shot and wounded in sectarian disturbances in 1824. Political sectarian battles were fought around Stewartstown in July 1829 and in 1830 there was bitter rioting at Maghera Orange marches. In 1845, Armagh's Catholic Archbishop called for a traditional Orange march to be re-routed from town centre. Crolly was not heard and the inevitable riot occurred with one Catholic killed.[19] This context of sectarianism and recrimination is part of the context in which Daniel O'Connell achieved Catholic Emancipation in 1829. It did not diminish the sectarianism. It was achieved in a sectarian Ireland in which the sectarianism was and continued to be pervasive and violent.

Agrarian violence was also prevalent. During the early 19th century rural protest movements grew, mainly known as White -

---

19 Rafferty, Oliver P., *Catholicism in Ulster, 1603-1983: An Interpretative History* (Dublin: Gill and Macmillan, 1994), p 117. Rafferty deals with Protestant-Catholic relations, including some harmonious relations in pp 112-119

boys, though various other names were used. This violence es-
calated in the 1830s, 'with what amounted to episodic warfare
over payment of church tithes'.[20]

The tithe was much resented by non-Church of Ireland
members. The Rockites, one of the secret organisations, 'burned
down Protestant churches, expressing a reaction to Protestant
proselytism, the Orange Yeomanry and the new constabulary'.[21]

In the second half of the 1820s many of these secret societies
were in the O'Connell camp, perhaps following a new leader
who gave them a different kind of political identity. This was remarkable given that some of his followers had formed vigilante
groups against the Whiteboys. O'Connell formed the Catholic
Association which was not only the mobilisation of popular politics but a mobilisation for democracy. O'Connell helped de-
mocratise Irish Catholics.

The improvement of Catholic rights had been the objective of
aristocratic laypersons. By 1823 a Catholic Committee had been
replaced by the New Catholic Association, directed by O'Connell.
The following year O'Connell came up with the idea of supporters giving a farthing a week. Known as the 'Catholic rent' it
aimed to raise £50,000 annually. This not only helped to democ-
ratise Catholics, it terrified the landlords and O'Connell was on
his way to becoming 'King Dan'. By organising the rent on the
basis of parish boundaries, the clergy became key figures. Even
when the British government outlawed the Catholic Association
in in 1825, the priests stayed loyal to O'Connell. In a Waterford
by-election, O'Connell and clergy-led opposition to the domin -
ant Beresford family, supported an alternative candidate and
won. The victory dented the Protestant Ascendancy and though
a significant moment, O'Connell had to wait until 1828 before
he could contest a Westminster election. The election took place
in Co Clare where the sitting landowner had resigned to take up
another key post. Rank and property were again called into
question as crowds marched into Ennis on election day with
priests urging them to vote 'for God and O'Connell'.

---

20 Foster, R. F., *Modern Ireland 1600-1972*, (London: Penguin Books,
1988), p 292
21 Ibid, p 295

The process for Catholic Emancipation had begun in 1778. By 1812 there was sympathy in the House of Commons but vested interests, especially by successive monarchs had blocked it. By organising the people O'Connell had mobilised a democratic force constitutionally. His mass rallies were non-violent and empowered Irish Catholic people. Often described as monster rallies, they were remarkable for their peaceful character. Furthermore, 'Nationalism, or even anti-Unionism, was not a necessary part of this'.[22] Liberal Unionists were emancipationists. Nevertheless, it was a Catholic organisation which could and did lead to alienation and opposition.

O'Connell became the focal person in Irish politics and was known beyond Ireland. He took the Clare election with a huge majority but was barred from taking his seat in parliament. However, the British government could not ignore O'Connell and his mobilisation of popular politics.

Momentum for Catholic Emancipation was gathering but there was little expectation that the Prime Minister, the Duke of Wellington and the Home Secretary, Robert Peel, would give way. They had consistently opposed it. On 11 December 1828, Wellington still wanted to bury the controversy, which greatly reassured the Orangemen. Just over a month later on 5 February 1829, the King's speech to parliament contained the explosive information that the government planned to 'review the laws which impose civil disabilities on His Majesty's Roman Catholic Subjects'.[23] The Emancipation Bill came before the House of Commons and was passed by 353 to 180 and then passed through the Lords by 213 to 109. On 13 April 1829, King George IV gave the Bill his reluctant assent. The emancipation was far from complete. A Catholic could not become Regent, Lord Lieutenant or Lord Chancellor. The Oath of Supremacy was abolished but there was an oath of loyalty to the Crown. The main achievement was that Catholic MPs could sit at Westminster.

'Catholic emancipation brought into existence the Catholic nation, with a distinct identity and national purpose.'[24] This replaced the Protestant Ascendancy or nation, though the alien-

---

22. Ibid. p 297
23 Tanner, op cit , p 237
24 Stewart, op cit, p 150

ation of Protestants was never overcome. It remains a tragedy that no side in the Irish division has been able to promote the whole of the people of Ireland. Yet O'Connell's achievement was significant, and all the more so because it was achieved without violence. It was a political and moral victory, won not by physical force but by moral force. In 1840, O'Connell launched his campaign for the Repeal of the Union, again holding monster rallies. In calling for Repeal he was not looking for Irish independence but the restoration of the Irish parliament. Though using the same moral tactics, O'Connell found a more united government unwilling to move. He had to climb down over a monster rally called for Clontarf in 1843, with the government ready to put soldiers in the fields and on the roads. O'Connell was not prepared to forsake his principles of non-violence and pulled back.

The Repeal campaign did not succeed and O'Connell is remembered only as the Liberator with reference to his achievement of 1829. The result is that O'Connell is not in the premier division of Ireland's heroes. They tend to belong to the physical force tradition and less has been made of O'Connell even though his achievement was greater, not just because of emancipation, but that he was also the 'architect of the modern Republic of Ireland'.[25] Even Catholic emancipation of 1829 has not been commemorated with the same enthusiasm as other more violent events. All of this says a great deal about the dominance of a culture of violence in Ireland. But someone who could bring up to one million people onto the roads of Ireland without violence, has a unique place in Irish history and is a counter-cultural figure in relation to the physical force and violent culture of both sides in the Irish conflict and to the government's use of violence and, at times, state terrorism.

Physical Force Tradition
O'Connell's failure to repeal the Union and his retreat from Clontarf brought about a shift in Irish politics. By 1843, when O'Connell had claimed the Repeal of the Union would be achieved, a more revolutionary form of politics had appeared in

---

25 Ibid p 152

the formation of Young Irelanders. This was a group of young
Catholics and Protestants, intellectually well equipped but more
prepared to use violence. The leaders included Thomas Davis,
William Smith O'Brien, John Mitchel and Charles Gavan Duffy.
By 1847, they had formed the Irish Confederation, also the year
when O'Connell died in Italy. In 1848, Europe was gripped by
revolution which had overthrown the French monarchy and
which was greeted by Irish bonfires and the hope that a blood-
less revolution could happen in Ireland. Smith O'Brien even
hoped that the French would intervene in Ireland to assist an
uprising. The famine was devastating Ireland at the time and
someone like Smith O'Brien became disillusioned by government policies. The British government introduced a security net
and made treason-felony a new offence which meant speaking
in such a way as to encourage rebellion. Later Smith O'Brien
was transported to Tasmania. The Young Irelanders may well
have disagreed with O'Connell's non-violent approach, impat-
ient of his perceived acquiescence with the British government,
though being both Catholic and Protestant, they did argue for
'an inclusive non-sectarian approach to politics'.[26]

The latter led to a political split with O'Connell over the government proposal to introduce non-denominational colleges.
Not for the first or last time did division occur over religion and
education, O'Connell supporting the bishops in their opposition
to the non-denominational idea. 'The disagreement presaged a
wider rift over violence'.[27] By the mid-1840s, the nature of the
Young Irelanders revolution was becoming clearer. By 1848,
'The rhetoric was militaristic and republican; an insurrectionary
ethic founded in an almost psychotic Anglophobia.'[28] Smith
O'Brien led a rising in 1848, forming a National Guard by
March, was arrested, tried and released by May and led the rising in July. Further arrest followed, then a commuted death sentence when he was transported to Tasmania. Smith O'Brien was
unconditionally pardoned in 1856 after which he left politics.
Some of the young men who had been involved in the aborted
rising of 1848 founded the Irish Republican Brotherhood a

26 Kinealy, op cit, p 160
27 Foster, op cit, p 315
28 Ibid p 316

decade later and around the same time the Fenian Brotherhood
was founded in New York.

Much of this was based on a belief that the British government would never grant Irish independence unless forced by
violent revolution. The logic of violence appears to run from
1798 through the 19th century to the rising of 1916 and to the
IRA campaign of the decades following 1969. The logic and consequences of violence have not always or rarely been thought
through critically. Much of it has been turned into legend with
romanticised heroes and there is little appetite to dismantle the
legends. At the same time the physical force tradition taking
firm root in the 19th century was a response to British government self-interest and unwillingness to seriously consider Irish
independence. The famine may be more complex than the often
simplistic readings but it was easy for even disillusioned intellectuals like the Young Irelanders to see it as British genocide.
British colonial policies produced the physical force tradition
and that included the physical force tradition in the Protestant
community. The sectarian patterns of the 17th century took a
different form in the 19th century but sectarianism and its logic
of violence was more pervasive than ever. The formation of
physical force groups were a concrete expression.

• Peep O'Day Boys and Defenders

Both groups have already been mentioned and their formation in Co Armagh. Ireland was already characterised by violence and bloodletting, and much of it would be discredited today
as gang warfare. It was such a fight that birthed both groups in
1784. Ironically the founders of both groups were Protestant
farmers, but given the existing tensions in Co Armagh sectarian evolution followed. The Defenders expanded throughout Ulster, forming
lodges in local communities. As the name suggests they were formed to
defend the Catholic community against Protestant attacks. Another
ironic twist is that they were royalists pledging loyalty to King George
III. The United Irishmen were republican, Presbyterian founders
of modern Irish republicanism. The Catholic Defenders were
royalists and loyalists! Later the Defenders did join the United
Irish cause though they failed to turn up in a meaningful way
when the 1798 rising began.

The Peep O'Day Boys 'were very much an Armagh phenomenon'.[29] Unlike the Defenders they did not spread as much throughout Ulster. But they did form the basis of the Orange Order formed after the Loughgall battle between themselves and Defenders. The Orange Order became an all-Ireland institution. Before this Armagh experienced tit-for-tat violence and a serious increase in sectarian and violent activity. A Catholic church was burned in Portadown in 1789 and after a Protestant magistrate had convicted and executed two Defenders, brutal vengeance was taken by Defenders. They attacked the home of a Protestant schoolteacher in Forkhill, 'cut out part of his tongue, inflicting the same torture on his wife and her 13 year old brother, Nathaniel'.[30] What might be called mutual ethnic cleansing followed with the flight of south Armagh Protestants. The Boys responded by 'papering and wrecking', sticking pieces of paper on Catholic doors and ordering them to leave. If they refused their homes were wrecked. Many Armagh Catholics did leave for Mayo where the next generation suffered again from the famine. The activity of the Boys was blatantly sectarian.

... they assaulted a priest near Tandragee; they attacked a chapel on the Obins estate near Portadown, where they destroyed a stone crucifix purchased on the continent by the landlord; they destroyed the vestments and chalice of the parish priest of Forkhill. Defender violence was initially reactive in character, shaped by the intimidation of one confessional community by another.[31]

It was largely the violence of the Boys that pushed the Defenders towards the United Irishmen. Battles and bloodshed continued between them and in 1795, a Peep O'Day Boy, Dan Winter was instrumental in the founding of the Orange Order.

The violence of both sides was sectarian and equally brutal. The physical force antecedents were all too real in late 18th century Armagh, and not surprisingly the 20th century saw south Armagh as an IRA stronghold and Orange marches in Portadown remain a controversial flashpoint.

- Whiteboys, Oakboys and Steelboys

The Boys and the Defenders were not without precedent.

29. McBride, op cit, p 414

30 Tanner, op cit , p 191

31 McBride, op cit , p 418

Various organisations emerged in the mid-18th century as part of agrarian violence and rebellion. In 1762, a 'council of war' near Fermoy was attended by 'several hundred Whiteboys. A bay gelding was beaten and then shot in what appeared to be a symbolic action against a local magistrate who had sentenced a Whiteboy to a prison sentence.'[32] The Whiteboys were resisting the tithe demands of landowners and the enclosure of common land. Much of their activity was in destroying fences. Their violence was mainly against cattle and horses. Their activity can be observed in three phases.

Originating in Tipperary and spreading to Cork, Waterford and Limerick, they were aggrieved by enclosure of common land and the tithe of potatoes. From 1769 to 1776, the grievance was over a corn tithe and evictions over high rents. The third phase was from 1785 to 1788 provoked by 'the financial exactions of the clergy of the Established Church'.[33] Organising marches from parish to parish and holding swearing-in ceremonies in Catholic churches, not only mobilised Catholics but also anticipated Daniel O'Connell's mobilisation of popular politics towards Catholic Emancipation.

The Whiteboys appear to be a Munster phenomenon but to the dismay of the authorities, similar organisations appeared in Ulster. These spearheaded 'explosions of organised protests, led by the 'Hearts of Oak' (1763) and 'Hearts of Steel' (1770-72)'.[34] They were viewed as insurrectionist movements and thought to be extremely dangerous by those in power.

The Oakboys originated in the Brownlow estate at Lurgan and in Markethill, Richhill and Tandragee, a Co Armagh phenomenon. The organisation spread through much of Ulster and terrorised clergy of the Established Church and landowners for a summer month in 1763. Mass demonstrations of up to 20,000 people appeared, much of it as a tax protest against things like tithes and fees payable for marriages, funerals and baptisms. Presbyterian tenant farmers were often involved.

---

32 Ibid, p 312
33 Ibid, p 317 McBride offers an extensive analysis of all three organisations, including motivation and political significance in pp 312-341. The brief descriptions here are based on McBride.
34 Ibid, p 318

The Steelboys insurrection was much more violent and sustained. It lasted from 1770 to 1772 and was mainly concentrated in Antrim and Down, Presbyterian heartland.

The Steelboys terrorised large parts of east Ulster, burning houses and haystacks, maiming cattle and ruining crops, as well as levying contributions on local people to fund their activities. The general background to the Steelboy revolt was an economic downturn caused by three successive crop failures (1769-71) and a simultaneous reduction in the foreign demand for linen.[35]

This was a social revolution against the economic system and land ownership of the time. It was the era of Protestant Ascendancy and tenants and workers were looking for forms of justice and liberty. There was economic prosperity for the elite, agricultural prosperity and whilst linen was involved in mid-Ulster much of the activity represented agrarian unrest against wealthy landowners identified with the Established Church.

The movements were characterised by 'military or quasi-military discipline, together with a hierarchy of officers'.[36] Uniforms were adopted and there was 'marching at order'. In the north, Oakboys and Steelboys reflected the Protestant militia, complete at times with horns, drums, fiddlers and bagpipes. There were levels of violence, enough to suggest to Ian McBride that there were 'Rites of Violence' in the behaviour and practice of these organisations. People were killed, perhaps as many as 200. The state hanged up to 85 people and in Ulster 20 Oakboys and 24 Steelboys were 'killed in action'. McBride suggests a total figure of 70 as reasonable. Organisational activity killed men and animals and torture was used. A Whiteboy informer had part of his tongue and leg cut off and similar atrocities were committed against tithe-farmers.

The social and economic systems and structures of the time did disadvantage the ordinary people. Power and wealth was held by the elite, whether Established clergy or landowners. The Protestant Ascendancy was itself a form of violence against linen workers and tenant farmers.

Agrarian rebellion is understandable from a people who

35 Ibid, p 318
36 Ibid, p 526

want life and liberty. The dilemma is between violent and non-violent responses. Ireland already had its culture of violence by the 18th century and it was sectarian violence. In Ulster the agrarian revolt was intra-Protestant since Presbyterian tenant farmers were with the Oakboys and Steelboys against the Anglican establishment. Yet how much does violence achieve? Whiteboys, Oakboys and Steelboys killed people and animals, but what was achieved? Yet there is the desperation and despair of people suffering from a seemingly intractable social, economic and political system. It was the end of the 19th century and 1903 before George Wyndham's Land Act finally resolved the agrarian issue. And this was after the land war of the 19th century.

The Peep O'Day Boys and Defenders were the physical force successors of the earlier 18th century organisations. That did mean more violence, especially in Ulster. By the end of the 19th century violence was well established in Irish culture and it was deeply sectarian. The mobilisation of popular Catholic politics which had begun with O'Connell's non-violent achievement had alienated Protestants. By 1834 Presbyterians had found common cause with Irish Anglicans over against the growing confidence of Catholic religion and politics. By the end of the 19th century, Catholicism and nationalism were identical. So too was Protestantism and unionism. There were of course a few exceptions, Catholic unionists and Protestant Home Rulers. O'Connell's non-violence was already eclipsed and the new 20th century was to be engulfed by political turmoil and some of the most brutal violence ever.

CHAPTER THREE

What is worth commemorating a century on? 1912-1916

Commemoration is not an exclusively Irish preoccupation. It happens elsewhere and many nations have their list of commemorative days and rituals. Because of the history of conflict and violence, commemoration in Ireland is contested. On either side of the historical divide there are chosen traumas and selective events, including chosen victories to be remembered. Perhaps the smallness of Ireland and the closely knit nature of Irish society personalises memory. Some relative, however far back, was there. Or 'I have a sword in the attic that was used by family in the 1798 Rising' a neighbour informed me. Even if no relative was there, the tribal memory has been passed on and has become part of our personal and collective story. Commemoration becomes woven into our identities and since the commemorations are contested, our identities continue to be oppositional, even antagonistic. The perpetuation of memories will continue to be divisive unless we find some way to walk through history together, enter into each other's chosen traumas and victories. This of course will include being prepared to acknowledge a largely fictionalised past, confronting legends more often than facts, and recognising that 'facts' are always interpretations, forever open to revisions. We might prefer our prejudices to engaging in such a struggle with history.

Marianne Elliott in her fine book on Robert Emmet posed a challenging question in the penultimate page:

> Irish nationality has consisted disproportionately of the celebration of heroic sacrifice and legends like that of Robert Emmet. Is it perhaps fear of what would be left that deters many from questioning such legends.[1]

This not only applies to the Emmet story, but to any part of our historical story, nationalist and unionist. If we stripped away the layers of fiction and legend, what would be left? And that

1 Elliott, Marianne, *Robert Emmet: The Making of a Legend* (London: Profile Books, 2003) p 235

might have a devastating impact on our respective identities. Would truth, or the honest search for truth, be too much to handle? What would be left to commemorate? One might be tempted to think that in a more globilised era, with technology and travel and post-modern worldviews, Irish young people will have less interest in commemorating a past, or some version of it. Yet in Northern Ireland, children born since the ceasefires are likely to be more sectarian than the earlier generation of their parents. If true, it begs the question which selected stories are being passed on? Which legends are children being told? Sectarianism includes yesterday's memories which can be kept alive by commemoration. After 1994, children were not born with sectarian genes. It was passed on and they were educated, even nurtured into it.

This is not an argument for ignoring history but for a more robust and critical telling of the story(ies). A serious reflection in the *Scotsman* newspaper suggested that the gatekeepers of history have reduced Scotland's past to a collection of statistics without a story, and that Scottish children are not being taught their history. This is traced back to post-Act of Union in 1707, that when Scots 'got absorbed into the Union, and especially as the prospects of empire opened up, it was really a new nation that arose with a new history – this history being before it, not behind it. So there was no point in studying the old history'. Interestingly Michael Fry, the author, writes that Scotland has always been a contested country, with different kinds of history. Teaching and learning history is, he believes, 'an exciting aspect of Scottishness in the 21st century with the aim of redefining what Scotland is and Scotland means'. He, therefore, hopes that there will be an end to the long neglect of the nation's history at its schools.[2]

The neglect of history in the educational curriculum, however contested it is, is a diminution of identity and a distortion of memory. Commemoration is not to be abolished, but engaged in a shared, robust and critical way.

In the vast tracts of historical time, a century past is only yesterday. In Ireland, north and south, a decade is looming during

2 Fry, Michael, 'End the neglect of our own heritage in schools' in the *Scotsman*, Saturday, 10 April 2010

which the centenaries of a number of highly significant events will be commemorated. The decade from 1912-1922 was a decade of upheaval and change in Ireland. Beginning north, the Ulster Covenant in 1912 and ending with the partition of Ireland in 1921 and the end of the civil war in 1922, these bookends and events in between shaped the rest of the 20th century in Ireland and the legacies of the decade continue to shape the politics, attitudes and relationships of the present. It was a violent decade and the legacy of violence remains, if not always in action, then still pervasive in mindsets. What erupted in 1969 in Northern Ireland was, in a real sense, the unfinished business of the decade. It began with the militarisation of politics and we approach the centenaries of the decade's events with the fragile hope that the gun is being removed at last from Irish politics. The events of 1912-1922 were dominated by the gun and violence and continued, more especially in the politics of the northeast and, even after ceasefires and decommissioning of weapons, remain.

Between 2012-2022, the events will be commemorated, but how? The events are significant and cannot be ignored. It was a decade of massive change in Ireland, but how will we commemorate violent events in a context of relative peace? How will we commemorate the violence? It will not be possible to remember the events and their impact without remembering the violence that was integral to them. To walk through this decade of change together will require actual engagement with each other's violence and a shared, rigorous ethical evaluation.

Ethical Remembering
As we approach the centenaries of 1912-1922 there are questions about what we shall remember. Selective memory is a problem and widely practised. On the 90th anniversary of the 1916 Rising in 2006, the Irish government took control of events. The dominant role of government may have been to put down a marker for 2016 and the centenary commemoration, letting Sinn Féin know that it was not in charge and not the custodian of the 1916 memory. Whatever shape or form the 2016 commemor - ations will take there will be two different versions of 1916 commemorated, one by government and the other by Sinn Féin.

Who creates history and why is it written in a particular way
and in different ways? The same will be true in 2012 on the cent -
enary of the Ulster Covenant. Loyalists may well have their version and the mainstream unionist parties another. Whether or
not the Protestant churches, heavily involved in 1912, will want
to have any role, remains to be seen. Their endorsement of the
gun in politics then may make them very cautious, if not extremely nervous, especially if loyalists propose re-enactment of
gun running, albeit in wood!

Selectivity will undoubtedly exist, with the temptation to
play down the violence of the decade. The larger question is not
what we will commemorate, but how? When the decade of commemoration begins we will be fourteen years into the Belfast or
Good Friday Agreement. How fragile is the process of peace?
Will it be strong enough to handle or survive ten years of commemorations that shaped the present in Ireland? In the context
of the peace process, with relationships and political systems
relatively better, but by no means all they should be, how will
commemorations be expressed? Given that the world has
changed beyond recognition since 1912-1922, we live in a very
different Europe largely at peace with itself and in a global context where globilisation impinges on every aspect of our lives,
which means that Ireland is not the Ireland of then, how shall
we commemorate? Old unionist and nationalist/republican
rhetoric will sound like a foreign language. Carson and Pearse,
Craig and de Valera are long dead and do not speak to a post-
modern world. They do not fit into this new global one and we
have no way of knowing how they would respond to our contemporary geopolitics and our global economy. It is pointless
speculating, even claiming that they were big men, heroes big
enough for the 21st century, but how do we know? They belonged to another time, if not to another planet, such is the
world in which we now live. Will any contemporary Irish politician fit into the world of 2112 and 2116? It would be foolish to
try and answer, even speculate.

In a very real sense we are on our own during the decade.
The onus will be on us to commemorate in our current context.
We have no other context and we cannot dress up in the clothes
and styles of then and travel Ireland by steam train for the next

decade.

It's not only about selective memory or frozen memory, some of the histories will be rewritten because we now have new information. There is no final, definitive version of any period or event in history. Like science and theology, new light keeps appearing and the stories of the centenaries will be told differently from those of the 50th anniversaries. Those who want a hegemonic narrative will insist on their fixed dogma but truth demands otherwise.

The greatest challenge to remembering the events of a decade 100 years later, will be to struggle with ethical remembering. There is nothing new in this. Ethics are not being invented for the centenaries. They were around during 1912-1922. When Francis Sheehy-Skeffington took a pacifist stance and opposed violence during the decade, he was practising ethics. When Presbyterian minister, J. B. Armour took a stance for Home Rule on the grounds of justice, he was taking an ethical stance. On the other hand, when Carson organised an illegal army and gun running, were his actions ethical? When Pearse called on young men to shed blood for Ireland, their own and anyone who was in the way, and seized power and imposed a government on the people of Ireland in 1916, was he behaving ethically? There are ethical evaluations and judgements to be made because they were being made then for better and for worse. How we commemorate or remember between 2012-2022 will include ethical remembering if our remembering is to have any integrity.

In a book that followed the 90th commemoration of 1916 and focused only on the Rising, Seamus Murphy wrote a critical essay on 'Easter Ethics'. He did not deal with the Rising in complete isolation, but made connections with some of the events which followed and were a consequence of the Easter Rising. He articulated an ethical framework helpful, if adopted and applied to 1912-1922.[3]

• *Context is Important*

Context is important to ethical remembering but not every-

---

3 Murphy, Seamus, *Easter Ethics in 1916: The Long Revolution,* edited by Gabriel O'Doherty and Dermot Keogh, (Cork: Mercier Press, 2007) pp 329-351

thing. Painting in a context for the events of 1912-1922 can become a tail chasing exercise, because having identified a context there is another context behind the context. Nevertheless, to identify an immediate context to the decade is important and helpful.

These are of course three centuries of history and these have been explored in the opening chapters. These are violent precedents and earlier expressions of physical force traditions. There is colonial experience, ascendancy and disestablishment, land league and reform, '98 Rising and Catholic Emancipation. Home Rule was first introduced in 1886 and opposition to it grew steadily as did aggression for it. Guns were around before 1914, Risings occurred, the Irish Republican Brotherhood existed and the Orange Order was involved with guns from at least 1893. Political parties were being formed, such as Sinn Féin and Ulster Unionists, both in 1905 and the Irish Parliamentary Party had experienced the Parnell affair and his death only to struggle under the leadership of John Redmond. There is enough context to give meaning to the events of 1912-1922. They did not occur in a vacuum but emerged from dynamics and forces which shaped them and propelled them. There was also enough of a culture and ethos of violence in Ireland to inspire the violence of the decade.

- Ethical Analysis
  History and the writing and revision of history are never ethically neutral, nor are acts of commemoration. There are always critical and ethical questions to be raised. As well as paying attention to context, Murphy's ethical analysis includes three significant dimensions.[4]

These were the personalities, characters and motives. Given that this history is British as well as Irish, there were personalities on both sides of the Irish sea and ethical evaluation is required in relation to the nationalist and unionist leaders as well as key British politicians. Who were Carson and Craig, Collins and de Valera, Asquith, Bonar Law, Lloyd-George and Churchill and what were there motives and characteristics?

---

4 Ibid, pp 332-333

The actions and politics of the time also need critical and ethical evaluation. Carson was leading the Ulster Protestants in a particular direction and pursuing politics of violence. Pearse was leading armed insurrection and justifying it by mystical theology. Lloyd-George was a war-time Prime Minister with global concerns and war policy, though troubled by an Irish question. Collins and de-Valera had two different visions of Ireland, one a democracy and the other a Republic, and in 1921 they were not the same. With all of these personalities, how much was political nous, deviousness, double-talk, transparency?

Ethical analysis will ask questions about consequences and outcomes. What were the consequences of Ulster resistance, gun running and a readiness to fight the British to remain British? Did Carson and Craig really think about consequences? What were the outcomes of the Easter Rising? Had Pearse thought those through or was he simply taking his armed cue from the Ulster loyalists? Did both events of 1912 and 1916 make part-ition inevitable? Did the Rising guarantee a war of independ-ence and make a civil war, treaty divide inevitable? Was the out-come of the Covenant a sectarian state in Northern Ireland which ensured the violence of 1969 and the following years? There is no avoiding these questions if remembering is to be ethical. And there is perhaps the most discomfiting question of all, was the violence necessary or justified in 1912-1922 and 1969-2004? Is violence always inevitable or the only option, and is there always another way?

• *Ethical Values*

The ethical values in play during the decade and during the later violence in Northern Ireland can be drawn from a fourth basis. In Covenant and Proclamation there was a central appeal to faith. Whether the faith expressed in the two foundational documents of both parts of Ireland was warped and distorted, shaped by imperialism and nationalism is a critical ethical ques-tion that needs to be asked. Was this in fact authentic faith in the Ireland of the time or was it skewed by ideology and the churches themselves? There was another source of ethical perspective. 'The ethical framework of liberal democracy is concerned with representative democracy, human rights and the rule of law.'[5] These liberal democratic values provide a framework for ethical evaluation of the events of 1912-1922 and the latter decades of the 20th century.

Murphy suggests that the leaders of the Rising were not democrats in practice: they were nationalists first, and their understanding of democracy was subordinate to their understanding of nationalism.[6] The same could be said of the leaders of Ulster resistance, though they would not have wanted to use the term, nationalist. They were British nationalists and imperialists, though their historical understanding of covenant rooted in conditionality, allowed them to rebel against the British. Democracy was also subordinate to their nationalistic and imperial identity.

Carson and Craig had no intention of accepting the wishes of the majority of the Irish people. That had been overwhelmingly made clear in the 1918 British General Election. Their idea of self-determination was constructed within a separatist, anti-democratic framework. Neither Pearse nor de Valera had much time for democracy either. Collins returned with a negotiated Treaty signed by himself and others, not because Lloyd-George threatened immediate war if the Irish team did not. Rather as Collins said:

> I signed because I would not be one of those to commit the Irish people to war without the Irish people committing themselves to war … I can state for you a principle which everybody will understand, the principle of government by the consent of the governed.[7]

Collins was aware that he had signed his death warrant, but for what was left of his life he stuck with democracy, while others stuck with the Republic, ignoring democracy and plunging the country into a violent civil war. When the consent of the people was sought in the June election of 1922, 80% of voters backed candidates who supported the Treaty. Democracy had spoken,

---

5 Ibid, p 313
6 Ibid, p 334
7 Feature article by Stephen Collins in the *Irish Times* on 'Sharing Collins Legacy of Democracy', Saturday, 21 August 2010

but by 22 August, Collins was shot and killed in West Cork. It appeared that the militarists despised democracy and democratic politicians. Later in the 20th century the physical force traditions of loyalism and republicanism still showed no commitment to liberal democracy, human rights and the rule of law, and neither did the unionist hegemony. The practice of western ethical values in Ireland has been a struggle, often with violent consequences.

Hatred has been an unethical value during the violence of the decade and later events. Sectarian hatred and violence had been a virus endemic in the north-east of Ireland since the early 17th century. The virus lay behind the riots of Belfast and Derry since the early part of the 19th century and infected the resistance of 1912 and the violent clashes and killings that followed partition in 1921 in Belfast, Derry and Lisburn. The endemic virus of sectarian hatred, still present, calls for serious ethical critique then and now.

Hatred was also a driving force in events of the decade in the rest of Ireland. Even though the Dáil had been in existence since 1918, there was no electoral or even parliamentary mandate for the war of independence. It started as a 'private enterprise of local volunteers starting to shoot RIC men. It was inspired by and in line with the model of the Easter Rising: individuals feeling called to kill and be killed for Ireland, without authorisation by any elected body'.[8]

If a sectarian virus of hate existed in the north, the south was inflicted by a romantic revolutionary virus, no less possessed of hatred. In keeping with late 19th century European national - isms with its lust for war and violence, Irish nationalist rom - anticism generated high levels of hate. 'Hate tends to war, and war encourages hate.' It also 'undermines tolerance, acceptance of the other, and acceptance that we are not all going to hold the same values.'[9] The problem with a virus is that once it takes hold, it can take a long time to work itself out of the system. The romantic revolutionary virus kept breaking out from time to time, not least in 1969 and like the sectarian virus, with which it was combined in the decade and in 1969, it almost appears to be

8 Murphy, op cit , p 340
9 Ibid , p 342

a life-long condition. Pluralism and tolerance were not on the map in 1912-1922, and, whatever the rhetoric about civil and religious liberty in Covenant and Proclamation, there was an ethical failure to build a pluralistic and tolerant society. That failure came home to roost again later in the century.

The reality of so much violence raises the most serious ethical questions of all. What is disturbing is that loyalist and republican opted for violence rather than democratic parliamentary and constitutional politics. The guns and illegal army of the Covenant undermined constitutional politics and negated the talking and negotiation which is the normal part of such politics. The 1912-1913 option for militaristic politics, and the British failure to deal with it, encouraged the 1916 leaders to follow the pattern and undermine further the way of democracy and constitutional politics. Both events undermined normal politics and the anti-Treatites did the same in 1922. There was no pursuit of the common good and that is an ethical deficit.

The precedents for non-violent, constitutional politics were also ignored. John Redmond was a constitutional parliamentarian, who led a weakened but still viable Irish Parliamentary Party. Redmond was at the heart of the third Home Rule Bill, put forward in1912 and agreed in 1914. Yet the sectarian and romantic revolutionary virus has virtually removed Redmond from a noble place in the history of Irish politics. His achievements have been downgraded by hatred and violence and by the politics of militarism. That calls for ethical critique.

One of the greatest achievements in Irish political life was Catholic Emancipation in 1829. It was achieved non-violently and solely through constitutional political means. Daniel O'Connell was committed to non-violence and constitutional politics. Yet O'Connell is not really in the pantheon of Irish political heroes!

This is illustrated by a story related by Murphy that when Sean T. O'Kelly became President of Ireland in the 1940s, he had O'Connell's bust removed from the foyer of Aras an Uachtaráin and dumped in the basement. Years later when de Valera was asked about the relegation of O'Connell in post-independent Ireland, he is supposed to have said:

You must think, you must consider our feelings at the time. We firmly believed that the Irish people could only be 'jolted' from their lethargy and Irish freedom and liberty achieved by force of arms. How then could we promote the memory of the man who achieved so much by parliamentary means with no loss of life? To praise him would have made it impossible for us to justify armed insurrection.[10]

It is an extraordinary statement that lacks ethical perspective, either the ethics of liberal democracy or faith-based ethics. That two of the greatest constitutional politicians in Irish history should be relegated and rejected as they have, to justify and maintain the justification of the use of violence and militarised politics, betrays a crisis in ethics.

Just how critical and ethical the commemorations and remembering will be during the decade of centenaries, and in any acknowledgement of the most recent phase of violence, remains to be seen. Ambivalence or amnesia would not deserve to be called ethical. We may even yet prefer to undermine liberal democracy, acquiesce in unethical religion, leave the door open to a future resort to violence, or push along the painful and fragile road to an ethical reconciliation in Ireland.

The Ulster Covenant: 1912
Before 1912, British governments led by William Gladstone had attempted to introduce Home Rule to Ireland. After the Act of Union in 1801, Ulster Protestants became its stalwart defenders. When the repeal and revolutionary movements collapsed in the 1840s, there was little real threat to the Ulster Protestant sense of identity. In the 1880s things changed and by 1886, when Gladstone introduced the first Home Rule Bill, the Protestants of Ulster organised to defend the Union. Irish nationalism was also re-emerging and the Home Rule Party was capturing the Catholic vote. Irish unionism was the response, which later became Ulster unionism.

Gladstone offered Ireland the possibility of self-government in 1886 and 1893, which Protestants saw as a threat to their way of life. The threat led to a revival of the Protestant Orange Order, but when the Nationalist Party in 1885, led by Parnell, won 17

10 Ibid, pp 343-344

out of 33 Ulster seats, and Gladstone introduced his first Bill the following year, Protestants were alarmed. A Loyalist Anti-Repeal Union was formed bringing together Protestant landowners, businessmen and churchmen (and they were men!). Randolf Churchill encouraged Protestants 'to play the Orange card' and Ulster Protestants were called in a huge public meeting to resist. The slogan 'Ulster will fight and Ulster will be right' was born. Tensions were such in 1886 that there were sectarian riots in the Belfast shipyards and in Belfast 32 people died with many injured. Unionist clubs were formed and links established with the Conservative Party in Britain, and an Ulster Defence Association was also formed, suggesting that armed resistance was a considered possibility.

By 1893, Gladstone tried again with a Second Home Rule Bill and again failed. With the Irish Parliamentary Party falling apart after Parnell's scandalous relationship with Kitty O'Shea and his death, the immediate danger to Ulster dissipated. Though Gladstone also died shortly afterwards, the Liberal Party remained committed to Home Rule for Ireland. For Gladstone it had been a moral issue as much as a political one.

In the 1906 general election, Home Rule was played down and the Liberals had a landslide victory with 400 members elected and a majority of 270. The proposal of an Irish Council to deal with some internal affairs was not enough and John Redmond was under pressure from the newly formed nationalist organisation, Sinn Féin. But the Liberals were untouchable in Parliament, at least until the House of Lords committed political suicide by rejecting Lloyd George's budget in 1909. This was an unprecedented act and led to another general election in January 1910, which if the Liberals won, would lead to reform of the Lords. In effect, it would lead to the removal of the Lords veto on government Bills and that would mean no obstacle to another Home Rule Bill. The Liberals needed Irish nationalist support, especially after the election when they returned without their large majority. Asquith was Prime Minister with the support of Redmond and the Irish Party, the absolute veto of the Lords was abolished, and Irish nationalists could look forward to a third Home Rule Bill.

The Bill was introduced in April 1912, affirming the sup -

remacy of the Westminster Parliament, providing for 42 members at Westminster (80 in 1893), an Irish senate of 40 members and a House of Commons of 164 members.

An Irish Executive was to be headed by a Lord Lieutenant who had 'power not only to approve or veto legislation, but also, and more dangerously, to reverse a decision, and thus to postpone legislation indefinitely'.[11] Section 3 of the Bill addressed the Ulster Unionist slogan, 'Home Rule is Rome Rule', by prohibiting legislation that would 'discriminate either in favour of, or against, any form of religious practice'. In particular, the Irish Parliament was prevented from legislating to 'make any religious belief or religious ceremony a condition of the validity of any marriage.'[12] Protestant fears had been heightened by the earlier *Ne Temere* Papal decree and the fall out from the McCann case which caused the bitter break-up of a mixed marriage. More than heightened fears, this had led to intense Protestant anger and proved the Rome rule point. Irish nationalists on the other hand felt humiliated by religious prohibition in the Bill.

Meanwhile in London, the Liberals spent little time discussing the Ulster problem and even convinced themselves that 'Unionist opposition was artificial'.[13]

The Ulster Unionist Council had already expressed opposition and resistance before the introduction of the Bill. The leaders of the resistance were Sir Edward Carson, a Dublin lawyer and MP for Trinity College Dublin from 1892, who became Solicitor-General for England in 1900.

Carson was committed to maintaining the union and was an Irish unionist before becoming caught up in the Ulster problem and what became an Ulster Unionist cause. Ulster's cause, he came to believe, was the 'cause of the Empire'.

James Craig was the Presbyterian son of a whiskey distiller and had become an Ulster Unionist MP at Westminster in 1906. He was an activist and administrator and 'He was obstinate and

11 Jackson, Alvin, *Home Rule: An Irish History 1800-2000,* (London: Weidenfeld and Nicholson, 2003), p 110

12 Ibid, p 110

13 Adelman, Paul and Pearce, Robert, *Great Britain and the Irish Question, 1800-1922* (London: Hodder and Stoughton, 2001) p 115

single-minded and determined at all costs to resist any attempt
to force Ulster into a self-governing Ireland'.[14] He, not Carson,
was the first to call for armed resistance to Home Rule.

Massive military-type demonstrations expressed implacable
opposition to Home Rule. The largest was on Easter Tuesday in
Belfast, just two days before Asquith introduced the Bill. It was
a march-past of 100,000 Ulstermen in military formation. Bonar
Law and Carson were the main speakers joined by 70 British
conservative MPs. The drilling and training of volunteer soldiers had preceded the demonstrations and the Ulster Unionist
Council had formed the Ulster Volunteer Force supported by
local Protestant JPs and advised by army officers. The UVF became highly organised throughout Ulster with county divisions
and regiments, a corp of nurses and dispatch riders. There were
as yet no arms but preparations for these were being made with
monies available since at least 1910.

The UVF was an illegal army and Unionist leadership also
defied a ban on weapons by gun-running in April 1914, bringing in 35,000 weapons and 5 million rounds of ammunition
from Germany. These were landed mainly at Larne and spirited
away by the Volunteer Motor Car Corp, without any interfer-
ence from the authorities. In terms of law, a treasonous government was waiting in the wings to take over if Home Rule was
imposed on Ireland.

There is no question that Ulster Unionist resistance was militant and the militancy continued on 28 September 1912 when
the Ulster Covenant was signed by 218,000 Ulstermen, some it is
said in their own blood, invoking their own blood sacrifice theo -
logy and martyr complex. Ulster Day was an act of militant and
massive resistance. It was also a highly charged religious occasion. Religious services were held early in the day throughout
Ulster with highly politicised sermons being delivered. Free
Bibles were also distributed on the day and the most popular
hymn was 'O God our help in ages past, our hope for years to
come'. This was not sung as an expression of personal and
spiritual religious confidence, but as a political affirmation, a
militant unionism with God on its side and the expectation of
political deliverance from the conspiracy of Home Rule. Ulster

---

14 Ibid , p 117

resistance had an integral religious dimension and it brought leaders and people together in a common oath of armed political resistance legitimised and blessed by God.

Among the first seven signatories of the Solemn League and Covenant were the leaders of the three larger Protestant churches, pledged to 'using all means which may be found necessary to defeat the present conspiracy to set up a home rule parliament in Ireland'. Everyone had known from at least 1910 that unionist and Orange military activity was taking place and that money and plans were in place to obtain weaponry. Carson knew it was all illegal and even told the Ulster Protestants, 'Don't be afraid of illegalities.'[15] The Protestant church leaders in sermons and signing of the Covenant clearly concurred and the churches gave their moral blessing to the militarisation of politics in the early part of the 20th century. They were rooted in an empire theology which identified God with empire and which had been expressed by an earlier Methodist editorial which proclaimed the crown rights of Christ and the crown rights of empire as one. Giving moral legitimacy to the gun in Irish politics was consistent with imperial theology. It is both the theology and the ethics of violence that require a critical evaluation, not necessarily in hindsight, but because alternative theology and ethics were around at the time.

Interestingly, the covenant text does not begin with theology, but with 'the material well-being of Ulster, as well as of the whole of Ireland'. Ulster was the industrial part of Ireland and therefore the economically prosperous part of Ireland. Proximity to the ports of Glasgow and Liverpool helped, as did geographical and cultural identity with Glasgow in particular. Ulster militant resistance to Home Rule was rooted in its imperial identity and economic wellbeing and the fear of loss of both. Home Rule, it was feared, would dismember the empire and cripple Ulster's industrial economy.

The Covenant also claimed 'equal citizenship' with the rest of the United Kingdom, but in Orange Ulster the issue was not equality but superiority, and during the 19th century riots and up to 1912, that was a racial superiority. Home Rule 'certainly

15 Irvine, Maurice, *Northern Ireland: Faith and Faction*, (London: Routledge, 1991), p 81

threatened a fatal blow at the master-race syndrome'.[16] The Covenant was not only opposed to Home Rulers, it feared subversion of 'civil and religious freedom', meaning Protestant civil and religious freedom, and it assisted a superior religious and racial identity.

The document itself was modeled on a 17th century Scottish covenant, indeed a series of Scottish and Presbyterian covenants underpin the 1912 document. The Protestant churches approved the Covenant with its Calvinist/Reformed tradition and in doing so supported the primacy of material success, racial superiority and the physical force tradition, all blessed by God. At the same time what options did church leaders and local clergy have? The depth of feeling and power and the intimidation that followed often threatened clergy posts and livelihood. Some who supported Home Rule did lose their parishes while others may or may not have had the choice but to bless the guns at special services. Ethics and social morals lost in 1912. And yet the Covenant remains in the minds of many Protestants as a foundational document, a kind of constitution of Northern Ireland, and Carson as a founding hero. Yet by 1921 and partition, Carson saw it as defeat, had deep doubts as to whether it was all worth it, left Northern Ireland, visited infrequently, and finally returned when his body was brought back for burial in St Anne's Cathedral, Belfast.

The Easter Rising: 1916

The drilling, training and arming of up to 100,000 Ulster Volunteers produced a similar response on the nationalist side. As many joined the Nationalist Volunteers and Germany also supplied the arms which arrived in Howth. The physical force tradition was embedded on both sides and there was the potent - ial for a civil war. Asquith discredited the speeches of Carson and Law as a 'Grammar of Anarchy', and Redmond assured him that the unionists were playing 'a gigantic game of bluff and blackmail'.[17] That was a dangerous delusion, and whatever about Redmond, Asquith had no real grasp of the reality of

16 Lee, Joseph, *The Modernisation of Irish Society, 1848-1918*, (Dublin: Gill and Macmillan, 2008 revised edition), p 138

17 Adelman and Pearce, op cit , p 120

Ireland. Not a few of his successors have shared the same problem.

Joseph Lee in the 1973 edition of his book believed that the
Orangemen were responsible for bringing the gun back into politics. He has since modified this view fearing that it gave the impression that politics since the Union were conducted without
regard to the power of the gun. He now believes that Irish politics were, in fact, conducted within the framework prescribed
by the power of the gun – the British gun. British troops in
Ireland were the precondition for British rule. In light of this he
now believes it more accurate to say 'not that Ulster unionists
brought the gun back into Irish politics, but rather that the arming of the Ulster Volunteer Force brought an alternative to the
British gun into Irish politics'.[18]

An alternative to the British gun in Irish politics is not how
Irish history is read, but it is a pertinent reminder that Britain
has an enormous responsibility for the militarisation of Irish
politics. Indeed, what Ireland has suffered from is the militarisation of British politics in Ireland. When the Unionists armed
themselves in 1914, it was an alternative to the British gun. The
British militarisation of politics in Ireland goes back centuries,
which is neither to engage in a blame game nor to condone the
Irish physical force traditions, but to acknowledge the current
part played by Britain in the modern Irish story. In commemorating a decade of events this needs to be acknowledged.

In this context, it is also true that nationalists not only responded to the arming of unionists, but also responded to the
Covenant with the Easter Rising. Every nationalist effort to respond to the British military presence had ended in failure and
defeat. O'Connell's constitutional achievement of Catholic
Emancipation was the one outstanding success in the face of
British military and political presence. Risings and revolutions
had been crushed. The physical force tradition had achieved
nothing but a series of crushing defeats and put downs. Now
the nationalists looked at the Covenant of 1912 with all its illegalities and treasonous subversion of British governance and
system, including its military system, and saw that unionists

---

18 Lee, op cit, p x

had won. A people in Ireland had been prepared to fight the British, albeit to remain British, using all 'those devises of sabotage and civil disobedience at which the Irish are so fatally adept' and were successful.[19] The crisis of 1912-1914 had shown that Carson and Craig had been prepared to use non-constitutional means, even armed resistance, to defeat a constitutional and democratic Bill and not only get away with it but neither a British government nor its armed forces in Ireland were prepared to or dared to arrest Carson and Craig for their activities. That encouraged the nationalists. If the unionists could defy and achieve, then so could they. Arms and physical force could achieve independence for Ireland. Years later when 'Eoin MacNeill was asked what the decisive factor was in bringing about the Easter Rising, he replied with one word "Carson".'[20]

This may be oversimplified, but the influence of the Ulster crisis should not be underestimated. Contemporary lamppost banners in summertime Belfast still proclaim Carson as 'founder of the people's army'. The banners are a reminder of what Carson actually did militarily with all its tragic consequences for later history. Pearse was already committed to a mystical physical force tradition before leading the Rising in 1916, but he and others were undoubtedly encouraged by Carson's role. He had, after all, defied illegally the British system.

In 1914, the first War intervened and Redmond, on the basis that this was a war to defend the rights of small nations, persuaded the majority of Irish volunteers to become involved in the war. The 10,000 remaining Volunteers were opposed to an imperial war. The AOH in the USA fully supported Germany. Irish opinion was divided and this led to the leaders of the more militant Irish Republican Brotherhood preparing for a rising. A Military Council was formed in 1915 and preparations were made for a nationwide rising at Easter 1916. Pearse especially, but also Plunkett, MacDonagh and Ceannt were leading architects. When the rising happened it reflected earlier risings in its less than effective strategy. There were not enough arms and a

---

19 Stewart, A. T. Q., *The Shape of Irish History* (Belfast: Blackstaff Press, 2001), p 166

20 Ibid, p 167

lot of confusion about timing. There was even a countermanding order all of which destined the rising for failure.

> Even before a shot was fired, the leaders regarded the rising as a heroic gesture, and one that would probably end in their death. But the rising was less about realism than about idealism and symbolism.[21]

The rising was a piece of street theatre. It began on Easter Monday, 24 April 1916 and ended five days later when Pearse and Connolly officially surrendered. As with all violent conflicts, the non-combatants suffered most with 230 civilian deaths, 64 insurgents and 132 soldiers. The execution of 15 leaders by the British swung public opinion in favour of the republicans and the most successful failure in Irish history was born.

The most outstanding personality in the rising was Pádraig Pearse for whom military success or failure was an irrelevancy. Underpinning the rising was Pearse's theology of blood sacrifice. 'To die for Ireland – was a noble end in itself and would help to stimulate Irish national consciousness.'[22] In a very real sense Pearse was right, at least in relation to his theology. Dying for Ireland, shedding blood in sacrifice of one's life, he believed had redemptive qualities and his death along with others in 1916 did raise national consciousness. Ireland's honour had been redeemed and the blood sacrifice legacy continued into the 20th century violence in the north and still lingers.

Pearse has been described as the rising's 'high priest' whose 'life and views did rather more fully echo the central themes of the Easter Rising nationalism as the subsequent faithful were to interpret them'.[23] Educated by the Christian Brothers and at the Catholic University College Dublin (UCD), Pearse himself was an educationalist. In 1908 he founded St Enda's school in Dublin with himself as head teacher. Thirty of his boys were in the GPO with him during Easter week 1916. The school was 'explicably Irish nationalist' and its primary aim was to 'embody true Irish

21 Kinealy, Christine, *A New History of Ireland* (Stroud: Sutton Publishing, 2004), p 201

22 Adelman and Pearce, op cit, p 129

23 English, Richard, *Irish Freedom: The History of Nationalism in Ireland* (London: Macmillan, 2006), p 268

national identity'.[24] Pearse was not alone in his goal of building a strong national youthful virility. Baden-Powell had the same goal and founded the Boy Scouts in the same year, 1908. He actually wrote to Pearse asking him to set up Boy Scouts, presumably within St Enda's, but Pearse declined. Pearse was not alone in his views of blood sacrifice either.

He was a complex character, celibate, devoted to the Virgin Mary and avoiding intimacy with women. He may even have been transsexual, given his frequent dressing as a woman, and perhaps homosexual, even inclined to paedophilia. On a visit to the west he asked to sleep with the young sons of the household and was asked by friends not to publish a poem with paedophile overtones. Pearse was upset by this, not understanding why there could be objections 'to a poem celebrating the joys of savouring the kisses of a particularly beautiful boy'.[25]

Clearly Pearse was a complex personality but it was as the 'spiritually-orientated cultural nationalist and devoted Catholic' that he developed his romantic nationalist dream, his 'imagined Ireland' and his role in the sacrificial struggle to take it forward.[26] It was in the mythology of heroes such as Cúchulainn and the blood saturated imagery of the eucharist that shaped Pearse's theology of the rising. It was for him a symbolic act, an intentional dream, above all a 'blood sacrifice' shed on behalf of Ireland.

The 1916 Rising in Dublin was suffused with this kind of Christian inspiration. It was timed to coincide with the most momentous day in the Christian calendar. The chief ideologue of the conspirators, Pádraig Pearse, a portly schoolteacher, intentionally thought of the revolt in Catholic terms as a religious sacrifice, freely offered, from which inestimable benefits would flow, though not necessarily in their own time.[27]

Any centennial commemoration of the rising will need to critically evaluate the mythical and Christian underpinnings of blood sacrifice and dying for Ireland. As noted earlier, Pearse

---

24 Ibid, p 269
25 Tanner, Marcus, *Ireland's Holy Wars: The Struggle for a Nation's Soul 1500-2000* (New Haven:Yale University Press, 2003) p 281
26 English, op cit , p 269
27 Tanner, op cit , pp 280-281

was not alone in his theology of violence. Pearse's Christian faith, or his Catholic interpretation of Christian faith, allowed him to provide the moral basis for physical-force nationalism. The British war poets, from within their not dissimilar Protestant interpretation of Christ's death, were advocating a romantic call 'to die for the English national myth as a form of eternal service and cultural redemption'.[28] Rupert Brooke was embracing 'cleansing violence' and he found the war 'exhilarating and terrible'. His obituary in 1915 recorded that 'He was all that we would wish England's noblest sons to be in days when no sacrifice but the most precious is acceptable, and most precious is that which is most freely proffered.'[29]

The French poet, Charles Peguy, was of the same mind seeing the defence of Catholic France as divine mission, another national myth, like that of the English and Irish ones, requiring willing sacrifice on its behalf. Peguy, Brooke and Pearse were all singing from the same hymn sheet, seeing violence as serving a national myth of redemption and that serving the myth with death 'meant eternal joy and beatification'.[30]

The later British war poets, Owen and Sassoon, became dis - illusioned by this myth of blood sacrifice and their poetry is much more critical. Pearse had a ready made Irish myth of Cúchulainn, the child-hero redeemer who loses an earthly battle, yet wins the battle for glory. Though killed by his enemies he wins eternal triumph. Ironically the loyalists in the most recent phase of Irish violence invoked the myth of Cúchulainn as defender of Ulster against the Irish and as an inspiration for their own sacrifice. In terms of the myth the loyalists had a better claim than Irish republicans!

Pearse merged the myth with the death of Jesus and saw blood sacrifice as strong and redeeming. Dying for Ireland was like the death of Jesus, an act of atonement and redemption. The shedding of blood for Ireland was 'a cleansing and sanctifying

---

28 Moran, Sean, Farrell, *Patrick Pearse and the Politics of Redemption: The Mind of the Easter Rising 1916* (Washington: The Catholic University of America Press, 1994) p 185

29 Ibid, p 187

30 Ibid, p 189

thing'.[31] Pearse also believed that his own death, like that of Robert Emmet's in 1803, was for 'a divinely ordained purpose – a sacrifice for Ireland like Christ's on the cross'.[32] He even claimed that Ireland could learn from the European war 'the transforming power of bloodshed and death'.[33] Connolly apparently shared the Pearsean vision, quoting the Christian Testament Letter to the Hebrews with reference to blood sacrifice and redemption: 'Without shedding of blood there is no redemption'.[34]

All of this imagery was at the heart of the traditional interpretation of Christ's death and eucharistic theology. It still is, and a critical question to be asked in the centennial commemoration in relation to the power of the romantic religio-mythic power of violence in Ireland, must be, are the traditional interpretations of Christ's death and the imagery of eucharist authentic, desirable and worth keeping? Or given that they are inherently violent do we need to subvert them and articulate a more peace-orientated interpretation of Christ's death and eucharist?

The blood sacrifice theme still lingers as a romantic virus in republican and loyalist psyches. It suffuses the violence of 1969-2004 and still lingers in the mindsets. It is also alive and well in the British acts of remembrance and in the language of 'supreme sacrifice' applied to the military victims of the wars in Iraq and Afghanistan.

The militarisation of politics in 1912 and 1916, both rooted in blood sacrifice, left a violent legacy still to be subverted and changed. It may well be that both 1912 and 1916 were a rejection of modernity and the threat of its culture of reason to what was perceived as Irish or British (Unionist) values and culture. At any rate these significant events were a hinge of history on the island when 'the force of reason in politics gave way to myth and unreason'.[35] Almost a century on the myths and unreason

---

31 Ibid, p 194
32 Ibid, p 199
33 Ibid, p 199
34 Ibid, p 200
35 Ibid, p 202

have not gone away. The romantic virus is still in the air, modern -
ity has given way to post-modernity; dreams have not been
realised, blood has been shed without glory. The world has
changed and the violence and politics of 1912 and 1916 belong to
a very foreign land. How we commemorate will be challenging
and interesting.

CHAPTER FOUR

What is worth commemorating a century on?
1916-1922

The decade from 1912-1922 was indeed a decade of change. It shaped Ireland for the rest of the 20th century and still casts a long shadow into the first decade of the 21st century. The events themselves also left a bitter-sweet legacy. The Republic of Ireland secured and built on its independence. For the Ulster Unionists, Home Rule as total independence had been avoided, a form of Home Rule within a United Kingdom framework had been achieved. In one sense the north had secured its independence from what was perceived at the time as Rome rule. The bitter legacy shaped Irish politics and family relationships. A sizable minority of losers were left feeling abandoned in the Unionist north while the majority set about systematically ensuring that they would remain losers and know their place. Meanwhile, with all the rhetoric of domination and superiority, the northern majority remained fearfully insecure, not only not trusting the Catholic minority, but equally distrustful of their political masters in Britain. The culture of violence was too deeply ingrained on all sides to go away and the north remained a tinder box waiting to explode. Not surprisingly it did in 1969 and in some senses the legacy of the decade of change had come home to roost or returned to haunt the island of Ireland and Northern Ireland in particular.

The events of the decade need to be seen as a whole. They are inextricably linked together. A common thread, not least a thread of violence, holds the events together, which is why a decade of commemorations or of centenaries needs to be viewed whole. At this point in the 21st century we dare not and cannot be selective in our commemoration. From Ulster Covenant to Civil War and the events in between, Catholic, Protestant, nationalist, unionist and dissenter, all need to engage with the entire decade, otherwise memory and identity will be skewed.

The Battle of the Somme 1916

Every year on 1 July in east Belfast, Orangemen and some women march to commemorate the Battle of the Somme. It has been commemorated in this way for decades. The controversial Orange march to Drumcree Parish Church near Portadown on the first Sunday in July each year has the same purpose. The events commemorate the thousands of young 36th Ulster Division soldiers who died in a horrendous battle in 1916. It was, of course, in the same year as the Easter Rising in Dublin and both events have shaped respective psyches connected by the common theme of blood sacrifice.

Commemoration has been divisive, with the impression created that Ulster Protestants were the main victims, at least from Ireland, in the first World War. Nationalist Ireland, for the best part of 90 years airbrushed the even greater numbers of nationalist war dead from history and historical remembrance. Dying for King and Empire did not fit with nationalistic ideology, nor with the struggle for independence from the very state whose army thousands of nationalist Irishmen joined. Though there is no comparison between the numbers who died in the Rising and Somme, one death was one too many, both events cannot be separated and in 2016 both commemorations will hopefully be observed by all on the island of Ireland.

The Rising and Somme both occurred in the larger European context of militarism and violence. Long before 1916, European societies had been moving progressively into this militarised environment. What was happening in the 19th and early 20th century made the likelihood of war inevitable.

Europe began the 20th century dominated by three emperors, all cousins and connected by bloodline to Queen Victoria. George of England, Nicholas of Russia and Wilhelm of Prussia, were not only cousins but increasingly involved in a power struggle leading to confrontation with each other, with Wilhelm in particular dreaming of domination. There was not a little demagoguery related to personality deficiencies and maybe even some mental imbalance. In a world of social elitism those with power ruled and dreamt of expansionism to already existing empires. War was natural and it mattered not how many of the ordinary majority population of Europe might die in such a

war. They were fodder for imperial designs and wholly expendable. The ruling classes even saw war as a way of controlling the
unruly masses.

It was also the age of nationalism, a very modern invention,
and one which now dominated political and military thinking.
Nationalism was the new religion and 'the relentless advance of
nationalist ideologies, through which the "nation-state" had
come to be seen as the highest form of human political organisation' contributed powerfully to the militarised culture.

> ... many people willingly embraced military, and militaris-
> tic, ideals. Political groups on both left and right asserted the
> benefits of military organisations and discipline, and, all across
> Europe, men were increasingly to be seen in uniform.[1]

The tone of Christian faith, expressive of European Christendom, also contributed to the militarised culture and war enthusiasm. Uniformed organisations for young men were formed in
which drilling and marching were important aspects. The Boys'
Brigade was about training boys in true manhood, a version of
'muscular Christianity', and although the Boy Scouts were more
secular, it was about directing energies into 'patriotic military
activities'.[2] Churchgoers sang fervently popular hymns like,
'Onward Christian soldiers, marching as to war', the cross was,
as Constantine intended centuries before, a military symbol of
victory with a warrior Christ at the head of an army. Imper -
ialism, nation-state politics, Christian faith and patriotic youth
provision all fed into the culture of militarism, violence and ad-
venturous enthusiasm for war. Before the great war began,
paramilitarism emerged in Ireland, first with the Ulster
Volunteer Force in 1913, followed quickly by its shadow, the
National Volunteers. Germany armed both illegal armies and,
when the first World War was declared, both Volunteer forces
were regularised when thousands joined the fight against the
Germans who had armed them in the first place. Now men
divided by competing and antagonistic national ideologies,

---

1 Jeffery, Keith, *The First World War and the Rising: Mode, Moment and
Memory in 1916: The Long Revolution,* Doherty and Keogh (editors),
(Cork: Mercier Press, 2007) pp 87-88
2 Ibid, p 88

fought and died on the same side on different Somme sites, but together in the 1917 battle at Messines ridge.

It was a time when war was in the air and violence was cent - ral to the culture. In this context Ireland was to experience the Easter Rising and lose thousands of its young men on battle-fields such as the Somme, Messines and Gallipoli.

For varied and complex reasons, over 140,000 Irishmen vol-unteered for the British Army. John Redmond, the Irish national-ist leader, had committed the Irish Volunteers to join the British cause in a speech at Woodenbridge, Co Wicklow. It was also, he believed, for 'gallant little Belgium'. Many volunteers did join but Redmond's stance had split the movement. The members of the Ulster Volunteer Force who joined were facilitated to form what amounted to their own unit, the 36th Ulster Division. The many more nationalists who joined were not allowed this privi-lege, but joined to form two largely, though not exclusively Nationalist formations, the 10th and 16th Irish Divisions.

The Battle of the Somme began on 1 July, 1916, and was one of the most bloody actions of the entire war. The 36th Ulster Division went over the top on the first day and suffered huge losses. Some 5,500 were killed or wounded leaving many homes in Protestant areas of Belfast grieving. On 12 July, Belfast came to a standstill with silence observed and the annual Orange pro-cessions had already been cancelled in the north. The losses were great and Unionists soon contrasted their loyalty and sac-rifice with what they saw as the treachery of rebels in the Rising. The Somme became embedded in unionist memory and the tradition of commemoration. It became a key focus in the Orange-Unionist calendar, monopolised to a great extent while the nationalist dead of Ireland were forgotten. Some 50,000 Irishmen died in the Great War, the majority of them nationalist. Those who returned, many with the highest awards for bravery, were despised and at times spat upon in their own local commu-nities. Unionists had their loyal war heroes, especially the dead and they were happy to ignore the rest of the Irish war dead. What did provoke their antagonism and fears was the southern nationalist indifference to the finest traditions of Ulster union-ists. The Somme, as unionists saw it, was being ignored and that was the indifference to, even disparagement of their traditions.

More immediately relevant was the extraordinary insensitivity of home rulers and Sinn Féin alike in accepting Cardinal Logue as arbitrator in the disputed Ulster constituencies in the general election of 1918. This confirmed unionists' deepest suspicions that home rule meant Rome rule. And it cast considerable doubt on the nationalist commitment to the separation of church and state, one of the specialisations of function characteristic of the modernisation process.[3]

Elsewhere in the United Kingdom the huge losses of war were remembered with grief and sorrow. That too was present in the north of Ireland but with an added dimension. It was a fervent celebration by the unionists because the 'losses sustained by the 36th (Ulster) division at the battle of the Somme in 1916 represented a sealing with blood of the political union with Great Britain, a kind of parallel "blood sacrifice" (if that is what it was) to that of Easter 1916.[4]

The Somme was an act of loyalty and sacrifice which placed the British government under obligation. The Ulster covenant had been signed only a few years earlier, some signing with their own blood, and covenant was a contractural agreement which loyal Ulstermen could ignore if the contract was not kept by the British. Now Ulstermen had well and truly sealed the covenant with their blood, literally and no longer symbolically. In time it was to be perceived that 'blood sacrifice' had given birth to partition. It was the blood of the dead that had finally liberated them from Home Rule'.[5]

In a sense the Rising and the Somme represent the Irishisation and Ulsterisation of the Great War. Whatever happened on the global scale was viewed through the frame of the Irish and Ulster problem. Both events became sacred reference points for either side in the struggle to gain independence or maintain the British connection. Each side had its theology of blood sacrifice and each had God on its side.

---

3 Lee, Joseph, *The Modernisation of Irish Society 1848-1918*, (Dublin: Gill and Macmillan, 2008) p 172
4 Jeffery, op cit, p 95
5 Tanner, Marcus, *Ireland's Holy Wars: The Struggle for a Nation's Soul*, 1500-2000 (London: Yale University Press, 2003) p 323

Belfast unveiled a war memorial in 1929 with the Latin words on it, 'For God and Nation'. The Gaelic Athletic Association, in 1922, had unveiled a statue to Archbishop Croke in Thurles with the same words inscribed.[6] There is no doubt that different nations were intended, but were they also referring to different Gods, or did God have a split personality, or was the divine two-faced?

A theology of violence was writ large in both unionist and nationalist camps. So too was 'blood sacrifice'. Pearse had described 1914-1915 as the 'most glorious in the history of Europe. Heroism has come back to earth'.[7] Blood sacrifice was part of patriotism. Writing of the war he said:

> It is good for the world that such things should be done. The old heart of the earth needed to be warmed with the red wine of the battlefields. Such august homage was never before offered to God as this, the homage of millions of lives given gladly for love of country.[8]

There was an insanity about such violent sentiments and Pearse was not alone. On the British side there were Brooke and Binyon. Nearer home a Belfast Methodist described war as a 'kind of purgatory. It is a painful but salutary remedy for softness, slackness and sensuality.' The Church of Ireland Bishop of Meath, Keene, saw the fiery trial as a 'purifying discipline'. The Catholic Primate, Cardinal Logue wrote of 'the imperishable glory which Irish Catholic soldiers have won for their country'.[9] Blood-letting and blood sacrifice were noble things, required by God for peace in the war against Germany or liberation for Ireland from the oppression of Britain.

The theme continued when in 1921 a memorial tower was dedicated in Thiepval, France, to the memory of the fallen of the 36th Ulster Division at the Somme. The Protestant church leaders were prominent. The Church of Ireland Primate, Archbishop D'Arcy, Presbyterian Moderator, Dr Lowe and Methodist President, W. H. Smyth, conducted the worship, leading the

---

6 Jeffery, op cit, p 96
7 Ibid, p 91
8 Ibid, p 91
9 Ibid, p 92

same hymn that had become an anthem on Covenant Day, 1912, 'O God our help in ages past'. Whatever the original Hebrew poet had meant, by 1912 and 1921, God was with the Ulster Protestants. Dr Lowes' sermon was a blend of empire theology, sacred violence and a warrior, partisan God. He compared the men of the 36th Ulster Division to the men of Derry who had closed the gates against King James II in 1689, an appeal to the Ulster Protestant violent tradition. Of the Somme slaughter he said: 'They fought and alas many of them fell in the cause of freedom, the cause of the empire and the cause of Ulster, because the cause of Ulster is the cause of freedom and the cause of the Empire.'[10]

Ulster here appears to be the centre of the Empire if not the centre of the universe and the blood sacrifice of the Ulstermen at the Somme was required by God 'our help in ages past'. Seemingly God requires a lot of drastic and ultimate human help as well.

Those who died in the Rising and the Somme were shaped by the culture of militarisation that had possessed Europe and by the religious culture of blood sacrifice at the heart of which was a medieval interpretation of the blood sacrifice of Jesus, both required by a violent God. In 2016 both events should be commemorated in Ireland and loss of young life grieved. But the shared theology of Rising and Great War needs serious critique as does war and violence as methods of resolving conflict and issues of power. The myth of violence, including blood sacrifice needs to be demythologised and the God who requires it, debunked and deconstructed. Such a God, fatally wounded at the Somme, in modern Irish history and killed off at Hiroshima and Nagasaki, needs to be finally laid to rest. Whatever other memorials we have or will create for 2016, let there be no memorial to the violent God of death.

On the Way to Partition
The Great War changed everything in Europe, though not the Irish or Ulster problem. Home Rule had been passed by the British House of Commons, but had been shelved because of the

---

10 Tanner, op cit , p 323

war. Irish political dynamics continued throughout 1914-1918. A revolutionary movement was taking shape in Ireland as the 1916 Rising became the most successful failure in Irish history. Carson was a member of the British cabinet which gave him a big advantage over Redmond. A policy of partition was forming in London and Prime Minister, Lloyd-George was even suggesting that Home Rule should be implemented even before the war was over. His idea included the exclusion of six Ulster counties, Antrim, Armagh, Down, Fermanagh, Londonderry and Tyrone. Redmond accepted the reality of partition but did not agree with Carson's demand that partition be permanent. Lloyd-George called an Irish Convention in 1917, representative of all Irish interests, but when it met in July, Sinn Fein refused to participate and the unionists refused to move their position. The convention did manage to agree on a home rule parliament for all Ireland, but by this stage the Convention was an irrelevance. Meanwhile, Sinn Féin had breathed new life into the nationalist movement and by the time Redmond died in 1918 his authority as a nationalist leader had been lost. Michael Collins had emerged into a leadership role, especially in relation to the Volunteers and his experience of 1916 'led him to believe that only guerrilla warfare would defeat the government forces'.[11] The Ulster crisis of 1912 had encouraged nationalists to believe that they too could form an illegal army, create an equally illegal government, face down and defeat the British military presence and achieve Irish independence. The intransigence of the unionists throughout and the British government's stalling and continuing oppressive governance in Ireland strengthened the determination of Collins and a physical force tradition to fight for independence. After all, the rights of Ireland were as valid as the rights of little Belguim for which a greater war was being fought. Somehow the British did not make that connection. The island in the middle did not see that on either side of them, little Belgium and little Ireland had the equal right to be free.

The demise of the Irish Parliamentary Party and the rise of Sinn Féin were all too obvious. Between 1917 and 1918 a series of by-elections confirmed the shift in Irish politics. In a context

11 Kinealy, Christine, *A New History of Ireland* (Stroud: Sutton Publishing, 2004) p 210

of violence and intimidation, Sinn Féin took the seat in South Longford in May 1917. Two future Irish Taoisigh (prime ministers), de Valera and Cosgrove won seats in East Clare and Kilkenny. The Volunteers and Sinn Féin were in the ascendancy, armed force and politics combining. Not everything though was going their way. In 1918 there was failure to win by-elections in South Armagh, Waterford and East Tyrone. A boost was provided by the British government's decision to extend conscription in April 1918 to Ireland, which Sinn Féin bitterly opposed and which also led to the Catholic Church coming out strongly against conscription. The opposition was such that the government postponed the implementation of conscription in Ireland and instead arrested seventy three leading members of Sinn Féin in the pretext of 'Pro-German intrigue'.[12] The government had actually abandoned conscription but damage was done and Sinn Féin's political authority was enhanced. When a general election was held over Christmas, 1918, Sinn Féin was well placed for a landslide victory. The Party won 73 of Ireland's 105 seats on a manifesto which had stressed the 'unbroken history of Irish resistance to British rule', a theme of the anti-conscription campaign.

> It is based on our unbroken tradition of nationhood, on a unity in a national name which has never been challenged, on our possession of a distinctive national culture and social order, on the moral courage and dignity of our people in the face of alien aggression.[13]

There was truth in this but it was not the truth about one million Protestant Irishmen and women in the North and that was the problem. Even then Ireland was not a monoculture and the 'unbroken tradition of nationhood' only reached back with the rest of Europe to the 19th century. The recent phenomenon of nationalism, currently tearing Europe apart and slaughtering millions was now claimed to be an unbroken tradition in Ireland.

Nevertheless, Sinn Fein's 1918 electoral victory was signifi-

---

12 Ferriter, Diarmaid, *The Transformation of Ireland 1900-2000*, (London: Profile Books, 2004) p 183
13 Ibid, p 183

cant, also because 75% of Irish adults now had a vote. Before 1918 it was only 25%. The number of those entitled to vote in 1918 had trebled. Sinn Féin's share of the vote was 47.5% which did not go unnoticed by unionists, especially when Sinn Féin was to argue later that the creation of Northern Ireland was undemocratic.

In Ulster, Cardinal Logue had played a controversial role in facilitating the process of choosing candidates, giving the Irish Parliamentary Party four constituencies and four to Sinn Féin. This confirmed unionist fears that Home Rule really was Rome Rule. Unionists did well in the election increasing their representation by eight, taking a total of 23 Ulster seats.

The seats won in the 1918 general election were all Westminster seats but Sinn Féin refused to take them. Instead they constituted Dáil Éireann on 21 January 1919, elected de Valera president and declared independence. The British government did not recognise the Irish parliament and said it was a 'dangerous association'.[14] Towards the end of 1919 a newspaper could describe the country as an 'invisible republic' with an 'underground government'. The latter it believed had used all methods, including violence, to emerge as the government of Ireland.[15]

The new Dáil made its first appointments. Arthur Griffith, founder of Sinn Féin was deputy president to de Valera, Countess Markievicz, the first woman to be elected to the British parliament, though she did not take her seat, was appointed Minister of Labour and Collins was put 'in charge of the military campaign to resist British intervention'.[16]

The Dáil proceeded to do three things. It ratified the 1916 Proclamation, asked the international community to recognise Ireland as a republic and produced a Democratic Programme.

The 1916 Proclamation had been shaped by two movements, the physical force tradition, especially of the Irish Republican Brotherhood, and the socialist doctrine of James Connolly. It began in the 'name of God' and immediately named the 'secret revolutionary organisation' and 'her open military organis-

14 Ibid, p 184
15 Ibid, p 187
16 Kinealy, op cit, p 211

ations'. The right to freedom had been asserted 'six times in the past three hundred years ... in arms'. Furthermore, 'Standing in that fundamental right and again asserting it in arms in the face of the world, we hereby proclaim the Irish Republic as a Sovereign Independent State ...'

God, physical force, violence and independence were affirmed and asserted and in the minds of the authors, they were indivisible. The question though remains, who is this God of physical force and violence of both Ulster Covenant and Easter Proclamation? Is this the warrior God of 19th century nationalism, the God of empire, an ideological God invented by patriots obsessed by violence? It may well be that people obsessed by violence projected their own violence, fear and inability to resolve conflict by any other means onto the Christian idea of God. Or maybe the accepted Christian idea of God was violent and in the churches was the theological norm.

The second half of the Proclamation did contain a remarkable vision of social justice and had Connolly's fingerprints all over it.

> The Republic guarantees religious and civil liberty, equal rights and equal opportunities to all its citizens and declares its resolve to pursue the happiness and prosperity of the whole nation and all its parts, cherishing all the children of the nation equally ...

Whether Connolly would have acknowledged it or not, it was a social vision with its roots in the Judeo-Christian tradition. Ancient Israel's basic credo, its primary story of Exodus liberation, the radical prophetic tradition of Amos, Jeremiah and Isaiah, Jesus' core vision of the kingdom of God and Paul's proclamation of liberating social justice at the heart of a letter like Romans, all had an egalitarian streak, an equality commitment and a justice praxis. The Proclamation was also anti-sectarian in its sentiments, oblivious of the differences, cultivated by the British divide and rule policy. The vision did include the Protestants of the north-east. But what of the social vision was ever realised? Sectarian violence destroyed it from the start. The vision of social equality and equal cherishing of all, built into the Democratic Programme was soon also left behind as a Dáil without Labour influence, devoid of working class member-ship, became more obsessed with power and holding onto it than with social vision and policy. It may be asked if the chil-dren of the nation have ever been cherished equally, north or south? Social and political conservatism, reinforced by influen-tial churches conspired to keep Irish people divided and to ensure that the social vision of equality would not be realised. After 1921 it could not be blamed on the British. Once in power in Dublin and Belfast, the Irish politicians mirrored the British and showed themselves equally adept at divide and rule, and perpetuating sectarian religion and politics with violence. The physical force traditions also remained and retained the right to assert or defend their rights, however they saw it, to inflict violent destruction, division and injustice on Catholic and Protestant people who, as always, were mainly the non-combat-ants and innocent. Violence not only destroyed lives, it de-stroyed creative, social vision which ultimately did disable human social well-being in Ireland.

The War of Independence
The new Dail was struggling to govern against the backdrop of a war, known either as the Anglo-Irish war or the war of inde-pendence. It began in Soloheadbeg, Co Tipperary, on 21 January 1919, with the killing of two policemen, members of the Royal Irish Constabulary (RIC). It was carried out by Irish Volunteers who increasingly became known as the Irish Republican Army (IRA). Directed by Collins, the IRA became embroiled in a guer-rilla war characterised by ambushes, assassinations and raids on RIC barracks. Flying columns were created and according to an IRA newspaper were entitled to use 'all legitimate methods of warfare against the soldiers and policemen of the English usurpers and slay them if necessary to overcome their resist-ance'.[17] Legitimate methods were not defined but the flying columns soon became ruthless and efficient in their methods. The British responded with equally brutal methods through the formation of the Black and Tans and the Auxiliaries.

The Black and Tans were so called because of the colour of their uniforms. They consisted of men already brutalised by the

17 Ferriter, op cit, p 221

Great War experience and came to Ireland with anti-Irish stereotypes and a lack of discipline. Their methods included harass-
ment and reprisals and the shooting of farmers' livestock to supplement their rations and diet. Their most notorious reprisals
were in Balbriggan, Ennistymon and Cork. Brutally they set fire
to houses and, in one case, shot a young husband and then
threw him into the blazing house.[18] The 'Tans' engendered intense hatred and an increasing spiral of violence deepened the
brutality of the war. Two particular events stand out.

Bloody Sunday occurred in November 1920. Collins gave orders, as a result of his intelligence network, to assassinate British
officers in their beds. Fourteen British officers were assassinated,
not all of whom were intelligence agents as supposed. The
'Tans' took indiscriminate revenge by firing into a crowd in
Croke Park for a GAA match, killing 12 civilians. Collins' brutality in the morning was matched by the army brutality in the af-
ternoon. A week later, near the West Cork village of Kilmichael,
between Dunmanway and Macroom, a flying column ambushed a party of Auxiliaries. Seventeen Auxiliary cadets were
killed, some after being clubbed and then shot. 'Only one
Auxiliary survived, crippled and comatose.'[19] From the IRA
perspective it was 'a brave, daring, and even brilliant ambush
but it turned into a massacre'.[20] It was an annihilation intended
to shock and send a message to the British that they could be defeated. But it was summary execution and it defined the morality or immorality of the war. A few weeks later the Black and
Tans took revenge by torching much of the centre of Cork.

The Black and Tans were later described as 'the greatest blot
on the record of the coalition and perhaps on Britain's name in
the twentieth century'.[21] Since 1916, British policy had been repressive and hard line and often illegal. As an emerging liberal
democracy, Britain had no credibility in the world because of its
actions in Ireland. The lesson that guerrilla warfare could not be

---

18 Ibid, p 234
19 Hart, Peter, *The IRA and Its Enemies: Violence and Community in Cork
1916-1923* (Oxford: Clarendon Press, 1998) p 23. Hart devotes an entire
chapter to the ambush, ch 2, pp 23-38
20 Ibid, p 37
21 Ferriter, op cit, p 255

defeated militarily lay far ahead in the 1990s. It took a similar timespan for the IRA to realise that guerrilla methodology could not defeat an army of 40,000 soldiers and 10,000 armed police in Ireland then or in the most recent phase of violence in Northern Ireland. Meanwhile British military activity in the war of independence was successful in 'manufacturing Sinn Féiners in Ireland'.[22]

The brutality of the 'Tans' and Auxiliaries was matched by that of the IRA. British abuses were mirrored by flying columns. Kilmichael became a highly venerated IRA victory but as Peter Hart has shown, a brave ambush 'became a cowardly massacre which involved the deliberate killing of already surrendered soldiers'.[23] In Cork alone, between 1917-1923, over 700 people died, 400 killed by the IRA. Of the total dead, one third were civilians. The IRA 'deliberately shot over 200 citizens, of whom over 70 were Protestant, one of the reasons for the reduction by 34 per cent of the Protestant population of the south from 1911 to 1921'.[24] There was a brutal sectarian dimension to the IRA brutality. Protestants were abused and demonised by the use of pejorative names, which justified killing them. In April/May 1922, ten Protestants were shot dead in the Bandon valley. James Buttimer, a Dunmanway Methodist, was awakened by shooting and banging at the door. After pleading with a group of armed men he was shot in the face, 'his brains and teeth blown out'.[25]

Two others were already dead in the Main Street. Others escaped but killings continued the following night. In all, ten Protestants were dead. In the previous two years 'Scores of Cork Protestants had been killed as "spies" or "informers" ... Hundreds went into hiding or fled their homes as a wave of panic, fanned by threats and rumours, raced through West Cork.[26] The latter flight occurred after the Bandon valley murders. Trainloads of refugees passed through Cork, many to Belfast and England. Cork had produced an unprecedented

---

22 Ibid, p 234
23 Ibid, p 227. See Hart, op cit , p 23
24 Ibid, p 227. Quoting Hart's research
25 Hart, op cit , p 273
26 Ibid, p 277

Protestant massacre, which some thought were reprisals for attacks on Catholics in the north. The killings had included Thomas and Samuel Hornebrook and Herbert Woods, all executed and whose bodies have never been found.[27]

It is difficult to know if the Cork massacres were reprisals for the sectarian violence in the north in 1920 when Catholics were expelled from the Belfast shipyards and factories. August riots had resulted in 30 deaths in Belfast. Or were the sectarian riots and killings in Belfast a response to the violence of the war of independence? The question may be facile. The reality was that Munster, Leinster and Belfast had spiraled into vortex of violence, much of it indiscriminate and not a little of it nakedly sectarian. But then religious and political sectarianism was at the heart of the Irish problem and while British divide and rule policy exploited it, sectarianism was and is an Irish disease, the cause of many Irish deaths in the 20th century, most of them civilian and innocent.

Partition

As the violence increased, Lloyd-George and the coalition government were preparing what they hoped would be a constitutional settlement. The architect was a Conservative MP, Walter Long, who originally proposed that Ireland should have two parliaments, subordinate to Westminster. The Ulster parliament was to be responsible for 9 counties. He also suggested a Council of Ireland, consisting of 20 members from each new parliament with the task of developing an all-Ireland parliament. Long had been a former leader of the Ulster Unionists, but his Government of Ireland Act 1920, disturbed the new Ulster Unionist leader, James Craig, who had just succeeded Edward Carson who had resigned. Craig feared that the inclusion of Cavan, Donegal and Monaghan would weaken a Protestant government in Belfast. A nine-county Northern Ireland had been proposed back in 1914, but then it was realised that such an entity would leave a vulnerable Protestant majority, which might be easily overturned.

The Ulster Unionists, who had not originally wanted self-government within the United Kingdom, eventually came to see

---

27 Ibid, p 279

the advantage of the new proposals, particularly in the light of the IRA's violent campaign throughout Ireland. 'We see our safety in having a Parliament of our own', wrote Captain Charles Craig (brother of the Ulster Unionist leader), 'We feel that we would then be in a position of absolute security'.[28]

The acceptance, though, was based on a six-county state which left the Unionists with an untouchable majority. The Unionists successfully lobbied for the smaller, more secure alternative and the Government of Ireland Act included the six-county option. On 23 December 1920, the Act easily passed through the Westminster parliament and it became operative in May 1921.

Twenty-six southern counties became Southern Ireland and elections were held in both parts of Ireland.

Southern Ireland	Northern Ireland
Sinn Féin 124	Unionists 40
Independents 4	Nationalists 6
	Independents 4

On 7 June, 1921, the Northern Ireland parliament met, elected James Craig as Prime Minister and on the 22nd, King George V, officially opened the new parliament in Belfast City Hall. The King's speech made clear that it was never intended to last. He appealed 'to all Irishmen to pause, stretch out the hand of forbearance and conciliation, and to join in making for the land which they love a new era of peace, contentment and goodwill'.[29] It was a call for reconciliation, which included political reconciliation.

On 16 August, Sinn Féin convened the second Dáil. The Dáil lasted less than a year. Sinn Féin had nothing but contempt for the Act and the great paradox now was that the Ulster Unionists were the Home Rulers and Sinn Féin was rejecting it.

Was partition inevitable? The war of independence had not helped. The British state violence, along with that of the IRA and the northern unionists perhaps did make the government of Ireland Act inevitable. The violence was so intense, brutal and

28 Adelman, Paul and Pearce, Robert, *Great Britain and the Irish Question 1800-1922* (London: Hodder and Stoughton, 2001) p 138
29 Quoted in Kinealy, op cit, p 213

sectarian that no other solution may have been possible at the time.

Yet, it has been suggested that the Act was 'essentially constructed to solve the Irish problem as it stood in 1914 and not in 1920'.[30] If that was the case then the Act was not likely to be an effective solution. Dated solution or not, 'a separate Belfast administration had been created with great care and thoroughness by civil servants during 1920 ...' Dublin Castle passed its experience and resources onto 'a successor administration for Belfast'.[31] Partition was dismissed as an irrelevance by nationalists, who may even have thought it would go away, and was copperfastened by Castle civil servants collaborating with the Ulster Unionists. In a sense both unionists and nationalists ensured that partition would last.

The other great paradox of partition was that it 'was the first step in the dismemberment of the British Empire'.[32] Partition meant that the British government was able to off-load the sectarian religious and political problems of Ireland, exacerbated by the Act of Union in 1801, to Dublin and Belfast. That led to sectarian violence in the north through vicious killings, mainly of Catholics and described as a pogrom. It led to a brutal civil war in the south when Irishmen turned a brutality and a bloodlust on each other worse than anything the British had committed. Britain's oldest colony was divided and convulsed by violence, Irishmen on Irishmen, south and north. British imperial violence and sectarian violence had brought Ireland to a less than satisfactory place. As the establishment in Britain feared, India was next out of the Empire, albeit almost three decades later.

Anglo-Irish Treaty and Civil War
Between July and December 1921, intense negotiations took place and at 2.30am on 6 December 1921, the Anglo-Irish Treaty was signed. The twenty-six counties were to be known as the Irish Free State, becoming self-governing as a dominion of the British Empire. Naval bases were retained by Britain in Irish

---

30 Quoted in Adelman and Pearce, op cit, p 139
31 Foster, Roy, *Modern Ireland 1600-1972* (London: Penguin Books, 1988) p 503
32 Kinealy, op cit , p 215

ports and members of the Dublin parliament still swore an oath
to the Crown. The major Irish concern was unity even though
partition was already a reality. The British were determined to
keep Ireland in the Empire. Collins was sent by de Valera to lead
the Irish delegation to London and de Valera's own absence
from the negotiations has remained controversial. Collins
would be the fall-guy.

Neither the Irish nor the British wanted the resumption of a
military war, realising as both did that neither side could win.
Collins and his team returned to Dublin believing that the terms
of the Treaty were the best they could have got. It was 'a com-
promise between dominion status and the elusive republic'.[33]
They agreed in the early hours of 6 December after Lloyd-
George had threatened 'war within three days' if they did not
sign.

In the Dáil the Treaty was debated from 14 December 1921 to
7 January 1922. De Valera was totally opposed to the Treaty and
made many interjections. Collins made, what his biographer described as, 'easily the best speech of Collin's life and one of the
greatest statements of political rationality in Irish history'.[34] In
emotional and heated debates, dead men and children yet un-
born were invoked and whether or not they would approve of
the Treaty. Collins reflected that few 'have spoken as to whether
the living approve of it'. He ended his speech with the stirring
words:

> Dont let us put the responsibility, the individual responsibil-
> ity, upon anyone else. Let us take that responsibility our-
> selves and let us in God's name abide by the decision.[35]

When the decision came the Treaty was carried by 64 votes to
57, a small majority. The cabinet had voted for it by 4 votes to 3.
The anti-Treaty members retained the name Sinn Féin and led
by de Valera they withdrew from the Dáil, believing that the
Treaty was a betrayal of the Republic proclaimed by Pearse in
1916. In June 1922, a general election endorsed the Treaty.

33 Ferriter, op cit, p 240
34 Peter Hart quoted in Aldous, Richard (ed), *Great Irish Speeches*
(London: Quercus, 2007) p 71
35 Ibid, p 74

Collins was still in charge of the Irish Republican Brother-hood and persuaded half of its members to join the Free State army. The anti-Treaty half established themselves in the Four Courts, Dublin. On 28 June, the Free State army began a bombardment of the Four Courts. A civil war had begun 'more brutal and more destructive than the earlier Anglo-Irish war ...'[36] By 20th August, Collins was killed in an ambush in Co Cork. A few days earlier, Arthur Griffith had died of a brain hemorrhage leaving the Free State without its key leaders. The new leader, William Cosgrave, interned many of the anti-Treaty forces and executed nearly eighty. By December the Irregulars were defeated but kept fighting until April when their leader Liam Lynch died. His successor, Frank Aiken, called for a unilateral ceasefire and for the dumping of arms. Almost a thousand people had been killed. 'In the final six months of the civil war, the Irish government had executed twice as many people as were executed by the British during the turbulent years between 1916 and 1921.'[37] Even when the war had ended executions still continued and by the beginning of 1923, some 12,000 anti-Treaty soldiers were still imprisoned.

> The civil war that followed in 1922-3 looms larger in Irish history than the 'Anglo-Irish' war, because it was both more traumatic and more influential ... By contrast, the civil war created a caesura across Irish history, separating parties, interests and even families, and creating the rationale for political divisions that endured.[38]

By September 1922, the partition of Ireland was a constitutional reality with a Free State constitution and Northern Ireland formally excluded from the Free State by Article XII of the Treaty. The north had its own killing fields. Sectarian gun battles ensued. The new police Specials, B Specials, produced another 'bloody Sunday' in Belfast when they fired into nationalist areas with rifles, revolvers and machine guns. This happened on the 10 July 1921 and by the end of the week 23 civilians were dead, 17 Catholics and 7 Protestants. Many more were in-

---

36 Adelman and Pearce, op cit , p 145
37 Kinealy, op cit, p 219
38 Foster, op cit, p 511

jured and more than 200 Catholic homes were destroyed. The sectarian brutality of the north and the human cost can be measured by the statistics from July 1920-1922.

453 killed: 257 Catholics, 196 Protestants
8,750 Catholics driven from employment
23,000 Catholics driven from homes[39]

When RIC Dstrict-Inspector Swanzy was murdered by the IRA on leaving a Lisburn church on Sunday, 22 August 1920, loyalist mobs took revenge on Lisburn Catholics. Shops and pubs were looted and homes were burned. The entire Catholic population of Lisburn, up to 1,000, fled to west Belfast. Meanwhile loyalist violence spread to east Belfast and the small Catholic enclave in Ballymacarrett was the target. The police and army were inactive and no one was ever charged for the Lisburn destruction. By 1922 the British government was alarmed and put pressure on the two Irish governments to reach an agreement. Craig and Collins did meet and a Pact agreed on an end to the boycott of Northern goods, the re-employment of Catholics driven from the shipyard, an end to IRA activity in Northern Ireland and the establishment of a Catholic-Protestant police force. The Craig-Collins pacts did nothing to change the violence.

After a decade of violence Ireland was partitioned. Both states had been born in violence and after partition, not only were there two confessional and arguably sectarian states, they continued in anarchy, lawlessness, civil war and a pogrom. The violence in the north remained with periodic outbreaks until a prolonged phase erupted in 1969. Both governments behaved after partition in repressive ways and in many ways mirrored the repression of the British in Ireland during the decade.

It was a decade of change, huge change, that still shapes community life and relations in Ireland. It was also a decade of violence and the difficulty with the centenaries is how we commemorate violence. These events were major defining moments in modern Irish history which should be commemorated in a shared and cohesive way, but it would be an unethical use of memory to commemorate these political events and ignore the

39 Source: Kinealy, op cit , p 227

fact that all of them were surrounded by, and steeped in, violence. It is true that violence and war were pervasive and core to European psyches at the beginning of the 20th century. It was the European ethos at the time but that cannot justify the use of violence by all sides in Ireland during this significant decade.

As much of Europe struggled to build liberal democracies the tension in Ireland was between the values of liberal democracies and those of narrow nationalisms. Nationalism and liberal democracy have different priorities and values, the former locating ultimate value in the concept of nation, the latter seeing individual persons as the 'only locus of moral significance'.[40] Unionists and nationalists were more committed to their brands of nationalism: the cause mattered more than people, and the latter were expendable. Or in the violent language of nationalism, British or Irish, the cause is sacred and people are called to make the supreme sacrifice. The big ethical problem was, most of those who died in the decade were civilians, what later 20th and 21st century warfare obscenely called 'collateral damage'.

Committed ultimately to nationalism, unionists and nationalists not surprisingly ignored democratic majorities. The Treaty was passed by the cabinet and Dáil and the following general election returned majority pro-Treaty candidates, but Sinn Féin in the name of the violent and sacred cause ignored the democratic majority. Unionists likewise had no intention of accepting the democratic wishes of the Irish people in the 1918 general election and the democratic wish for home rule. At the same time they ensured a six county rather than a nine county Northern Ireland with an untouchable ruling majority. Orange or green nationalisms were the driving forces, no matter how many might die for Ulster or Ireland, and liberal democracy was suspect to say the least.

Commemoration is the wrong word for the events of 2012-2023. It would be unethical to commemorate violence and unethical to pretend it didn't happen. Acknowledgement is a better, if not more ethical word. We can acknowledge 1912 - 1923 as a decade of change and violence, and should acknowledge it as a decade

---

40 Murphy, Seamus, *Easter Ethics in 1916: The Long Revolution*, op cit, p 335

of change and violence. And unionists and nationalists need to acknowledge the decade together. It will mean acknowledging the events and the symbolic relationship between all of them, and acknowledging the mirror image violence we turned on each other. Ethical remembering will also mean a shared commitment to never again allow violence become the means of settling differences. Between 1912-1922 we were obsessed by violence, in love with it, even possessed by it, including a God of violence. Ethical remembering and acknowledgement can be liberating.

CHAPTER FIVE

Blame it on the Babylonians, They started it!

The decade of change in Ireland was steeped in violence. The unionists used it to defend their cause, the nationalists to assert and hopefully achieve their cause. All of it left a romantic virus in which violence was all-pervasive, heroes were martyrs for the cause and the supreme sacrifice was to die for Ireland or Ulster. The theology of blood sacrifice was as pervasive as the violence. Europe had entered the 20th century with its leaders straining for war convinced of its cleansing effect and its redemptive power. The warrior God and the holy war were at the heart of the elite European consciousness. This same consciousness controlled the masses and millions went to their deaths for it. Ireland was not outside this ethos. In Ireland also there were nationalists, orange and green in love with violence, committed to the God of violence and believing in its redemptive power.

The roots of violence were not in Europe, nor in modern European consciousness. In fact the roots of violence pre-dated the birth of Europe and stretched back millennia to the ancient city-states of Babylon. The origins and roots of violence lay in a very ancient myth, myth with the capacity to reinvent itself repeatedly right down to the present. The myth of redemptive violence or the myth that violence liberates goes back very early in the human time-frame. Before tracing it back to the Babylonian city-states it is important to appreciate the nature and power of myth.

The Reality of Myth

In our scientific world, myth has been dismissed as fairytale, make-believe and definitely untrue. Our literalistic world of facts has no place for myth. An Oxford Dictionary defines myth as 'a widely held story or belief which, on examination turns out to be entirely untrue'.[1] The popular expression 'it's a myth' is intended to convey that it is untrue, not to be believed. The assumption behind this is that only those things which are literally or historically factual are true. Only the factual is true. But this is

---

1 Price, Bill, *Celtic Myths* (Harpenden: Pocket Essentials, 2008) p 12

a very narrow understanding of what is true. There is something more profoundly true in the Amerindian's preface to his tribal creation story. 'I don't know if it happened this way or not, but it's true.' Beyond the narrow limitations of our scientific worldview there are more things true than we can imagine. Imagination produces myth and myth is story. It is profoundly more and 'we must understand myth as meaning in story form'.[2] We create myths or tell stories to make meaning, make sense out of some life experience.

The Belfast-built *Titanic* sank in 1912 on its first voyage, the unsinkable ship holed by an iceberg. The disaster occurred in the same year as the Ulster Covenant and the forthcoming centenaries may well be dominated, perhaps for commercial reasons, by the *Titanic*. The Titanic has cast a spell over many people for almost a century. There is an unquenchable fascination with its story, and its story has grown and been re-imagined a number of times. At a basic level there is the iceberg, no doubt taking shape and forming before the ship was built in the Belfast shipyards. Titanic story poses a perennial question, why is nature so often hostile to human endeavour? But as Ellwood points out, other questions of meaning arise:

> … why the arrogance of those who considered the ship unsinkable, the heedlessness of not providing enough lifeboats, the pride of kind which so divided the passengers into classes hardly aware of one another as real people? All those issues we find explained over and over as myth.[3]

In 1997, James Cameron produced the famous movie, *Titanic*, and here was another level of meaning.

> The movie *Titanic* added another theme to cosmic and general human sources of evil – the hero myth, with its implication that one way to understand evil is the mythic way, that is through the medium of story. This film frames evil, both natural and human, as adversary a hero must overcome.[4]

---

2 Ellwood, Robert, *Tales of Darkness: The Mythology of Evil* (London: Continuum, 2009) p.3
3 Ibid, p 3
4 Ibid, p 3

Who knows if the main characters played in *Titanic* ever existed or not; or if the storyline really happened? Probably not, but is it untrue? The story is profoundly true at another level of meaning. There is deeper truth here in our human struggle with evil. The movie *Titanic* is a myth and true. Story and meaning then are essential to myth.

> Myths, like modern fiction or art in general, can be seen as a way of attempting to describe what may otherwise be inexplicable and to provide, at least to some extent, meaning and understanding amidst the complexities and vicissitudes of life.[5]

The reality of evil in the world cannot be explained rationally, yet we must find some kind of meaning in the face of evil. The imagination creates story, a way of getting behind what cannot be explained in rational terms. The same can be true of goodness and not just evil. Or clans and tribes and ethnic groups have their creation stories and sometimes their end stories. No one was there at the 'beginning', no one witnessed the forming of the universe, so stories are told and imagined. The creators of such myth know that they are not literally or factually true, but they are told to give meaning to that which is beyond human knowing, they are true in a much deeper sense.

Myth, as philosopher Paul Ricoeur pointed out is 'a species of symbol ... Myth is symbol in narrative form'.[6] A good example is the Hebrew myth of Adam and Eve. It provides symbols of human experience. It 'not only offers an explanation of evil, but points to exile as an ultimate metaphor for the human situation'.[7] It is not a historically true story and the Hebrew storytellers knew that better than children of the modern Enlightenment do. The story is profoundly true as every person's story, this is who I am and what the world is really like.

Myths are powerful stories full of powerful metaphors and symbol-laden. They provide pointers of meaning to ultimate and complex questions. Sometimes they are creation myths and sometimes foundational myths, stories told about how a group of people came together to form a society. 'Myths demonstrate a

---

5 Price, op cit, p 13
6 Ellwood, op cit, p 7
7 Ibid, p 7

system of ethics and morals'.[8] Myths provide ways to live and values to live by. They provide us with a window or way of looking at the world. They try to offer explanations as to why things are as they are, and may suggest to us that this is the nature of things. This can be both positive and negative. Myths wrestle with answers to questions often beyond the reach of human consciousness. Myths reach out for truth beyond the capacity of rational minds. It requires imagination to create or re-create myths and also to appreciate them. Religion expresses itself more in myth than our scientifically shaped minds and Enlightenment rationality realise. To make sense of God and evil we need to recover the power of myth and to be at home with mythology.

The Myth of Redemptive Violence

The original myth emerged from the Babylonian city-states. It was a creation myth at the heart of which was violence. In fact, it claimed the creation of the world and humans came out of violence. Violence and war are realities and this is how things are. But it was not always the way.

The human story may have developed over five thousand years without domination of war and violence. The earliest evidence for human societies goes back to 9,000 BCE. Mesopotamia was the heart of early human civilisation and even as population increased and animals were domesticated, there is no evidence of overt warfare. Even when tools were invented they were used for hunting and domestic living, with nothing to suggest that they were weapons of war. 'Most strikingly, there is very little evidence of warfare between 9,000 and 4,000 BCE, and not a great deal until around 3,000, after which it proliferates dramatically'.[9] Even in the fourth millennium, war and violence did occur but did not dominate human existence. It is remarkable that 'Civilisation began four to five thousand years before the first evidences of war'.[10] Wink points up the evidence that archeologists have unearthed cities, unwalled, undisturbed and unplundered and that in Neolithic paintings there are no war-

8 Price, op cit, p 17
9 Wink, Walter, *Engaging the Powers: Discernment and Resistance in a World of Domination* (Minneapolis: Fortress Press, 1992) p 36
10 Ibid, p 36

riors or heroic conquerors, battle axes or swords. This is not to
say that there were no clashes or that blood was not shed, but it
does point to a largely peaceful existence. 'Egypt flourished
without a standing army for the first 1500 years of its history.'[11]
Not only were these early societies relatively peaceful, they
were also basically egalitarian. And this seems to be the evidence from Old Europe, the Near East, Mexico and the
Amerindians. Neither were these societies matriarchical or pa-
triarchical, ruled by women or men. There is evidence of sexual
equality, partnership societies, co-operation rather than compe-
tition and what Wink has described as 'actualisation hierarchies
(where leaders serve the communities) rather than domination
hierarchies (where communities must serve the leaders)'.[12] This
is not a retrospective reconstruction of paradise or utopia. All of
human history has been a history of struggle and the myth of a
Fall is not a myth created out of an historical moment, still less a
moment experienced four to five thousand years after the earliest evidence of human civilisation. The myths of a human Fall,
including the Hebrew one (Genesis 2-3) are stories about who
we are and what life is like.

Around 3,000 BCE in the city-states of Sumer and Babylon
something radical did take place and relative peace and egali-
tarianism gave way to war, violence and patriarchy. The city-
states became autocratic and standing armies appeared with
new bronze weapons and horses.

> Their social system had become rigidly hierarchical, authorit-
> arian, and patriarchal. Some of these warrior peoples wor-
> shipped their weapons. Others revered divinities of war,
> whose will decreed the massacre of their male victims and
> the sexual subjugation of their female victims.[13]

Hierarchy, patriarchy, warfare, warrior gods and the subjug-
ation of women all appear to have developed together after 3000
BCE, and all appear to be connected. In relation to women the
earliest known law code came from Mesopotamia around 2,300
BCE and seeks to violently control women. Prior to that women

---

11 Ibid, p 37
12 Ibid, p 37
13 Ibid, p 39

could take two husbands, but after 2,300 BCE they were stoned, presumably to death, if they tried to take more than one husband, and if they spoke disrespectfully to a man, the mouth was crushed by a fire brick.[14] The domination system at the heart of the city-states was controlled by violence and women too were kept in their socially inferior place by violence. The rise of the city-states was about the rise of male supremacy, male violence and inferior status for women, the poor, slaves and captives. This called for the creation of new myths to explain why things were as they were, to 'define reality' and to make sense out of violent, domination systems.

In this context Babylon came up with a creation myth, the Enuma Elish. The earliest known version of the myth dates to around 1250 BCE from tablet texts found at Ashur, Nineveh, Kish and Uruk. 'In fact the epic is primarily a celebration of the Mesopotamian city of Babylon and its city god Marduk'.[15] The myth has multiple levels of meaning, one of which was to 'justify the rise of Marduk from his status as a minor Sumerian deity to chief of the Babylonian pantheon during the reign of Nebuchadnezzar I in the twelfth century BCE'.[16] The Enuma Elish also marks a change in Babylonian mythology reflecting a change in the ethos of society. A society characterised by 'cultural principles centred on fertility and the balance of male and female roles' was giving way to a 'much more patriarchal and hierarchical perspective ...'[17] It is above all a violent myth justifying violence to defend, achieve or assert in the name of a warrior god.

The Enuma Elish begins with a description of the beginning of time. The skies above and the earth below are not yet named.[18] Apsu and Tiamat, the god and goddess gave birth to the gods. The younger gods make so much noise that the older gods plot to kill them and restore peace and quiet. The plot is discovered and Apsu is killed. Tiamat looks for revenge. Ea and the younger

14 Ibid, p 40
15 Leeming, David, *The Oxford Companion to World Mythology* (Oxford: Oxford University Press, 2005) p 122
16 Ibid, p 122
17 Ibid, p 42
18 The essence of the myth is helpfully told in ibid, pp 123-124

gods are terrified and seek help from Marduk, a huge powerful god with four heads, who has already irritated Tiamat by causing great waves and noise. Tiamat began to form an army of monsters, which really terrified the younger gods. Marduk will only agree to help the younger gods if they make him their new king, give him absolute and undisputed power in the assembly of the gods. They agreed and so Marduk approached Tiamat, caught her in a net and as storm god he filled her grotesque mouth with wind, then pierced her bloated body with an arrow, split her skull with a club and scattered her blood. He then stretched her dead and violated body and from that act of violence created the universe.

The purpose of myths is to make meaning, to explain the way things are. In Mesopotamia there had been an earlier Sumerian creation myth in which the female aspect was import - ant in terms of fertility and irrigation. These were important in an agricultural society. The new myth has a male storm god create the world out of the dead body of violated and defeated feminine power, Tiamat. This all-dominating male god is essential to Babylonian national priorities and security. Babylon must confront threats to its hegemony and control, defend its territory and assert its supreme power. Marduk is a victorious, warrior god, an all-powerful male god whose hierarchical power is superior to the watery chaos of the feminine Tiamat.

Out of the act of violence and dead body of Tiamat, Marduk creates the skies and the earth, the planets and the stars and proper order is established. Out of Tiamat's dead son Kengu's blood, humans are created to do the work the gods would normally do. Humans too are created out of violence and to be violent. This is how things are, its the nature of things. Marduk has brought social and political order to the otherwise chaotic social and religious systems, a temple is built in Babylon and Marduk is celebrated and worshipped as the supreme deity.

The Enuma Elish portrays creation as an act of violence, chaos is prior to order, violence established order and peace. Evil is prior to good, violence is inherent to god and humanity. Humans are created out of violence to serve a violent god. 'Our very origin is violence. Killing is in our blood.'[19] The god is male and male is supreme and male humans serve the will of the god

19 Wink, op cit, p 15

and sacrifice themselves for the god and the higher order, good and peace.

At the beginning of the Babylonian new year the Babylonians re-enacted this original battle. The King was Marduk's representative on earth, god's representative and during each new year ritual the King played the part of Marduk. A priest would stroke the King's face and pull his ears. The new year ritual was cultic, religious and military, a combination that remains along with the myth of redemptive violence. Politics is divinised and salvation is politics and peace is through violence and war.

Paul Ricoeur, the philosopher, has described the Enuma Elish myth as a 'theology of war founded on the identification of the enemy with the powers that the god has vanquished and continues to vanquish in the drama of creation. Every coherent theology of holy war ultimately reverts to this basic mythological type'.[20]

The roots of violence, then, are in this Babylonian myth. Violence did not originate in modern Irish history, but modern Irish history has been shaped by a Babylonian story, the same myth that underpinned the wars of the bloody 20th century and which has shaped the theology of 'supreme sacrifice' or 'blood sacrifice'.

> The ancient mythic structure has been vicariously called the Babylonian creation story, the combat myth, the ideology of zealous nationalism and the myth of redemptive violence. The distinctive feature of the myth is the victory of order over chaos by means of violence. The myth is the original religion of the *status quo*, the first articulation of 'might makes right'. It is the basic ideology of the Domination System ... Religion exists to legitimate power and privilege. Life is combat ... Peace through war, security through strength: these are the core convictions that arise from this ancient historical religion.[21]

---

20 Ibid, p 16 Wink's reference is to Ricoeur's book, *The Symbolism of Evil*, p 198 (New York: Harper and Row, 1967)
21 Wink, ibid, pp 16-17

It is the same myth that has underpinned every imperial system and its military and economic expansionism. It is the myth absolute of nationalism and nationalistic superiority. It is the myth of sexism and gender inequality and control of women's bodies and minds. The Enuma Elish is the 'ideology that rationalises the subordination of women in patriarchal societies by presenting their subordination as if it were a natural state'.[22] Faith communities have bought into the myth, colluded with it when they have blessed and legitimised wars, been ambivalent about violence and when they have been part of the subordination and control of women in society and church.

In the decade of 1912-1922, as with the rest of modern Irish history, the myth of redemptive violence has been all-pervasive through the repression of the British system and the repression and violence of Orange and Green nationalisms. From Covenant through Rising, Somme, Partition, Civil War and Belfast Pogrom, the Enuma Elish, myth of redemptive violence or ideology of zealous nationalism has been in the foreground. A warrior god has been at the heart of it and the churches have never really questioned it.

The myth of redemptive violence with its Babylonian origins and its supreme deity Marduk, given unquestioning obedience and for whom the supreme sacrifice is made eventually co-opted the god of the monotheistic traditions. Marduk was even replaced by the monotheistic, warrior God of Judaism, Christianity and Islam. It's the same Babylonian myth that 'enshrines the belief that violence saves, that war brings peace, that might makes right. It is one of the oldest continuously repeated stories in the world.'[23]

Irish Myths of Violence
Irish tradition is rich in mythology. It has taken its place among the best storytelling traditions in Europe. There are various books and cycles preserved thanks to the early Christian monks who wrote them down and were drawing on material much earlier than their written manuscripts. These 6th century monks

22 Ibid, p 17
23 Wink, Walter, *The Powers That Be: Theology for a New Millennium* (New York: Doubleday, 1998) p 42

saw no conflict of interest between their biblical and theological writing and mythology. They obviously had a greater appreciation of myth than contemporary Irish people. An imaginative storytelling tradition recognised a good myth when it heard one, including the mythological genre in the Bible itself.

> ... the monks were committed to their Christian point of view and made certain Christian adaptations, but they were Irishmen, clearly intent on preserving Irish culture. Furthermore, Irish-Celtic culture had been less disrupted than that of the rest of the British Isles by the arrival of Romans and Christians ... Finally, the hereditary *filidh* continued to preserve and orally transmit the ancient stories well after the establishment of Christianity.[24]

The official storytellers preserved the myths which the Christian monks committed to writing. These included heroic mythology and the best known are a cycle of tales known as the Ulster cycle or the Red Branch cycle. The Ulster cycle includes the great Irish epic narrative of the *Táin*, the Cattle Raid of Cooley, drawn from the Book of Dun Cow and the Book of Leinster. Irish mythology is rich in heroic narrative, also tragic in which we encounter people such as Cúchulainn, Conchobar, Fergus, Queen Meabh, Finn and Oisin. As well as the Táin there is the Fenian cycle and the heroic stories of Finn. These are myths saturated with violence, heroic and tragic myths, which though not historically or factually true, nevertheless reflect something of early Irish culture and values. It has been asserted that 'mythology embodies a system of symbols encoding the rules of society'.[25] This sociological reading of mythology would suggest that the societies reflected in the Ulster and Fenian cycles were shaped by violence and a violent ethos. It might even be said that the myth of redemptive violence was all-pervasive and that the dominant culture was one of violent heroes and violent action.

The myth of the Táin is about a cattle raid and the great war

---

24 Leeming, op cit, p 204, The *filidh* were the poets of Ireland whose responsibility was to preserve the history and love of Ireland. They were also the sacred bards who told the stories of an Irish heroic past.
25 MacKillop, James, *Myths and Legends of the Celts* (London: Penguin Books, 2005) p XXVII

that developed over the Brown Bull of Cooley began with bed-time talk between Queen Méabh and her lover over the value of their possessions. When Méabh realised that her possessions were inferior to her husband's she was determined to own the brown bull from the Cooley peninsula. 'The bull always stands for power and virility and is associated, in Ireland especially, with sacred kingship'.[26] The Táin is a myth about politics and power and hegemony. Standing between Méabh and the brown bull is Cúchulainn, who predominates the Ulster cycle. His name means 'the hound of Culann and 'Cú (hound) was a common designation for a warrior in early Irish literature'.[27] The myth locates him in Co Louth with earliest roots in a small Celto-British tribe who settled there. According to the myth, Cúchulainn single-handedly defends Ulster against the mighty army of Queen Méabh of Connacht.

Cúchulainn's violent character emerges early in the myth with his boyhood exploits. A fierce hound which guards cattle is let loose and Cúchulainn on his way home and hitting a ball with a hurley stick, encounters the savage beast.

> When the hound saw the boy come racing over the green to-wards him, it let out a blood-curdling howl that rolled and echoed across the plain. All who heard it froze with dread but Setanta didn't even break his stroke at the sound. The hound leapt forward to tear the child apart, its massive jaws wide open. Setanta hurled the ball with all his strength down its gullet and so great was the force of the ball that it carried the animal's entrails out through its body. Then Setanta seized the hound by the hind legs and dashed it against a rock so hard that its body broke in fragments that scattered the ground.[28]

Culann, the smith, who owned the hound, was heartbroken at its brutal death. Setanta promised to find him another and meanwhile Setanta himself would look after the cattle. The

---

26 Leeming, op cit, p 370

27 Ó hÓgáin, Daithí, *The Lore of Ireland: An Encyclopedia of Myth, Legend and Romance*, (Suffolk: The Boydel Press, 2006) p.137

28 Heaney, Marie, *Over Nine Waves: A Book of Irish Legends* (London: Faber and Faber, 1994) p 78

druid then said that his name would be changed from Setanta to Cúchulainn, the hound of Culann. Clearly this was a young man destined for heroic and violent deeds.

In the Táin, Cúchulainn's body becomes transformed into a kind of battle-frenzy.

He shakes from head to foot and revolves within his skin, his features turn red, one eye becomes monstrously large while the other becomes tiny, his mouth grows huge and emits sparks, his heart booms in his chest, his hair becomes spiked and glowing and the 'warrior light' comes from his brow. This description is obviously an echo of ancient ideas concerning the inspiration of a warrior.[29]

The warriors are the heroes in this early Irish society. The Táin has a story of him taking up arms at seven years of age, smashing seventeen chariots, hurling an iron ball at an attacker's forehead, killing him and then cutting off his head. After many more killings and violent exploits 'the whole company gazed in wonder at the boy who had triumphantly taken up arms and defeated the most formidable warriors though he was only seven years old.'[30]

Meanwhile, Méabh decided to invade Ulster and take the brown bull by force. Taking command of the army she marched with Fergus as her chief scout and guide. When the Red Branch warriors were overcome by Macha's curse and became as helpless as women in childbirth, complete with birth pangs, Méabh attacked. Only Cúchulainn was immune to Macha's curse. The Queen's scouts entered Ulster only to be beheaded by Cúchulainn. She sent soldiers and up to 100 per day were killed. Then she sent her greatest champions to meet him in one-to-one combat, but all were killed. Eventually Ferdia was chosen to confront Cúchulainn, his foster-brother and equal in courage and skill. Neither wanted to fight but fight they did, hurling javelins till nightfall and wounding each other. The fight continued for days, brutal and bloody. Ferdia thrust his sword into Cúchulainn's chest. Cúchulainn calls for his powerful weapon, a barbed javelin that hacked its victim to pieces. The *Gae Bolga*, as

29 Ó hÓgáin, op cit , p 137
30 Heaney, op cit, p 89

it was known, 'drove into Ferdia's belly and the barbs opened out, filling every crevice and cavity of his body'.[31] There was no victory though for Cúchulainn, only despair and grief, lamentation and mourning and Cúchulainn 'cursed the futility of the fight'.[32]

Cúchulainn's end is tragic. After a killing career as champion of Ulster, the children of one of his victims returned to seek vengeance. Méabh again engaged the Ulster warriors, but aware of treachery planned against Cúchulainn, he was ordered to remain at Eamhain until the war was over. With much of his strength gone he eventually joined the battle. A special javelin hit Cúchulainn and caused his intestines to fall out. He staggered towards a lake.

> He took a drink and washed himself and turned from the lake to die. On the shore, a little distance away, he saw a pillar stone and he struggled towards it and put his back to it for support. Then he took his belt and tied himself to the pillar so that he could die standing up, for he had sworn he would meet his end 'feet on the ground, face to the foe' ... the hero light still shone round his head.[33]

There Cúchulainn died and after some days his enemies approached his lifeless body. 'Then Cúchulainn's head was severed from his body and borne to Tara as a trophy and his body, still tied to the pillar, was left on the strand'.[34] The warrior hero became the victim of his own violence, violence that had become a brutal cycle which no one was able to break. Did the author(s) of the Táin see the 'futility of the fight', or is this the way things were. The Táin itself ends with the bull and violence still pervasive: The '... Bull of Cooley making his way home from Connacht with the carcase of his broken rival on his horns'.[35]

Finn MacCool has been described as 'The most celebrated hero in Irish literature and folklore'.[36] He was the warrior-seer, the leader of the Fianna. The cult of Finn is associated with the

31 Ibid, p 139
32 Ibid, p 139
33 Ibid, pp 151-152
34 Ibid, p 152
35 Dillon, Myles (ed), *Irish Sagas* (Cork: Mercier Press, 1968) p 104
36 Ó hÓgáin, op cit, p 238

Boyne Valley. The Uí Néill clan had driven the Leinstermen from the Boyne Valley. Under a new leader, Leinster engaged in a futile power struggle against the Uí Néill. Finn became 'a symbol of their efforts to regain possession of the Boyne Valley and that, as part of this, Finn was portrayed as having been a great leader.'[37] Prevalent in the Finn cycle of stories is the cult of war. Young trainee warriors were known as Fianna and so Finn 'was fancifully said to have been the leader of a mythical Fianna band long ago'.[38]

Many of the Finn stories are associated with the Fianna. They were warriors on the warpath, a band of warriors and hunters led by the mythical hero, Finn. They were also known as Fianna Éireann and sometimes as the Leinster Fianna. 'They stood apart from the rest of society and were charged to defend the sovereignty of Ireland against external enemies, both natural and supernatural'.[39] Rigorous induction ordeals were required for acceptance to the exclusive Fianna. Finn became their captain or leader and under his leadership

... the Fianna of Ireland came into a heyday of such glory that stories were told about them for centuries afterwards. Their exploits were so famous and the tales of their adventures so fabulous that over the ages they grew longer than life in people's imagination and Finn himself is remembered as a giant.

While Finn was their captain, he allowed only the noblest, the bravest, the swiftest, the strongest, the most honourable of men to join the Fianna. Under his command they stood ready to defend the state, support the King and protect the safety and property of the people.[40]

It was an act of violence that convinced the High King to appoint him to leadership. Finn was given a powerful spear and went into the ramparts of Tara to stand watch. Hypnotic music filled Tara's halls and soon everyone was asleep. Finn, as in-

---

37 Ibid, p 238
38 Ibid, pp 238-239
39 McKillop, James, *Dictionary of Celtic Mythology* (Oxford: Oxford University Press, 1998) p 196
40 Heaney, op cit, pp 166-167 From the Finn cycle

structed by the High King, held the spearhead flat against his forehead and therefore stayed awake. Aillen, thinking everyone was fast asleep, breathed a great tongue of flame to torch Tara. Finn deflected the flame, Aillen fled with Finn in pursuit. 'Finn threw Fiacha's magic spear at him and impaled him with it. Then he cut off Aillen's head and brought it back with him to Tara.'[41] Tara was safe and Finn was made head of the Fianna and 'the Fianna champions rose to proclaim their new captain'.[42]

Popular lore about Finn portrays him as a giant, with stories of him building the Giant's Causeway between Co Antrim and Scotland in a battle with another giant. Finn is said to have thrown the large boulders seen in Ireland in contests with other giants. Tales also have him tear up great sods of earth and throw them at a giant in England. Ireland's Eye, off Dublin, is said to have been thrown by Finn from Co Wicklow, creating the largest lake at Glendalough. So too is the Isle of Man a great sod flung from the north, thus creating Lough Neagh. Finn has been the star performer in stories for centuries, but the cycle is dominated by military activity involving Finn and his Fianna. Like Cúchulainn, Finn too died a violent death, according to one of the stories. It was also believed that 'one day he will return to save Ireland, just as Arthur, the "once and future King" will return to Britain'.[43]

The Cúchulainn and Finn myths are essentially Irish myths of violence. They are myths in which violence is pervasive, perhaps suggesting that in their respective times, this is how things were or are; we are naturally violent people and violence achieves, defends, makes peace. The earlier Babylonian myth is being replayed. The Irish myths have also replayed themselves in modern Irish history. Cúchulainn and Finn have become role models, warriors who sacrifice themselves for the cause and display generous heroism.

---

41 Ibid, p 166

42 Ibid, p 166

43 Leeming, op cit, p 136. It has been suggested that Finn and the Fianna are the Gaelic equivalents of Arthur and the Knights of the Round Table. Mythology from different locations does use a similar storyline or plot but with local adaptation. A shared mythological plot is found in the Epic of Gilgamesh and the Hebrew Flood story.

Cúchulainn stands in the Post Office in O'Connell Street, Dublin, as the great warrior and leader. He featured large in Pearse's theology of the 1916 Rising. The blood sacrifice that would redeem Ireland and cleanse the nation had its roots in the medieval violent interpretation of Christ's atoning death, symbolised in the Eucharist, and in the Táin where Cúchulainn the young warrior died the heroic death. Pearse saw his own approaching death in 1916, like that of Robert Emmet, death 'for a divinely ordained purpose – a sacrifice for Ireland like Christ's on the cross'.[44]

Combining the violent atonement of Christ dramatised in the Eucharist and the bloody heroism of the Táin, Pearse created a 20th century Irish myth of redemptive violence.

> For those who died with Pearse, but even more so for those who have followed, the twenty-two who have starved themselves to death for Ireland since 1916, Pearse's definition of their cause is not the propaganda of a revolutionary intellectual elite ... Pearse's language and ideas went beyond formalised rhetoric to posit a myth that served as an internalised belief system, which had precedents deep within the western tradition.[45]

The loyalists too in the latter part of the 20th century invoked the Cúchulainn myth. In east Belfast, Cúchulainn was portrayed on a wall mural as 'defender of Ulster against the Irish', thus justifying the loyalist paramilitary violence in defence of present-day Ulster against the contemporary Irish violence and murderous attack on their culture and traditions. Cúchulainn was no myth but a real historical person who fought and died for the freedom of Ulster. In loyalist minds the myth became historic - ised and literalised in much the same way that Hitler had historicised and literalised Wagner's dramatic and musical myths and used them to justify the cleansing of the nation from Judaism. But then has not the republican tradition in Ireland

---

44 Moran, Sean Farrell, *Patrick Pearse and the Politics of Redemption: The Mind of the Easter Rising, 1916* (Washington, DC: The Catholic University of America Press, 1994) p 199
45 Ibid, p 201

also historicised and literalised the Cúchulainn myth? Either way it is an abuse of the myth and a dangerous and violent use of mythology.

Those who apparently signed the Ulster Covenant in their own blood and the Ulster Protestants' blood sacrifice at the Somme are rooted in the same myth, however unconscious. The original Babylonian myth of redemptive violence was replayed in the British military and political repression in Ireland, in the militarised Ulster resistance of 1912-1914, Covenant and gun running, and in the Easter Rising and Somme of 1916, and in the subsequent violence up to the most recent phase of violence in Ireland. This has included the Protestant and Catholic violent god-myth at the heart of a medieval and Reformation interpret-ation of Christ's atonement symbolised and dramatised at the heart of the Eucharist. That perhaps is the most uncomfortable and challenging dimension of our shared history of violence.

Finn and his Fianna too have been replayed through our ob-session with violent heroism. Fenian was a distorted translation of Fianna invented in 1804, but quickly adopted by the Irish Republican Brotherhood formed in 1858, celebrated in militar-ised song in 'The Bold Fenian Men'. It became associated with violent activity and historicised myth again justified violence and killing. Ulster Protestants applied the word in an abusive and pejorative way to all Catholics, especially Republicans. It was the name the leading political party of independent Ireland used to describe itself, Fianna Fáil, 'Soldiers of destiny'. The Irish national anthem invokes the same ethos of militarised vio-lence through the 'Soldiers Song'. The British anthem is no less violent in its prayer to 'save our gracious Queen' and 'send her victorious'. This is no pietistic evangelical theology but violent theology articulating the violent god-myth. A significant woman in the Easter Rising and minister in the first Dáil, Countess Markievicz, founded a nationalist boy scouts, no less militarised in ethos than Baden-Powell's British scouts.

The Babylonian myth of redemptive violence runs deep. It has been at the heart of the modern Irish culture of violence. It might even be said that we are obsessed by the myth, in love with the myth of redemptive violence. The myth itself is at the heart of part of the Bible story in the violent God-images and texts of terror in both the Hebrew Bible and Christian Testament. The critique of this pervasive violence is also in the Bible itself expressed through counter-myths and counter-cultures. There is an alternative and in Ireland there always was. It is to these critical questions and exploration that we now turn in the following chapters.

CHAPTER SIX

Is this the word of the Lord?
Texts of terror in the Hebrew Bible

What are we to make of biblical texts that appear to have God sanction wars, genocide, gang rape and sexual violence against women, and place permanent exclusion orders on whole communities like the Moabites? Like it or not these are texts and storylines from the Hebrew Bible. They are nearly always edited out of the lectionary readings and so are never heard in public worship. Those who reject the use of the lectionary, often believing that they are open to the leading and guidance of the Spirit, are usually never guided by the Spirit to read of the slaughter of the Amalekites or the gang rape of an unnamed concubine. Everyone seems to accept there is a canon within the canon and practice a high degree of selectivity when it comes to the Bible, which is claimed to be inspired or the foundational document of faith. Christians have developed a well used escape route by claiming that the God of the Christian Testament is superior to the God of the Hebrew Bible and that Christianity has superseded Judaism. There is now a better and higher revelation of God, and Jesus is key to this supersessionism.

This well known escape route is problematic for a number of reasons. It is an expression of Christian triumphalism and profound prejudice, if not more often hate against Jews. It forgets that Jesus himself was Jewish, followed the Jewish God and only read the Hebrew Bible. It ignores the fact that the Christian Testament itself has violent texts and violent God-images and that Christian history has read, interpreted and used texts from the gospels and apocalypse in the practice of violence. It radically relativises all the Jewish foreground of the Christian faith, if not de-constructs it and further ignores that the Christian Testament assumes the thought-forms and authority of the Hebrew Bible. The supersessionist approach has also bought into Christendom Christology and its warrior Christ, only possible through eliminating the Jewish roots of the Christian Testament's Christological language. Jesus may not even be

who the Christendom creeds say he is! There is certainly one
very big reason why the Christian claim to supersede the violent
God-images of the Hebrew Bible is morally bankrupt. We conveniently forget that 'Christians, at least since the fourth century,
have not been peaceable, whereas Jews have never been violent
from the second century until this one'.[1] Jews have been non-
violent for almost two millennia while most of the same two
millennia has been characterised by Christian war and violence.
To describe the Christian claim to morally supersede Judaism as
blatant hypocrisy is a gross understatement. In relation to war
and violence, Christianity since the Jewish rabbi Jesus was
changed into the Constantinian Christ, has not a moral leg to
stand on, especially in regard to the practice of Judaism.

On the night before the battle at Milvian Bridge on the Tiber,
Constantine saw a cross in the sky with the words above it, 'In
This Sign Conquer'. It was a sign from the Christian God and
next day Constantine's troops went courageously into battle
and won. Presumably in the sign of the same cross Constantine
threw his rival to imperial supremacy off the bridge into the
Tiber where he drowned. This, 'the second-greatest story ever
told', after the Jesus story, shaped the history of Western
Christianity, after which '... the power of the empire became
joined to the ideology of the church'.[2] War and violence became
part of the ecclesiastical ideology.

When Cromwell massacred the people of Drogheda and
Wexford he justified it on the basis of texts from I Samuel in the
Hebrew Bible where God commanded the slaughter of every
Amalekite, including women and children. Cromwell's violent,
sacred texts were reinvoked on loyalist wall murals in Belfast.
Whether the cross or I Samuel, there is clearly a problem with

1 Yoder, John Howard, *The War of the Lamb: The Ethics of Non-Violence
and Peacemaking*, (Grand Rapids: Brazos Press, 2009) p 72. Yoder died
suddenly in 1997 and this book is a collection of his essays edited by
Glen Stassen, Mark Thiessen Nation and Matt Hamsher, leading interpreters of his thoughts. Yoder's reference to Jewish non-violence from
'the second century until this one' is therefore a reference to the 20th
century when violence became associated with the Jewish state of Israel
and its military forces.
2 Carroll, James, *Constantine's Sword: the Church and the Jews* (New York:
First Mariner Books, 2002) p 171

the Bible and interpretations of biblical texts and stories. We cannot seek for wriggle room though by placing the blame on violent interpretations of texts, though that is a serious problem. All reading of the Bible is interpretation and there is interpretation going on within the text itself, but texts of violence and terror remain as part of a book claimed to be sacred. Clearly there is also tension in the text and between texts best expressed by Jack Nelson-Pallmeyer.

> If I had to choose one word that best describes the character of God in the Bible, it would be violence. If I could choose a second word, it would be justice. Justice was important because the Exodus was understood to be a story of God freeing a people from oppressive, imperial rule.[3]

There is a tension between violence and justice. The former becomes structured injustice, a domination system, inflicting injustice on the many, especially the innocent or non-combatants. The Exodus was fundamental to ancient Israel's vision of justice, a liberation from the political and economic imperialism of Egypt, and yet the Exodus story as told in the Hebrew Bible contains violence. Egyptians were drowned! Was it just for a God of justice to drown Egyptians? There is an ethical tension in the way the story is told and remembered in the Bible and it suggests an ethical tension in Godself. Does the Bible ever get away from a morally ambivalent God? How do we resolve the tension between justice and violence in historical experience?

WRESTLING WITH TEXTS OF TERROR

The Warrior God

A dominant theme or image in the Hebrew Bible is that of the warrior God. A great deal of warfare and violence characterises the Hebrew scriptures and God appears to be the key activist. The war frequently appears to be God's War. If all reading is interpretation, then interpretation of war narratives is problematic, not least because the narratives as we now have them are already interpretations. The biblical texts themselves are interpretations, theologised and mythologised interpretations cent -

---

3 Nelson-Pallmeyer, Jack, *Jesus Against Christianity: Reclaiming the Missing Jesus* (Harrisburg, Trinity Press International, 2001) p 1

uries after an experience or event. The exact nature of the historical experience or event is beyond recovery. We have no way of
knowing what an historical Exodus looks like. To state the obvious, neither BBC nor RTÉ were there! The warrior God texts, including the Exodus, leave us with a number of interpretative
choices. Are we to take a 'mythologised' view of early Israel's
history or an 'historical' view? Should we read the texts as literal
history or theological history? Yet another reading strategy
would read those narratives as theo-myth.

Early Israel was surrounded by Near Eastern people steeped
in mythology. It was a familiar Near Eastern way of imagining
and expressing meaning. In the Enuma Elish and the Baal epic
there is war mythology in which the gods won the battle over
chaos. These myths are reflected in the biblical narratives, perhaps in subversive and counter-cultural ways, but it would be
surprising if ancient Israel did not have an appreciation of such
mythology and re-imagine it from a theological perspective.
Enuma Elish and the Baal epic are already theo-myths and the
creative imagination of Israel developed its own.

There may be something distinctive in Israel's theo-mythical
war narratives. Israel's neighbours did believe that their gods
would fight for them in warfare. 'However, they did not devel-
op a concept that the army was therefore not to fight. Rather, because the gods fought, the army was to fight all the harder.'[4] In
the war narratives of Genesis-Kings, there appears to be a radical difference. Exodus 15 is an early piece of war poetry centred
on the Exodus. The poetry affirms, 'The Lord is a warrior' (Ex
15:3). In the preceding chapter, narrative affirms that God will
fight for the Hebrew slaves and liberate them. They are to see
the deliverance of the Lord. 'The Lord will fight for you, and
you have only to keep still' (Ex 14:14). According to Lind, this
unique concept of Israel's holy war was first put forward in-
depth in 1901. God will fight, Israel will not. This was believed
to be a theological interpretation, emphasising divine help in
order to strengthen the community. Much later in the 20th cent -
ury, Von Rad's work on holy war made holy war and absolute

4 Lind, Millard C., *Monotheism, Power, Justice*, (Indiana: Institute of
Mennonite Studies, 1990) p 182

miracle inseparable.[5] Again this is theology rather than history.
There is a strong body of thought which understands the warrior God theme as God fighting excludes human fighting. 'The
salvation of the Israelites at the Red Sea is celebrated in military
language, but not as military action of the Israelites. Yahweh is
the victor'.[6] It is God who fights and the Israelites do not fight at
all. The warrior god theme is the denial of the efficacy or validity
of human violence.

The theo-mythical interpretation applies to the war narratives of the Hebrew Bible. Lind lists the more dramatic episodes.

1 Deliverance from Egypt, Ex 14
2 Joshua's battle for Jericho, Josh 6
3 Deborah's victory over the Canaanite Coalition, Judg 5
4 Gideon against the Midianites, Judg 6 v7
5 Samuel's battle with the Philistines, I Sam 7:5ff
6 David's battle with Goliath, I Sam 17
7 The King of Syria and Elisha, II Kings 6:15ff
8 Binadad and Elisha, II Kings 7
9 Isaiah's counsel to Ahaz, Is 7:1-9
10 Isaiah and Sennacherib, II Kings 19, cf Is 30:15; 31:1-4
11 Jehoshaphat against the people of the East, II Chron 20: 1-
307[7]

All of these battle narratives are written as theo-myth and the
most historical dimension is the historical context of Israel's existence, not the battles. Israel's story is always of a minority
power among great powers and empires. Theo-myth is being
applied to Israel's social and political minority experience. The
Deuteronomist was clear that Israel was the least of the nations
(Deut 7:6-8). In reality it was never in a position to fight with any
superpower or powerful coalition around it. To go to war with
Egypt, Assyria or Babylon would have been an act of collective
suicide. They were the least, the nobodies, the minority and to
take on any of the superpowers or their neighbours was a non-
starter. To read the battle narratives literally or as historical fact
is to fail to grasp the reality of Israel's minority experience and

5 Ibid, p 182-183
6 Yoder, op cit., p 68
7 Lind, op cit, pp 189-190

to miss the point of the narratives and poetry. This is mythologised history. The image of the warrior God is theo-mythical
imagination cast in the story form of Near Eastern neighbours
but radicalised through the rununciation of the use of horses
and chariots, military technology. Israel is to 'stand still' or 'stop
fighting' as it can be translated, 'and know that I am God'
(Psalm 46:10).

The warrior God tradition and the holy wars ended with the
establishment of the Davidic state. Now Israel had a King 'like
all the nations' (I Sam 8:5) which meant a standing army, horses
and chariots, and battles to be fought. The prophetic tradition
saw that development as a rejection of God's leadership or lord-
ship. Indulging in battles and violence as a small people meant
defeat, often crushing defeat. Those who have justified their
wars and violence by appealing to the warrior God, God on our
side, Ulster Covenant and Rising Proclamation, and to the biblical holy war narratives, have distorted and abused them, and
that includes the Zionist, Jewish and Christian fundamentalists
who apply them to the present Israeli-Palestinian conflict.

Pathological Images of God
Interpreting the warrior God in theo-mythical terms does not
satisfactorily overcome other violent God-images. Even though
theo-mythical narrative or poetry is claimed there are those who
are still uncomfortable with the military metaphors. These may
well be a bridge impossible to cross for some, but at least we
might still have to recognise that those theo-mythical writers
were using a literary genre common to their Near Eastern culture, and were using it in a radicalised way.

But this is not the complete answer to disturbingly violent
texts which seem to portray God in pathological terms.

A Leviticus text has God command the murder or execution
of disobedient children (Lev 20:1-2, 9). Deuteronomy has a similar command, this time for rebellious sons who are to be stoned
to death 'to purge the evil from your midst' (Deut 20:18-21).
Some of us would not have survived adolescence back then! At
least the local community was to do the stoning and not or not
only the father. It was very rough justice reminiscent of the kind
used against anti-social behaviour or informers during Ireland's

20th century violent troubles. Elisha, still spoken of as a 'man of
God' had really no sense of humour. When a gang of small boys
called him 'baldhead', he cursed them and 'in the name of the
Lord' summoned two she-bears out of the forest to maul forty
two of them.(II Kings 2:23-24). Not only a horrific form of child
abuse but God collaborated in the murder. There is no defence
of God in all this violence against children and young people.
This is a violent, dangerous and unpredictable God.

In religious syllabi children have been uncritically told the
story of Abraham being asked by God to sacrifice his firstborn
son, Isaac. Some courses have even been known to suggest that
at this point children should be introduced to the substitutionary theory of the atonement! Is it ethical to use a story like this or
a theory of Christ's death to traumatise children? Is it a moral
image of God requiring a father to murder his son as a test of the
authenticity of faith? Never mind the psychological trauma for
the father and the son, what about the mother who has no voice
and is not even asked?

It may be that the point of the story was being made at a time
when ancient Israel's moral awareness was developing beyond
the practice of child sacrifice not only of its neighbours, but also
its own practice. Through narrative ethics Israel may have been
rejecting the violent God-image and asserting that a moral God
does not require child sacrifice or any form of blood sacrifice. If
that is the case, then the ethical insight had not reached Ireland
in 1912, 1916 or in the century following.

If this is not the point of the story then we are left with a very
violent God who is not worthy of human loyalty or commitment. If, on the other hand, a non-violent God did not require
blood sacrifice, it is baffling to know why Christians have allowed a violent God's blood sacrifice of 'his only son' as a substitute for sinful humanity to dominate theology and liturgy for
the last 1,000 years. Have we become so possessed by the myth
of redemptive violence that it has shaped our primary image of
God and our dominant understanding of Christ's death?

Some of us belong to a generation which grew up with the
story of Noah and the Ark. Perhaps the telling of the story and
what impressed us most were the animals. We were never told,
because those who told us didn't know either, that in parts of

Genesis the animals entered the ark, two by two, but in other Genesis texts they went in by sevens! We never asked either what size of a boat it had to be to hold two or seven of every animal, insect or species on earth! But these were minor details. The really big problem was never raised. This was the destructive violence at the heart of the story when God destroyed all human and other life outside the ark because the earth was so filled with violence. Apart from one family in the ark, all others were destroyed because of their violence by an even more violent God. Even with a literal reading of the Noah story the angry, punishing and destructively violent God was never questioned.

It is now recognised that the flood story has numerous parallels in the ancient Near East, especially the earlier Epic of Gilgamesh. Recognising the mythical nature of the flood story, or rather its theo-mythical nature, still leaves us with a very violent God-image. But then, only when myth is literalised is violent human behaviour mirrored by God-images or humans imit - ate their literally violent God. The more profound truth of the Noah theo-myth is that violence always destroys.

Frequently in history religion has justified the expansionism of empires, which has in part been about the theft of land, gold and in various ways, people. People have been uprooted or displaced and land has been taken over by outsiders and settlers. It has always been the story of colonisation and empire building. Abraham is given vast tracks of land from Egypt to the Euphrates by God at the expense of ten named ethnic groups (Genesis 15:18-21). The Deuteronomists interpretation of a chosen people's experience is that of God bringing them into a land to enter and occupy it as God claims 'many nations before you' (Deut 7:1-2, 5-6). The implication is that all of these nations worship false gods and the chosen have been chosen by the true God, and therefore the displacement and colonisation is divinely justified, even authorised. Jewish writer, Regina Swartz, critically noted that 'over and over again the Bible tells the story of a people who inherit at someone else's expense'.[8] Taking another's

---

8 Quoted in Nelson-Pallmeyer, op cit., p 28 The quote is from Swartz's critical book, *The Curse of Cain: The Violent Legacy of Monotheism*, University of Chicago Press, 1997

land is legitimate, because they worship false gods and the one God has not only authorised it but been directly and actively involved in the violent displacement.

Not only do some texts portray God-ordained land theft but have God responsible for divinely sanctioned genocide. During the most recent phase of violence in Ireland, a loyalist mural included a text from Deuteronomy 7 '... when the Lord your God gives them over to you and you defeat them, then you must utterly destroy them. Make no covenant with them and show them no mercy' (Deut 7:2). In another text, the Lord commanded Moses to ensure that in the conquered land 'there was no survivor left' (Numbers 21:31-35). In Joshua 11:20, God orders utter destruction, no mercy but extermination. There are people rightly on trial at the International Hague Court for war-crimes against humanity which appear relatively low-key when placed beside God's acts of genocide against numerous ethnic groups in the Hebrew Bible. The book of Joshua makes particularly violent reading. Literalistic readings have turned these texts into mandates for colonialism and paramilitary killing. Read literally these are dangerous texts and the God they portray is much worse than any war-criminal. Not surprisingly, many who are not colonial masters, paramilitaries or war-criminals (those tried and those who won and were not) have put this genocidal God on trial and culturally declared him dead.

Yet archeology and history provide no evidence for the facticity of the narratives. What we do know is that ancient Israel was never and never likely to be a superpower, or even in control of its own destiny. The theo-myths emerge from the experience of an oppressed minority. The storyline is of a people struggling for justice in the face of violent injustice and oppression. Failure to recognise Israel's primary experience not only ends up with a literalistic reading of the texts, but a literalistic and unethical application of the violence to contemporary geopolitical situations.

These, therefore, are the texts of a dominated community, emerging out of hurt, pain and marginality. They are also texts of hope, longing for liberation and justice. There was never any possibility of Israel fighting such battles or achieving liberation and justice through such violent genocide. They simply did not have enough horses and chariots for that. The texts stand in Israel's powerful liturgical tradition of lament in which pain and hurt were voiced, often in raw, brutal terms, such as dashing the heads of the all-conquering Babylonian babies and children against the rocks (Psalm 137:9). At the heart of lament, arising from concrete, social and historical experience is hope, or the dream of a more just, liberated world. In this sense a book like Joshua reflects liturgical dream-time, which 'is understood as certified from heaven, and as that dream is certified from heaven, it has enormous credibility in the life of the community on earth'.[9] This is not history but theo-myth expressing the deepest yearning of a peasant community for liberation and justice. It did not happen this way. Israel did not nor could not exterminate oppressive and dominating neighbours. But Israel could lament in brutally raw language and dream dreams of freedom and justice. 'The dream of liberation and justice has credibility theologically because to deny it is to deny everything Israel knows about Yahweh, the Lord of the Exodus.'[10] Through theological or theo-mythical vision, liturgically expressed, Israel can re-configure the world, re-imagine reality and live out of a new liberated, just possibility for its world.

A Biblical Literalist

To read these texts of violence literally is to apply them literally. History is full of such readings and practice. The Bible itself has a story of a biblical literalist who set about a violent purge of his community in the name of the one violent God, and then became the victim of his own bloody violence.

In the 7th century BCE, a fundamentalist or literalist party emerged and carried out a bloody purge of the Jewish community. The key leader of this purge was King Josiah. He became king at eight years old after the violent assassination of his father. Violence as the Noah myth insisted is destructive and in this case it not only destroyed the life of Josiah's father, the violent trauma shaped the grieving boy and adolescent into violent person. He was only twenty when he began his own violent

---

9 Brueggemann, Walter, *Divine Presence and Violence: Contextualizing the Book of Joshua* (Eugene, Oregon: Cascade Books, 2009) p 26
10 Ibid, p 26

purge. Six years later he set about the renovation of Solomon's temple. A scroll was unearthed and Josiah believed he had received divine revelation. It turned out to be the lost fifth scroll of the Torah, or so they believed, and it inspired the young king with a violent disposition to strictly enforce the neglected laws. Josiah believed himself to be on a mission from God and he destroyed every sanctuary outside Jerusalem. Josiah embarked on a holy war, smashing altars and shrines and killing priests who sacrificed to any god other than Yahweh.

Josiah had discovered the book of Deuteronomy and read it literally. He brought his already pre-conditioned culture and mind-set of violence to the text, read the text literally and applied it literally. Violence, power and literalism merged and the question must be asked; was all this shaped by God or was Josiah's god shaped by the unholy trinity of violence, power and literalism? What we meet in this story is not only a violent religious reformer, but also a violent politician and militarist.

The young king saw clearly how the idea of a single all-powerful God in heaven implied the appropriateness of a single all-powerful king on earth – an idea that would exert a powerful appeal for kings and men who would be kings down through history, including Constantine and his fellow Christian emperors.[11]

Whether Josiah, Constantine or King James I and his fiction of the divine right of kings, what they held was a politicised, violent monotheism, one God, one true faith, one empire, one capital under one king, all of which means salvation. Unsurprisingly this is inherently violent and sees salvation or liberation being realised through violence. Josiah read the text literally and believed his violent purge was the road to his peo-

---

11 Kirsch, Jonathan, *God Against the Gods: The History of the War Between Monotheism and Polytheism* (London: Penguin Compass, 2005) p 73. The Josiah narrative is told in II Kings 22-23, which can be read as prophetic satire. Also in II Chronicles 34-35 which includes the story of his violent death. The books of Chronicles are the last books in the Hebrew Bible and are an extended re-description of Jewish history, though not history as we understand it. The books are a critical theological interpretation and written post-exile in the experience of Persian hegemony. Perhaps the final theological statement of the Hebrew Bible is witness to the remarkable tenacity of the Jewish people in the face of every imperial, domination system.

ple's salvation. Through his literalism and violence he was dead at forty. Positioned between two superpowers, Egypt and Assyria, he aligned the tiny kingdom of Judah with the Assyrians. The Egyptian army marched through his powerless kingdom, but he fought them at Megiddo in 609 BCE. He mounted his war chariot and led the charge but an Egyptian archer was too accurate. Wounded he was taken back to Jerusalem where he died, his violent internal purge a failure and his dynasty a failure. A quarter of a century later Jerusalem was destroyed by the new Babylonian superpower, a Davidic dynasty was extinguished, the temple razed to the ground and the key people of Judah exiled in Babylon. Whatever sovereignty Judah had was destroyed, a victim of violence and in a real sense a victim of its leader's violence. Not surprisingly the exiles reworked the Gilgamesh flood epic in Babylon and came up with the Noah myth which was profoundly true when it asserted that violence destroys.

Josiah was a biblical literalist, a violent zealot shaped by the trauma and violence of his childhood. In a succession of violent leaders which began with David and Solomon, when Israel wanted a king like other nations, Josiah put the finishing touches to the destruction of his own kingdom and ultimately his own life. It was not that Josiah took God seriously, he took himself much too seriously, including his own lust for power. What he thought was divine revelation and command, was like James I divine right of kings, a pious fiction, or god shaped by monarchical power and delusions of absolutism. Josiah was a biblical literalist who projected his own violence and power lust onto God. History, especially religious history, keeps repeating itself.

Violence Against Women

A disturbing feature of the Hebrew Bible is the inclusion of stories of violence against women which appear to have divine sanction. Given what we know of the culture of the biblical Near Eastern world, it is no surprise to realise that the entire Bible is set in a patriarchal context and reflects patriarchal concerns. The Bible represents the foundational documents of faith and there is the faith assumption that we learn something of God and the divine purpose from the documents.

Yet responsible faith is never uncritical and can therefore never approach the Bible in an uncritical way. Not everything in it is divine command or the word of God. Critical discernment is essential when reading its stories and texts. The truth is that a literalistic or flat reading of the Bible is impossible, theologically and ethically, or even in terms of coherence and consistency. Enough has been said above to realise that a literal reading of the warrior god images and commands to exterminate ethnic groups would send and has sent communities into an utterly destructive spiral of violence.

Critical discernment is a must when patriarchy is encountered in the biblical text. Abraham may be hailed as a paradigm or hero of faith but there is nothing ethical about his passing Sarah off as his sister for Pharaoh's sexual pleasure, in order to save Abraham's life. When the Eden myth was imagined by its Jewish storytellers, the woman's pain in childbearing and her husband's rule over her were never intended as divine commands or will for all time, but were the effects of sin in the story or its way of describing the dysfunctionality at the heart of life. This is our flawed existence and not how it is meant to be. Later Christian patriarchy and misogyny imposed male domination on the Hebrew myth to control and subjugate women, socially, politically and religiously.

The patriarchy of the biblical writers is also evident in the unnaming of women, the down-grading of women like Miriam to elevate the male Moses, and the violence that is justified by the text against women. The patriarchal culture is evident in both testaments, and there is no room for any Christian supersessionism in relation to gender issues.

Phyllis Trible has drawn attention to four major narratives of violence against women in the Hebrew Bible. Correctly she identifies them as 'texts of terror' and they are the stories of Hagar, Tamar, an Unnamed Woman and the Daughter of Jephthah.[12] Significantly two of the women have no names, but are victims of very brutal male violence.

The unnamed woman is a concubine from Bethlehem whose horrendous experience is narrated in Judges 19:1-30.

---

12 Trible, Phyllis, *Texts of Terror: Literary – Feminist Readings of Biblical Narratives*, (Philadelphia: Fortress Press, 1984)

The betrayal, rape, torture, murder, and dismemberment of an unnamed women is a story we want to forget but are commanded to speak. It depicts the horrors of male power, brutality, and triumphalism; of female helplessness, abuse and annihilation. To hear this story is to inhabit a world of unrelenting terror that refuses to let us pass by on the other side.[13]

Judges portrays a society without leaders in which chaos reigns. There is very little of God in the book and 'all the people did what was right in their own eyes' (Judges 21:25). It was a situation of social anarchy which always produces violence and vengeance. Violent chaos characterises the tribe of Benjamin (chs 19-21).

The concubine is a slave, owned by a Levite male, a person of some standing. She belongs to him, a piece of property for his own sexual purposes. Legally and socially she is nobody, lower than other women of the time. She appears to have slept with someone else which results in her leaving him. He follows her all the way to her family home, recovers his 'property' and sets off on the return journey. Lodging is required on the way. An old man living in Benjaminite country offers hospitality, and it is enjoyed by men only. The story becomes male dominated as a power struggle develops between the two men.

Festivities are lavish but are interrupted by 'a perverse lot' who demand the male guest to be handed over for sexual purposes. The master of the house cannot break the law of hospitality so he offers his virgin daughter and the concubine. Both the daughter and the concubine are powerless, pawns in a patriarchal ritual of hospitality. The concubine was thrown out and gang raped repeatedly 'all through the night'. When the doors were opened in the morning her lifeless figure is abandoned on the steps. Her master, unable to rouse her, puts her on a donkey and makes the journey home. On arrival he cuts her body into twelve pieces and scatters the pieces throughout the country.

'He took the knife' echoes a line from the sacrifice of Isaac. This time no angel intervenes and the brutal violence is complete:

---

13 Ibid, p 65

Of all the characters in scripture she is the least. Appearing at the beginning and close of a story that rapes her, she is alone in a world of men ... She is property, object, tool, and literary device. Without name, speech, or power, she has no friends to aid her in life or mourn her in death. Passing her back and forth among themselves, the men of Israel have obliterated her totally. Captured, betrayed, raped, tortured, murdered, dismembered, and scattered – this woman is the most sinned against ... Lesser power has no woman than this, that her life is laid down by a man.[14]

It is a brutally violent story followed by even more massive violence against women as four hundred women are captured to meet the demands of six hundred soldiers. The rape of one has become the rape in the end of six hundred as a further two hundred women from Shiloh are abducted and raped. In the story men respond to violence with greater acts of violence. 'Entrusted to Israelite men, the story of the concubine justifies the expansion of violence against women.'[15]

God is not named in the violent story of the concubine but is invoked and sanctions the orgy of killing and bloodletting that follows. That involved the massacre of over 25,000 Benjaminite men. Such slaughter threatened the future of the Benjaminite tribe, hence the abduction of six hundred women for the purposes of procreation and the continuation of a male line. Male power and violence always turns into violence and vengeance against women, and it is often sexual violence.

The story is part of the sacred text though probably never read, preached on or studied in the faith community. If read as part of public worship the response, 'This is the word of the Lord' followed by 'Thanks be to God' would be totally inappropriate. The rest of the Bible, whether ancient Israel or the early Christian community, maintains an 'overwhelming silence' in relation to the concubine's story. Yet women still suffer military, physical and sexual violence at the hands of men. Men still invoke God in the justification of their wars and violence and do what the men in the text did, project their fear and violence onto

14 Ibid, pp 80-81
15 Ibid, p 81

God. Patriarchy and misogyny belong to our age as much as they did in the centuries BCE, and they are part of the faith community still dominated by men. The silence needs to be broken and the ancient, violent story in the Bible read as present reality. It is a contemporary story of violence against women, a present tense text of terror still re-enacted in war zones and situations of violence. It is the story of violence against women still to be told of a violent Irish century.

Judges has another story of violence against the unnamed daughter of Jephthah (Judges 11). It is another brutalising story and portrays God as a violent land-thief as well as requiring violent human sacrifice. Jephthah is a 'mighty warrior' recruited to fight the Ammonites on behalf of Israel who has been accused of stealing Ammonite land. The Ammonite king proposes peaceful restoration of land but Jephthah will have none of it. The land is Israel's by divine action and sanction. If God gives victory in battle then Jephthah will offer a human sacrifice. '... and the Lord gave them into his hand. He inflicted a massive defeat on them ...' (Judges 11:32-33). The victorious warrior returns promising that whoever is first out of his door will be the human sacrifice. The first to appear is Jephthah's daughter, his one and only child. She buys time for two months of wilderness wandering to 'bewail my virginity'. When she returned Jephthah offered her as a human sacrifice. He had made his vow to God and above all God required that he keep it. When she emerged from the house, Jephthah 'tore his clothes' and grieved, but the story gives the impression that he mourned more for himself than for his daughter. 'As so often happens when a male warrior and a male deity plan together, the result is violence against women.'[16]

There are troubling images here which are still re-enacted in war zones and violent situations such as Ireland. In a patriarchal, misogynist world, male warriors do construct a male god who then sanctions bloody conquest, land-grabbing and whatever the land contains, gold or oil. The male and all-powerful god also sanctions violence against women, or somehow justifies it. Whether as victims of rape and torture or as 'comfort-

16 Nelson-Pallmeyer, op cit, p 30

women' violence is turned on women by brutalised men. The Judges' story does not make it clear if God is more pleased with mass killing and conquest, land thievery or the bloody sacrifice of an innocent young woman. All three happen and God seems to require all of them. It is a brutalised, unethical image of God from the sacred text. What kind of god requires such a vow from a father and remains silent in the face of such a vow being carried out?

> A vow led to victory; victory produced a victim; the victim died by violence; violence has, in turn, fulfilled the vow .... Moreover, in its presence even the deity to whom it was addressed remains silent. Under the power of the vow, the daughter has breathed her last My God, my God, why has thou forsaken her.[17]

The unnamed daughter has been completely forsaken by God and the faith community. Directly and indirectly, Jephthah is praised for his role. 'And the Lord sent ... Jephthah ... and rescued you out of the hand of your enemies on every side' (I Samuel 12:11). There is Sirach's litany of praise for great and famous men: 'The judges also with their respective names ... may their memory be blessed' (Sirach 46:11-12). The supersessionist Christian Testament also fails to raise a critical voice. 'For time would fail me to tell of Gideon, Barak, Samson, Jephthah .... who through faith conquered kingdoms ... became mighty in war, put foreign armies to flight. Women received their dead by resurrection ... (Hebrews 11:32-35). So Jephthah is a hero of faith, but his wife did not receive her daughter back by resurrection!

Is this the word of the Lord? Or do we need to look for the word of the Lord between the lines? Judges is part of the Deuteronomistic history. It tells the story of disloyalty to Yahweh from the founding of the monarchy to the Babylonian exile in 587 BCE. It was in exile that this history of covenantal infidelity was put together. This may be the interpretative clue, even a key as to how we are to read these many texts of terror and wrestle with their violent God-images. A literalistic reading of the texts is not possible. It in fact is a major distortion of the

---

17 Trible, op cit, pp 105-106

texts and provides divine sanction for our contemporary wars and violence. To read literally is to read through the lens of the Babylonian myth of redemptive violence and to allow it to colour and shape our violent culture. Read through the lens of exile experience a different voice is heard, one which shapes a different response.

> The *cry* is a proper voice of Israel in exile, a fresh admission of loyalty to *YHWH*, and a fresh readiness to obey *YHWH*'s commands .... the key programmatic concern of the Deuter-onomist in exile is *repentance*, that is, return to YHWH and YHWH's commandments ... that concern is articulated pri-marily with the recurrent use of the verb *shuv* ('turn, return') ... The term means to reverse course ...[18]

Israel's voice in exile is a cry of repentance, a turning around, a reversal of ethical direction to travel in a new and different way, more faithful to God's demand for justice, compassion, sol-idarity and non-violence. What we meet in these narratives of violence is not the word of the Lord, but 'Israel's religious com-promise and Israel's social barbarism and, of course in Israel's horizon those two dimensions of distorted reality are character-istically intimately connected to each other'.[19] This is why Judges affirms the social barbarism and violent anarchy at least four times. 'In those days there was no king in Israel; all the peo-ple did what was right in their own eyes' (Judges 17:6, 18:1, 19:1, 21:25). The Deuteronomist 'history' is expressed in theo-myth and re-imagined history and in both expressions we hear the cry of repentance. The brutalised violence and the violent God im-ages are not the divine will. The warrior God does not sanction war or violence. Blaming divine sanction or blessing for either is the worst form of idolatry. Violence against woman, military, paramilitary, domestic or social is an injustice against women's humanity and social idolatry as the deification of the male. The god of violence is a violent human construct and the projection of human fear and violence onto a deity. We read these brutal

18 Brueggemann, Walter, *An Introduction to the Old Testament: The Canon and Christian Imagination* (Louisville: Westminster, John Knox Press, 2003) p 128
19 Ibid, pp 128-129

texts of violence in their exilic (displaced, dislocated) context as a cry of repentance, a turning away from the ideology of violence to a different way of life.

CHAPTER SEVEN

But it's supposed to be Good News! Violent texts in the Christian Testament

The last chapter may have created the impression that the 'Jewish God' of the Hebrew Bible is different from the 'Christian God' portrayed in the Christian Testament. Christians do frequently make this distinction seeing the former as a bad and violent God, while the latter is good or non-violent. Or others will assert that the God of the Hebrew Bible is a God of justice, usually punitive justice, while the God of the Christian Testament is a God of love. It has been quite easy for Christians to make this claim. The texts of terror and violence in the Hebrew Bible are obvious and there are too many Christians who are quite happy to claim them through a literal reading and connect them to a nationalistic cause, war effort or violent revolution. A considerable sector within the Christian community in Northern Ireland has identified with such biblical stories of violence in support of militaristic opposition to Home Rule or to legitimise a defensive violent response to the terrorists of the IRA. For many Protestant Christians God is a punitive God and justice is primarily punitive and about law and order.

Significantly in this identification with the warrior God and justified violence against the enemy, there is often little if any emphasis on the non-violent teaching of Jesus. The focus is on his sacrificial death required by a punitive and violent God who requires the violent, substitutionary death of his Son as the penalty for sin. This violent God is consistent with the literal reading of the violent images in the Hebrew Bible. But what is also completely overlooked are the texts of non-violence and critique within the Hebrew Bible itself. These radical counter-texts will be explained in the next chapter.

A traditional reading of the story by most Christians, Protestant and Catholic, is that things were so bad in the Jewish narrative that God needed a new covenant and this was the purpose of Jesus, especially his death. It was for this reason that Christians, not Jews, invented the term 'Old Testament' and

'New Testament' implying that 'new' is better than 'old' and therefore puts a distance between Christians and Jews. The assumption is that the Jews misunderstood God's will, but Christians have got it with Jesus. A more extreme end of this line of thought is that the Jews rejected the Messiah and were responsible for the death of Jesus. There is no question that this has led to a history of anti-Judaism and has contributed to anti-semitism, a religio-racist prejudice that led to the Holocaust and the extermination of Jews in 20th century 'Christian' Europe. This superficial and supersessionist reading of the Christian story has cast Christianity adrift from its Jewish roots, even before the advent of Christendom in the 4th century which then made the Jewish faith illegal. By the 2nd century, Christians were cutting themselves off from their Jewish roots, distorting and denying their Jewish God and Jewish Jesus. By the advent of Christendom not only was theology or God-talk skewed, so too was christology. Supersessionism, anti-Judaism and anti-semitism have been dominatant in the subsequent Christian story and it is only post-Holocaust that Christianity has slowly begun to appreciate its Jewish roots and recover them in its reading of the Hebrew Bible and its understanding of who Jesus is.

The history of Christendom has not only been supersessionist, anti-Jewish and anti-semitic, it has been violent, and has conveniently ignored the long non-violent history of Judaism for practically all of the past twenty centuries. The next chapter will also show that the Jewish history of non-violence goes back to the 8th century BCE to Hosea and the 6th century BCE Jeremiah. Indeed a non-literal, theo-mythical reading of the violent texts puts them into a more theo-ethical perspective. The violence was never the command of God or sanctioned by God, but the projection of human violence and megalomania onto the deity.

But most Christians are still under the impression that the Hebrew Bible is a violent book and the Christian Testament is not. It is true that holy war is not so explicit or obvious in the pages of the Christian Testament. 'But does this mean that God has lost his taste for blood?'[1] Two thousand years of Christian or Christendom history would suggest not. The Christological dis-

---

1 Teehan, John, *In the Name of God: The Evolutionary Origins of Religious Ethics and Violence*, (Chichester: Wiley-Blackwell, 2010) p 161

putes of the early church councils which produced the familiar creeds were literally Jesus Wars. 'Ephesus and Chalcedon were battles for the political future as much as a war for eternal truths... The councils led to outrageous violence in many parts of the empire – to popular risings and *coup d'etat*, to massacres and persecutions.'[2]

But this is to fast-forward and skip the violence in the early Christian documents. That may be convenient but dishonest. There is violence in the Christian Testament, or at least there are numerous traditional interpretations of texts that are violent and have been used to justify Christian violence and war. When the great theologian of the church, Augustine of Hippo, who has been the major influence on Western theology, Catholic and Reformed, made a text from a parable of a feast, 'compel them to come in', the centre of his evangelistic theology, he sanctioned and legitimised coercion and violence in mission and evangelism. This violent theology, based on a partial proof-text, underpinned the marriage between imperial expansionism and Christian mission, which produced an imperial, coercive and violent form of missionary activity. It was violent and destructive in relation to indigenous cultures. Augustine's text from a Jesus parable was a compulsion text which has always suited the Christendom model of belief.

There are other Christian Testament texts, which when read literally or ideologically, portray violent and primitive God images and justify violence and war in the name of God.

Roman Imperial Violence

It is helpful to be aware of the violence of the empire because it dominated the world of the Christian Testament. Roman imper - ialism is in the foreground of the text from Matthew to Revelation and that means reading the Christian Testament as

---

2 Jenkins, Philip, *Jesus Wars: How Four Patriarchs, Three Queens and Two Emperors Decided What Christians Would Believe for the Next 1,500 Years*, (London:SPCK, 2010) p 25. Jenkins rightly takes the spiritualised gloss off early church history and shows that the Christendom process of creed-making was a very violent story of the early church's battles over 'right belief'. Violence was an essential part of defining 'orthodoxy', which raises critical questions about what was claimed to be 'orthodox belief', how it was defined and who defined it.

documents set in, living with and struggling to respond to a pervasive culture of violence. Imperial violence was frequent and
brutal and it deeply affected Palestine. Roman warlords and
legions dealt brutally and violently with any resistance or rising.
Crucifixion was the form of execution for terrorists. When there
was a rising or revolt the imperial military machine responded
with a vengeance. Galilee was a particular hot-bed for resistance
movements and rebels. When King Herod died, revolts were
widespread. Over a period of three years, a Roman general put
down these risings in Galilee 'with destruction of many villages,
slaughter and enslavement of people, and the crucifixion of
thousands.'[3] Only a few miles from Nazareth, where Jesus grew
up, the town of Sepphoris was burned and its population en-
slaved. This is the world of Jesus, the life-situation in which he
taught, healed, lived and finally became the victim of imperial
violence and execution. After Jesus' crucifixion things did not
get any better. About three decades later economic and political
conditions deteriorated with bands of zealots and extremists rising in revolt against the military and economic oppression of the
Roman empire. Galilee was reconquered and virtually destroyed,
and by 70 CE, Jerusalem and the Temple were razed to the
ground. Seventy years after that disaster another huge rising
took place led by Bar Kokhba. It was brutally put down by a
highly destructive war from 132-135 CE.

This is what happened to Judea and Galilee but Roman military and economic imperialism extended throughout the then
known world. Jesus lived in occupied territory dominated by
the world of imperial Rome. Paul worked in the great Greek
urban centres and they too were key strategic Roman cities of
control and domination. Nothing was outside the power of the
empire. The Christian gospels and letters were all written in the
shadow of empire and in the context of imperial military and
economic might. Pervasive state violence is the foreground to
the Christian Testament.

Richard Horsley draws attention to three immediate effects
of 'the "in your face" enforced violence and constant threat of
further violence.'[4] The effects are classic and recognisable in the

3 Matthews, Skelly and Gibson, E. Leigh (eds), *Violence in the New
Testament* (New York: T&T Clark, 2005) p 55

context and culture of Irish violence.

The imperial violence left a Galilean community seriously traumatised. Friends and followers of Jesus named in the gospels may well have lost relatives and friends. The village of Emmaus was obliterated. Village communities around the sea of Galilee were forcibly displaced so that the second capital of Herod Antipas could be adequately serviced. Traumatised communities are dysfunctional communities.

Such a situation of state violence produces 'patriarchal violence' when groups with a shared heritage turn on each other. When active resistance is an obvious suicidal act then violence turns in. The Jews and Samaritans shared considerable religious heritage but hated each other. Jesus' parable of the 'Good Samaritan' reflects the hostility and around 50CE Samaritans attacked and killed Galileans on their way to the Passover festival in Jerusalem. Retaliatory violence followed with attacks on Samaritan villages.

Horsley's third effect is more than pertinent. 'Imperial violence and the constant threat of more violence led to demonic possession'.[5] This condition features large in the gospel stories of exorcism and healing, Mark 5 being a good example. The story features not only a case of demon possession but its vocabulary is littered with Roman military and imperial words such as legion. It is now recognised that concern with demon possession and history and society controlled for the present by Satan reached unprecedented levels in Judaism during Roman imperial domination. Literalising or dismissing such language in the present is to ignore what was happening to a traumatised society in the past century or in the present. Demon possession 'was, among other things, a defensive (self-protective) response to the imperial (threat of) violence'.[6] Violent and traumatised societies produce psychosomatic illness leading, within Northern Ireland communities, to high levels of long-term illness, high drug dependency and to increased suicides. The healing stories and exorcisms in the gospels are related to the violent context,

4 Horsley's chapter 'By The Finger of God: Jesus and Imperial Violence in Skelly and Leigh, p 56-58
5 Ibid, p 57
6 Ibid, p 58

are a result of it and are in themselves a protest against imperial violence and the restoration of people to community in which there is wellbeing.[7]

Roman imperial violence did produce counter-violence. State violence did lead to violent resistance movements.[8] The most sustained results came from within the Judean and Galilean peasant communities. The upper classes in and around Jerusalem may have produced occasional resistance literature, but more often protested their power and privilege through collusion or collaboration with the Romans. There were voices of non-violence that not only condemned the imperial violence and oppression, but also the violent oppression of Jewish leaders and their collaboration with Roman power. This literature began back in Hellenistic times with the book of Daniel, especially chapters 7-12. In Roman times it is found in the Psalms of Solomon, the Testament of Moses and the texts from the Qumran community.

Resistance movements were often engaged in violent resistance. Frustration and despair led some Jewish intellectuals to assassinate prominent high priests. 'These intellectual "Daggermen" (*Sicarioi*) thus launched a kind of counter-terrorism to the imperial violence'.[9] Messianic movements did exist and were the inspiration for popular revolts in 4CE, 66-70CE and 132-135CE. The leaders of these violent revolts were hailed as 'kings' but in the writings of Josephus they are described in terms of liberation movements modeled on the actions of Saul and David who were proclaimed as 'messiahs' (II Samuel 2:1-4; 5:1-4). Messianic leaders or those with messianic pretensions do portray themselves in religious or moral terms. They do claim some kind of divine sanction or high moral ground. In religious terms they will, as did leaders of the movements in 1st century Galilee and Judea, read their sacred texts or sacred traditions literally and apply them literally. By ignoring the theo-mythical nature of the narrative they create a negative or violent myth in the present which can and does live on in popular memory. History, including Irish history, provides many examples. Christians have

7 Ibid, p 60
8. Ibid,p 58
9. Ibid, pp 63-68

put Jesus into this messianic category despite the fact he is represented in the gospels as debunking and rejecting the Davidic model, because of its violence.

Under Roman military imperialism, violent resistance and revolt stood no chance. The myth of redemptive violence was invoked on numerous occasions but each time brutally crushed by imperial power. Even the numerous non-violent movements of resistance, and there were many in the era of the gospels, were suppressed by large military forces.

It is not an exaggeration therefore, to read the Christian Testament in the foreground of state violence and counter-violence, and recognise behind the gospels in particular, traumat - ised and sick communities. From Genesis to Revelation violence is pervasive and these documents represent faith communities struggling to express hope and a radical alternative lifestyle, as did their ancestors of faith in the Hebrew Bible. But did they always escape from the violent Babylonian myth, or did they sometimes buy into it and project their own violence onto God?

Violent God Images?
All reading of the Bible is interpretation. Biblical literalists like to pretend that they are simply saying it as it is, the Bible says. But it never simply says. All read from a standpoint, through particular lenses, with various presuppositions. A text from the past will always and inevitably be interpreted and there may well be no interpretation which is ideologically free. The interpretative struggle, and it is that, is unavoidable. Biblical literalism is an interpretative strategy, and like all others struggles with consistency and coherence. But literalism's greatest challenge is with violence because it literally reads violent texts and literally interprets violent texts, and such texts or literal interpretative strategies exist in the Christian Testament.

Violent punishment appears to be in God's nature and purpose. We have already noted the tension in the Exodus story between God's violence and God's justice. A little people are liberated from oppression and injustice and enemies are drowned in the sea. Liberation comes through violence. Later Jewish trad - ition itself has expressed its discomfort with the drowning of Egyptians in the story of God asking the liberated to temper their celebrations by remembering that the 'Egyptians are also my children.' The Feast of the Passover is a memory of justice made present, a vision of just liberation. But it has also been read as a memory or commemoration of the defeat of Israel's enemies, which can also be remembered as present hope. This not only includes the drowning of the Egyptians at the sea, but God's killing of the firstborn Egyptians as preparatory for the journey of the Israelites to liberation. Remembered in this way these violent God-images carry over into the Christian Testament.

This strand of remembering is also present in the annual Feast of the Passover. In the gospels the crucifixion of Jesus takes place in or near the Passover feast when Jerusalem was crowded with pilgrims. It was a volatile occasion with heightened nationalism and anti-Roman feelings. After all it was a festival remembering the liberation of a people from Egyptian military and economic oppression. The parallels were all too obvious. The twin themes of justice and violence were present and the Romans took special security measures during this week. There is no direct evidence from the gospels that the violence of God strand was invoked by Jesus or any of his followers during Passover. Neither was it explicitly critiqued, though the altern - ative peace parade organised by Jesus on what we now call Palm Sunday, was an explicit rejection of Roman military violence and Jewish counter-violence, and any violent Davidic messianism. Undoubtedly for many the remembering of God's violence to overthrow Egyptians and to inflict the same on the Romans was all too real.

A song of Mary is found in Luke's gospel. It is a rich reflection on a much earlier song in Israel's history, the song of Hannah (Luke 1 and I Samuel 2). Both songs celebrate acts of God in the defeat of enemies. God has broken the bows of the mighty (I Samuel 2:4) and 'brought down the powerful from their thrones' (Luke 1:52). How God does this and whether or not a human physical force tradition is required is not stated. During the Samuel era, Israel did want a king like other peoples, which meant an army and a military tradition. Hannah's song may well reflect the counter-tradition of the warrior God which was also a tradition forbidding the use of armies and violence. Mary's song, clearly based on Hannah's, would be in the same tradition. Both could be read as motivation for using physical force and violence in the overthrow of oppressive powers. Yet the warrior God tradition forbids this, not least because taking on the might of the Philistines, Babylonians or Romans was futile, impossible and a recipe for self-destruction. Far from advocating the use of violence, unless read literally and without context, the song is a poetic vision of a reconfigured world with social justice at its heart. It subverts the imperial definition of reality, imagines an alternative world and keeps hope and justice alive in the midst of domination.

Violent readings do portray violent God-images. Our obsession with the myth of redemptive violence colours our interpretation of sacred text. A classic example is Jesus' parable in Mark 12 :1-12. It is the story of an absentee landlord who plants a vineyard, leases it out and returns to his far-off home. All of this was common practice in Roman-dominated Palestine. After harvest he sent a slave to collect the profits. The slave was beaten, a second ended up with serious head injuries, a succession of slaves sent in turn were badly beaten or murdered. Eventually he sent 'a beloved son', thinking he would be respected. The tenants thought that if they killed the heir, then the vineyard would belong to them. So they murdered the 'beloved son' and dumped his body as the final insult. The vineyard owner responds by coming himself, presumably with considerable physical force and kills the tenants. The vineyard is given to others who after this show of brutal violence will hand over any future profits.

A traditional and popular interpretation of the parable reads the story christologically. The 'beloved son' is identified with Jesus and the vineyard owner is God. It has been understood as a story of God's only Son being rejected and crucified and those responsible are the Jews. Nowhere does the story say this but it has been a dominant interpretation. Blaming the Jews has been a serious piece of Christian bigotry, hatred and prejudice against Jews. The interpretative assumption that the vineyard owner is God creates a brutally violent, vengeful image of God who punishes and kills off those who reject his Son. Incredibly this interpretation is as old as Christianity, is embedded in tradition and does not appear to raise serious moral and ethical questions for the faithful. In popular interpretative understanding the God of the parable is a violent God. The story itself does not say such things but it is the violent interpretation imposed on it.

Placed within the violent context of Roman imperial violence in occupied Palestine, the parable can be read differently. William Herzog in his book on the parables as subversive speech takes the imperial context seriously in his treatment of all the parables. Rather than interpreting the parable in Mark 12 christologically and profiling a violent God, Herzog gives it a more contextual title, 'Peasant Revolt and the Spiral of Violence'.[10]

The experience of Roman imperialism for most Palestinians was land-loss. Rich landowners, absentee landowners did not buy land but took it. It may have been taken as debt foreclosure, leaving people destitute or forced to work land for others which they had once owned. This was widespread practice and experience and when Jesus told a story like this, he would have had a knowing audience. Hitting back at the vineyard owner was what many wanted to do. Listening to this Jewish storyteller would have been an exciting experience, with enthusiastic audience participation. Often the humiliated and abused humiliate and abuse in turn. Victims of violence often become victimisers. But the punchline is in the question. 'What then will the owner of the vineyard do? He will come and destroy the tenants and give the vineyard to others' (Mark 12:29).

The parable is not about the killing of God's only Son and a violent God taking vengeance on those who reject Christ. In the context of Roman imperial violence it is a story about the utter futility of violent revolt. Herzog makes use of the obvious spiral of violence, then and now. Violent oppression by the domination system leads to revolt. The revolt leads to increased brutal violence and repression from the powers, which in turn leads to crushing defeat of the oppressed. Its a recognisable pattern of history. Other more radical and alternative ways have to be found to subvert the repressive domination system. Counter-violence is futile against a superior military power. It may even be described as a failure of subversive imagination.

---

10. Herzog, William R II, *Parables as Subversive Speech: Jesus as Pedagogue of the Oppressed* (Louisville: Westminster John Knox Press, 1994) pp 10ff

The vineyard owner in the parable is not God but the imperial system, the domination system of repressive landowners. There is no Christology in the parable but a story which represents Jesus' radical critique of the futility of violence through risings, revolts, rebellions and violent resistance, characteristic of life in the Galilee in which he lived. Liberating violence was and is a false hope.

The pervasive violent God-image became the basis through which the death of Jesus was interpreted. The violent God who punishes was not only read into the parables of Jesus, but eventually became the dominate interpretative prism through which the death of Jesus was understood. Blood sacrifice was required by God, which is the traditional interpretation of Abraham being asked to sacrifice Isaac. In the end God provides a ram since blood is required. The same assumptions have been made when reading the Cain and Abel story. God's anger needs appeasement so sacrifices are offered to fend off the anger of God. Abel's animal offering, shed blood, is acceptable to God which Cain's vegetables are not.

Key to a traditional Christian interpretation of the death of Jesus is the scapegoat ritual of the Day of Atonement. The sacrificial theme is expressed through the goat killed as a 'sin offering'. A second goat is sent away into the wilderness as a scapegoat carrying the sins of the people. The Leviticus 16 text is the creation of priestly writers in the Babylonian exile. If exile was understood as God's punishment of Judah's infidelity, then blood sacrifice and the scapegoat image are priestly responses, a way of appeasing a punishing and violent God.

Christians later took this imagery and applied it to Jesus' death. Jesus is the ultimate sacrificial lamb or scapegoat on whom the sins of the world are placed. 'Jesus stands between a wrathful God and sinful humanity. His death substitutes for our own'. Jesus offers the perfect blood sacrifice to appease the violent deity and that interpretation then became ritualised in the Lord's Supper or Eucharist. It was this interpretation and ritual that shaped the ideology and poetry of Pearse in the 1916 Rising and the early British war poets. Blood sacrifice cleanses and liberates.

Violent Atonement

The substitutionary or satisfaction theory of the atonement has dominated Western theology for the last 1,000 years. Shaped by Anselm, it was refined by Calvin and the reformers and is so embedded in Western theological thought and liturgy that it has not only become norm, but the interpretative key for Christian Testament texts. It has been read back into the early texts, imposed on them, leading to the assumption that this is the dominant Christian Testament way of understanding Jesus' death and atonement. Apart from Western theology over-emphasising the death of Jesus at the expense of his teaching, it has failed to realise that the dominant theory has embedded a form of violence, primarily God's violence, in its interpretation. Given that this violence of God has shaped social and political violence through its core idea of blood sacrifice, it is 'imperative to deal with the violence contained in the standard atonement theories'. As well as believing that violence is intrinsic to the atonement theories, Denny Weaver names the fundamental error of Christian thought.

> In fact, I believe it is arguable that the incorporation and rationalisation of violence in Christian thought and practice that entered the church in the fourth and fifth centuries is the most fundamental error in the entire history of Christian thought.'[11]

The roots of a violent theory of the atonement go back a long way beyond Calvin and Anselm. The violence is rooted in the Constantinian edict which has not only been the critique of the historic peace churches, but also led the founder of Methodism, John Wesley and others to see the Constantinian edict as the fall of the church.

There are, of course, other ways of understanding the death of Jesus, but the substitutionary and satisfaction theories have come to dominate and they raise ethical questions about God. How moral is a punitive, punishing, violent God and what does an innocent Jesus suffering at the hands of a violent, punishing God say to people trapped in abusive, oppressive and violent contexts? Many abused women have perceived this God to be

---

11 Ibid, p 316 footnote

abusive, which in turn legitimises male abuse and violence.

A major problem with these dominant theories of atonement is that they contradict the teaching of Jesus on non-violence. Does this mean that Jesus and God are in opposition to each other? It ought to be a core Christian assumption that Jesus is normative for Christian ethics and discipleship, and if that is so, then there is no avoiding the challenge to deal with atonement theories rooted in violence and violent God-images. If Jesus is for Christians the supreme clue to God, the primary disclosure, then our 'discussion of atonement is actually a conversation about our view of God'.[12] Furthermore, any discussion of atonement needs to embrace the life, teaching, death and resurrection of Jesus, otherwise our theology will be incomplete, if not skewed. The Christian claim to know God is centred on Jesus, and whilst no longer possible to make this an absolute or exclusive claim, it does mean that for Christians, Jesus is theological and ethical norm. Given that radical non-violence was at the heart of his teaching, about life and about God, then it does become imperative to articulate non-violent understandings of atonement, including non-violent liturgies of the Eucharist.

Central to an alternative approach is an understanding older than substitutionary or satisfaction theories. This is known as the *Christus Victor* understanding. Through his life, death and resurrection, Jesus was victorious over the powers of evil and violence. It is the language of victory and conquest but with a radical difference. The victory and conquest are non-violent. *Christus Victor* is characterised by a non-violent motif. There is violence at the heart of it but not God's violence, 'nor violence sanctioned or needed or used by God. The violence in normative *Christus Victor* comes from the side of the forces of evil that killed Jesus.'[13] This is the radical difference. The standard atonement theories contain divinely sanctioned violence. *Christus Victor* does not. Jesus is the victim of state violence, executed by the Roman imperial power. The empire is the embodiment of structural and human forces of evil. When that same empire became legally Christian in the 4th century, it could not ever bring

---

12 Ibid, p 317
13 Ibid, p 337

itself to acknowledge that Jesus was crucified by its representative, Pontius Pilate, or that the violence of imperial power was responsible for his death. Christendom eventually transferred the responsibility for violence to God and denied the real power of evil by inventing appeasement models.

The *Christus Victor* approach, more in keeping with the Christian Testament, locates the real source of violence, not in God but in the imperial power. The contrast is stark and intentional. 'In fact, it is the resort to violence that makes clear the differing *modus operandi* of reign of God and the rule of evil represented by Rome.'[14]

The Power of Apocalyptic

The *Christus Victor* understanding of the death of Jesus, which includes the whole Jesus story, does have a warrior God dimension. The violence that killed Jesus was not sanctioned or required by God, it was the violence of the state. The battle vision of *Christus Victor* is cosmic. It is a cosmic confrontation in which the forces of God and evil clash. Jesus did not call on a physical force tradition to fight the empire at Golgotha. He had consistently taught the futility of that approach and had put Peter to right when the latter used a sword. The imagery is mythical, the kind of language used in Revelation 12, which reflects a cosmic battle, a way of seeing the world from another dimension. This is the world defined not in terms of violence and counter-violence but an imagined world where the core issue is the triumph of good over evil, justice over injustice, non-violence over violence, love over hate. Literalise cosmic-mythic language and it has the power to transfer into brutal, divinely sanctioned violence among people. Apocalyptic language, another way of describing the theo-mythical, cosmic imagery, needs to be handled with extreme care.

Its roots lie in the Hebrew Bible, though it may well have been borrowed and modified from Near Eastern neighbours. Some vivid Persian imagination may lie behind it, which is not surprising given that returning exiles were subject to the latest imperial power of Persia. It came alive for the 'little people' of Israel when the Greeks dominated life and was given early ex-

---

14 Ibid, p 337

pression by Daniel. The real life context is in the world of 160-
150 BCE, a crisis that threatened Jews and Jewishness.
Antiochus IV was imposing his political and cultural domination on Jerusalem. It was a Hellinistic onslaught which threatened everything Jewish. The same crisis is reflected in I
Maccabees which tells the story of a Jewish rising led by a group
of brothers and their army. Apocalyptic Daniel (ch 7-12) pre-
sents the same crisis apocalyptically, in terms of a cosmic battle
that God will win, not with the help of Maccabean armies, but as
the warrior God who fights for the little people in another dimension.

Apocalyptic literature is crisis literature, produced in the
white heat of an historical crisis but which imagines the ultimate
outcome in another dimension. The real battle is not in
Jerusalem but in the cosmic sphere. Apocalyptic Daniel offers a
cosmic sweep of world history as successive empires are imagined in dramatic symbolism. They have feet of clay, however
beastly they are visualised. They have their day and cease to be.
Apocalyptic Daniel offers a subversive theology of empire
which is not world escapism but poetic or mythical imagery that
holds a people together in the face of crisis. 'This visionary language is a rhetorical strategy for articulating deep hope that lies
beyond the vagaries of historical reality.'[15] The approach is also
non-violent, but that is not how literalists have read it and used
it. It has become the language of prophets of doom who long for
the final showdown in history, somewhere in Israel, when Islam
will be wiped out, and ultimately Jews, though they are useful
at present. Christians alone will survive, taken up in the rapture,
or a thousand years peaceful reign will be inaugurated. Daniel
along with the book of Revelation became dangerous hand-
books of a violent God in the hands of militant and bloodthirsty
humans, usually men. But this is the distortion and corruption
of the apocalyptic genre. As crisis literature it 'represents a daring and courageous invitation to a hope in God who is not
ordered or domesticated or guaranteed by historical facts on the
ground'.[16] The biblical literalists with their obsession with vio-

15 Brueggemann, Walter, I (Louisville: Westminster John Knox Press,
2003) p 358
16 Ibid, pp 358-359

lence do not believe that and they are a danger to the peace of
the planet with their militaristic and violent visions of God's
present and future. It is when their warped apocalypticism
wants to become foreign policy or support US military advent-
urism that their take on the Bible is most obscene.

There is an apocalyptic text in Mark's gospel, not surprisingly
since Mark's gospel is war-time literature, written during the
Jewish-Roman war of 66-70 CE. Apocalpytic texts are also found
in I Thessalonians where a tiny faith community is living under
enormous imperial pressure. Some feel that the apocalyptic context is pervasive in the Christian Testament, that it was a major
interpretative key for the first generation Jesus movement. The
book of Revelation, though, is the most obvious example of
apocalypticism and the violence of its language has disturbed
many Christians, but fascinated others. Yet others are puzzled
because a clear reading of the text suggests brutal violence and
active non-violence in the same text and both appear to be God
and Christ images. Can both be literally true?

There are also those within the Christian community who
see so much violence in the book that they write it off.

Walter Wink concludes:

> The book of Revelation, however, despite its penetrating in-
> sights about the Domination System, is filled with a craving,
> not for redemptive violence, but something even worse:
> punitive violence to be carried out by God, of course, so that
> John himself keeps his own hands clean. We are a long, long
> way from Jesus here.[17]

The Jesus Wink has in mind is the Jesus of the Sermon on the
Mount and his radical, active non-violence, echoed by Paul in
Romans 13. Yet Jesus is central to Revelation and is portrayed
both as warrior king and non-violent Lamb.

The former image is expressed in a text containing a chilling
threat of violence. To the church at Thyatira, the Son of God
with 'eyes like a flame of fire, and whose feet are like burnished
bronze' (just don't get in the way of this figure) threatens a

---

17 Wink, Walter, *Engaging the Powers: Discernment and Resistance in a
World of Domination* (Minneapolis: Fortress Press, 1992) p 136

woman called Jezebel with brutal violence. 'Because I am throwing her on a bed, and those who commit adultery with her I am throwing into great distress, unless they repent of her doings, and I will strike her children dead' (Revelation 2:22-23). The lectionary does include this text along with the other letters to the seven churches in Asia Minor and the letters are popular texts with the free-style traditions. Yet there is no critique or even awareness of a chilling thread of violence from a threatening Son of God. Women are rightly disturbed by the image of a woman being thrown or shoved onto a bed for sexual purposes. The image is one of abusive sex, indeed rape. Killing children is an even more chilling image. Even if one reads the text symbolically, did the author have to use such brutal imagery? Jezebel has lived on as a pejorative, derogatory and abusive term for women and which has in turn sanctioned violence by men.

Revelation is littered with texts of violence, punishment and vengeance. There are judgement scenes which outdo Dante or perhaps provided Dante with images of everlasting fire and torment. One such text is Revelation 20:11-15. Those whose names are not written in the book of life were 'thrown into the lake of fire'. There are those for whom this text describes the literal end of those who are unredeemed.

If so, then it portrays God using massive violence on an unprecedented scale. In fact, according to Tremper Longman, 'no more fearful picture of a vengeful, violent God may be found than that described in Revelation 20:11-15.' As Longman sees it: 'Those who have moral difficulties with the genocide in the conquest of Canaan should have even more serious difficulties with the final judgement.'[18]

Longman has no difficulty with either the Canaanite genocide or the violent judgement. He does in fact take a progressive revelation approach advocating 'five distinct phases of divine warfare in the Bible'.[19] The first phase is 'God's fight against the flesh-and-blood enemies of Israel', which covers the Canaanite

18 Siebert, Eric A. *Disturbing Divine Behaviour: Troubling Old Testament Images of God* (Minneapolis: Fortress Press, 2009) p 184
19 Ibid, p 81

genocide. The last phase is 'the final battle' which justifies God's genocidal violence in judgement.[20]

All-time best sellers, eleven volumes of the 'Left Behind' series, combine 'conspiracy, romance, violence and Bible verses'.[21] Daniel and Revelation feature large in the 50 million copies sold. The world moves towards a violent doomsday scenario. The last great battle of Armageddon looms in those last days but just before the divinely authorised slaughter, the rapture will occur when God will snatch the faithful up to heaven before 'unleashing a seven-year period of global tribulation and terrible destruction on the earth'.[22]

Not only is rapture theology based on fear, it is a form of voyeurism and an addiction to war and violence by religious people. The millions who read those books and buy into this addictive theology of violence are people for whom war and violence have become entertainment. They have become entranced by it. But Barbara Rossing is right to describe it as 'The Destructive Racket of Rapture'.

Whether prescribing a violent script for Israel or survivalism in the United states, this theology distorts God's vision for the world. In place of healing the rapture proclaims escape. In place of Jesus' blessing of peacemakers, the rapture voyeuristically glorifies violence and war. In place of Revelation's vision of the Lamb's vulnerable self-giving love, the Rapture celebrates the lion-like wrath of the Lamb. The theology is not biblical.

Rapture theology is disasterous for the Middle East and it is even more dangerous for planet earth.[23]

---

20 Ibid, p 294 endnote 41 which lists all five phases. In fairness to Longman, endnote 43 emphasises his belief that 'God does not author - ise Christians to kill or engage in acts of genocide in the name of Christ'. That may be so, but it puts God in a category where the moral standards we adhere to do not apply to God. From a religious perspective, therefore, what moral norms do we have for moral behaviour? God is more violent than we are and can get away with it because God is God! This is not a basis for faith-based ethics.

21 Rossing, Barbara R, *The Rapture Exposed: The Message of Hope in the Book of Revelation* (New York: Basic Books, 2004) p XVI. Rossing's book is a devastating critique and exposure of this disingenuous distortion of the Bible which has its roots in fear. It is, she believes, a modern heresy which shapes the lives of millions of fearful Christians.

22 Ibid, p 3

23 Ibid, pp 1-2

Rapture theology drawn from Revelation adds substance to Nelson-Pallmeyer's conclusion on the book. 'It is filled with so much blood and gore that one needs a thick skin to read it'.[24] And yet Rossing believes that there is much more than violence in the book, there is non-violence which is paradoxically the imagery of conquest in Revelation and Lamb power. She believes that this key image of Revelation, the Lamb who was slain, has been highjacked by interpreters, especially the Rapture theologians-novelists. The crucial non-violence strand of Revelation will be explored in the next chapter.

The violent imagery, blood and gore remain and require acknowledgement and interpretation. If read and applied literally then this is the most violent book in the Bible, with some of the most violent images of God. If true, it would have been better if Revelation had lost the struggle to be included in the canon of sacred scripture.

The literary genre is apocalyptic and that provides the interpretative key. Much of the language is deeply symbolic and profoundly mythical. This is much more Lord of the Rings style literature and we would never dream of reading Tolkien literally. Apocalypticism deals with battles in a cosmic sphere. In relation to the every day struggle with an historical domination system, a superpower's violence and oppression, apocalypticism takes us behind the scenes, to the real battle portrayed in mythical, cosmic terms. Apocalypticism gives us a glimpse into the real reality of historical dynamics. The ultimate reality is the reign of God not imperial rule. The human cry and longing for justice, 'How long O Lord?', will not ultimately be disappointed. There are values like justice which ultimately count. Apocalyptic lang - uage is the language of hope in crisis and it was in some of the deepest crises that Israel turned to apocalyptic imaginings and symbols.

An apocalypse can provide support in the face of persecution (eg Daniel); reassurance in the face of culture shock (possibly the Book of the Watchers) or social powerlessness (the Similitudes of Enoch); reconciliation in the wake of historical

---

24 Nelson-Pallmeyer, Jack, *Jesus Against Christianity: Reclaiming the Missing Jesus* (Harrisburg: Trinity Press International, 2001) p 58

trauma (2 Baruch, 3 Baruch), consolation for the dismal fate of humanity (4 Ezra) or comfort for the inevitability of death (the Testament of Abraham). The constant factor is that the problem is put in perspective by the otherworldly revelation of a transcendent world and eschatological judgement.[25]

The judgment theme expressed is violent though mythical language in Revelation is the language of ending and new beginning. The book of 4 Ezra was written during the crushing defeat and destruction of Jerusalem in the Jewish-Roman war ending 70 CE. It was a way of articulating hope. End is never found but opens up the possibility for new birth and new beginnings. Written about 30 years later Revelation, through its apocalyptic and mythical symbols, proclaims hope in crisis and new beginnings beyond any end.

> ... apocalyptic hope is characteristically available in vivid images and venturesome symbols that offer no explanation, but simply bear testimony to newness that is beyond every human explanation.[26]

The tragedy is that millions of (fearful) Christians turn the vivid images and venturesome symbols into an obsession with militarism and an addiction to violence which threatens the very peace of the planet. They not only ignore and wish to destroy God's dream of *Shalom*, they ignore the Bible's devastating crit - ique of the violence in its own text.

---

25 Collins, John J quoted in Brueggemann, Walter, *Old Testament Theology: An Introduction* (Nashville: Abingdon Press, 2008) p 361
26 Ibid, p 361 Brueggemann goes on to say that apocalyptic literature 'is designed to nurture and sustain the buoyancy of hope ...'

CHAPTER EIGHT

The Bible critiques itself:
The Counter Witness

Recently a leader of one of the Loyal Orders in Northern Ireland complained that multi-culturalism and secularism, and by implication pluralism, were all conspiring to diminish Christianity. Christians were being given a hard time and political correctness was running wild. It is not unusual to hear such sentiments from conservative believers. Rooted in fear, what they are really demanding is a return to Christian hegemony and privilege, or turn the clock back to Christendom. It is a view which needs to be taken seriously but it still represents a failure to read the signs of the time. A continent, supposedly Christian yet responsible for the most violent century in recorded history, cannot expect its faith foundations to remain rock steady or occupy a place of hegemony and privilege. Not when there were so many fault lines in the faith structures. The violence and war of the 20th century has shaken the very foundations and institutional forms of religion which have been demoted by the people. The culture, if not cult, of violence and war with which the 20th century began was seriously crumbling after the First World War and collapsed after the Second. The religion that was so much part of it collapsed along with it.

Significantly, the Loyal Orders, whose leader complained about this loss of hegemony and vigorously called for its re-assertion by Christians, holds Constantine's motto: 'In this sign conquer.' The sign of course was the sign of the cross which doubles as a sword. But religious violence and war have had their day (well almost!). More than anything else they have de-privileged Christianity in the west by exposing perhaps its inherent violence. The sacred texts of violence have been exposed and the frequent violent interpretations. If we still read the Bible we can no longer do so uncritically. Brueggemann describes our current situation accurately.

The disestablishment of a triumphalist church in the West can hardly be contested. In the place of a consensus authority, we have within the church an amazing pluralism that is matched outside the church by vigorous, competing religious claims and by a profound secularisation of culture. It is especially evident that the Enlightenment establishment with which the church in its dominance had allied itself is equally disestablished ... What goes under the general term of postmodern signifies the breakup of any broad consensus about what we know or how we know what we know.[1]

This is where faith finds itself in the west, especially in Europe, but the good news may well be that anyone at home in the biblical world will not feel strange or fearful. The faith communities of the Hebrew Bible and Christian Testament were anything but hegemonic and lived in a world of many religions and many gods and lords. The Bible is a pluralistic book and there are a plurality of witnesses to God in the text. This means that there was no one way of talking about God or faith, or even one way of understanding Jesus. The entire biblical text is a witness to rich plurality in relation to God and life with God. Brueggemann makes this central to his massive book on *Old Testament Theology*. The 'several testimonies to Yahweh, in any particular moment in Israel's life, were often in profound dispute with one another, disagreeing from the ground up about the "truth" of Yahweh.'[2] He cites the example of the Priestly and Deuter - onomistic traditions in tension in the Hebrew Bible. The fact that both sets of writings, in profound dispute with each other, two different ways of reading Israel's story, are placed together in the canon of the Hebrew Bible is evidence of the pluralistic approach. 'Old Testament theology must live with the pluralistic practice of dispute and compromise ...'[3]

The same can be said for the Christian Testament. Harmonisation of the four gospels is impossible and to try or create a single agreed narrative out of the resurrection stories is a waste of time. Later Christendom created a theological hegemony for political reasons, even a hegemonic christology. But it

1 Brueggemann, Walter, *Theology of the Old Testament: Testimony, Dispute, Advocacy,* (Minneapolis: Fortress Press, 1997) p 709
2 Ibid, p 710
3 Ibid., p 710

was all directed by imperial power and a triumphalist church. This is not good news for those who want or need to believe that there is one timeless faith once and for all delivered to the saints. Even that is not historically factual anyhow. Faith has kept and keeps changing. Certainty is what we or the church invents, the latter out of a need to control and the personal out of fear and insecurity. In the light of the Hebrew Bible and Christian Testament, the process of dispute and compromise and pluralism are definitional for Jewish and Christian faith.

It is within this framework of definitional dispute that a response can be made to the texts of violence. That they do exist from Genesis to Revelation is not disputed, what is in dispute is their role in articulating God and the life of faith. Did the biblical writers intend the violence to be normative for God and life? Or did they tell it as it was? Were there those in the community like ourselves, with a fascination for violence, an addiction to violence and a lust for blood? There are millions of people of faith who reflect all of this in our contemporary world. Modern Irish violence, as elsewhere, has been underpinned by religious faith. Were the ancestors in faith around in biblical terms also and is it their faith we encounter in the texts of violence? It may be that violent humans project their fears and violence onto God and construct a violent God-image. It may well be that we all construct God in our very human image, more than we want to admit.

Unless one subscribes to a very mechanical, dictation theory of biblical inspiration (and that is all it is and can be, a theory) then there is no difficulty in recognising the human authorship of the biblical text, even with the guidance of the Spirit. The witness to God in historical and concrete events and an incarnational God (whatever exactly all this means) does imply that God does not bypass human experience and limitations. Dispute within the text follows and if human violence projects itself onto God and faith in action, then there ought to be no surprise if there are other texts which dispute the violence. There is, what Bruegge - mann would call, a counter-testimony or a counter-witness. Texts in dispute and definitive pluralism within the text itself does mean that we can acknowledge the texts of violence and the counter-witness. The Bible critiques its own texts of violence. There is a witness in both the Hebrew Bible and Christian

Testament to a non-violent God and active non-violent faith. What this does mean is that we bring a critical, ethical and discerning perspective to our reading and interpretation of the texts.

Counter Creation Myth

The Babylonian creation myth, the Enuma Elish has been explored earlier. In the myth creation is an act of violence. Order is established by means of disorder, evil precedes good and the gods are violent. In 587 BCE the elite of the small kingdom of Judah were taken into exile in Babylon. It was a catastrophic event which shattered the exiles politically, socially, psychologically and theologically. It was a profound politico-spiritual crisis and it shaped the Hebrew Bible as we know it today. The exiles found themselves unable to sing the Lord's song in a strange land (Psalm 137). Those who were left in the ruins of Jerusalem without city walls or temple, were also shattered and their laments are heard in Lamentations.

In Babylon the exiles felt that Yahweh had failed and the Babylonian god, Marduk, was supreme and superior. Part of the strangeness of the land was not just geographical but cultural and religious. Marduk was everywhere and in every New Year festival there was a re-enactment of the Enuma Elish. The creation myth was replayed and the violent god Marduk was affirmed. There was no way of avoiding the vividly ritualised myth and its assertion of Marduk as supreme god and god of violence and war.

In the face of this the Hebrews had no song to sing, but despair did not ultimately overwhelm the exiled community. Prophetic and priestly voices generated hope and exile became the most creative period in ancient Israel's history. Not only was most of the Hebrew Bible written, edited, redacted and conflated to its present form, but exiles found their singing voices again. Out of the catastrophe a new song was sung and in a counter-cultural move they developed a counter-myth to the Enuma Elish. Written poetically it was part of their new song, was meant to be sung and sung antiphonally as clear observation suggests. Out of exile came Genesis 1, the counter creation myth to the Babylonian one. It reflects their conquerors creation myth but with radical differences. The creation myth or poem of

Genesis 1 is diametrically opposed to and a direct rebuttal of the Enuma Elish.

Creation is not an act of violence and is not the work of a violent god. Creation is an act of goodness, the work of a non-violent God. The counter-myth portrays a good God who creates a good creation, indeed a very good creation, as the worshippers responded to the choir! Good is prior to evil and neither evil nor violence is part of creation. Marduk is a violent god, Yahweh is non-violent. In the Babylonian myth violence is not a problem, it is the essence of the way things are. It also requires the violent suppression of women and creates a social order in which women are subjugated by men and kept inferior. Furthermore, the Babylonian myth has humans created from the blood of a murdered god. 'Our very origin is violence. Killing is in our genes.[4]

The Hebrew counter-myth portrayed God as a non-violent creator. God is non-violent, creation is very good, humankind has freedom and responsibility to nurture and care for creation, women and men are created equal. 'This elemental assertion of the equality of men and women is at the tap-root of the Bible.'[5] Created in the image of God may well reflect a creative responsibility to care for the earth. Made in the image of God also means made in the image of a non-violent God. The human origin is not violence and killing is not in our genes. We are not naturally incapable of peace.

The counter-creation myth expresses a radically different theology and anthropology as well as a different relationship with creation to the Enuma Elish. The Hebrew myth is an essent - ially non-violent alternative to what the exiles encountered in Babylon. It is also significant that when they shaped the Hebrew Bible in its final form they put their counter-myth at the beginning. It was placed before a different creation story around 400 years older, but placed after the Hebrew exilic myth of creation. It suggests that the creative biblical architects wanted the themes of God's non-violence and human non-violence, along

4 Wink, Walter, *The Powers That Be: Theology for a New Millennium* (New York: Doubleday 1998) p 46

5 Brueggemann, Walter, *An Introduction to the Old Testament: The Canon and Christian Imagination* (Louisville: Westminster John Knox Press, 2003) p 35

with equality and earth responsibility to be normative for a life of faith.

> By its alternative depiction of God's non-violent creative power at the start of the biblical canon, Genesis 1 signals the Creator's original intent for shalom and blessing at the outset of human history ... As the opening canonical disclosure of God for readers of scripture, Genesis 1 constitutes a normative framework by which we may judge all the violence that pervades the rest of the Bible.[6]

Genesis 1 then, provides the Bible's own critique of violence in God and in life at the very outset. The creative myth of the Priestly tradition is an expression of 'exuberant liturgical tradition', which suggests that our liturgical language and actions ought to be non-violent as norm. Furthermore, the Hebrew creation myth at the beginning of the Bible has no connection at all with the 'creation versus evolution' argument. This argument misses the whole point of the poem and avoids the much more profound and deeper challenge of non-violence as constitutive of God and faithful, ethical living.

Hosea's Critique of Violence
Our own world is frequently reflected in the biblical world in that both appear to be driven by the ideology of violence. There is no shortage of violent texts in the Bible and violent ideology pervades the modern history of Ireland and has become a key theme in our everyday lives since 9/11. The world's only superpower has declared a war against terror supported by Britain and others. Given the real location of weapons of mass destruction many wonder where the effective terror really is. Such a war, as Northern Ireland proved, is unwinable and a global war on terror could go on for the rest of the century. The addiction to violence at the heart of the world's sole superpower and Al Queda, and the religious categories in which it is set give to the ideology of violence a mystique. People are driven by zealous ideals and the violence and counter violence, not only need each other, but are perceived as a sacred charge and responsibility.

---

6 Middleton, J. Richard quoted in Siebert, Eric, *Disturbing Divine Behaviour: Troubling Old Testament Images of God* (Minneapolis : Fortress Press, 2009) p 200

The violence itself becomes shrouded by mystique. It becomes a crusade with extremely grave and destructive consequences. As a religio-political text the Bible begins, as we have seen, with a critique of the violence associated with the divine and human. Genesis 1 subverts and critiques the mystique of violence.

The Hebrew prophet Hosea also makes a devastating critique of the mystique of violence. This may be as surprising to many as a contextual reading of Genesis 1 is. We are so in love with violence that we fail to see the Bible's own critique of its violence or to recognise that there is a profound dispute at the heart of the biblical stories. 'The power of his (Hosea's) ideas, and their systematic neglect by a people that claims to take inspiration from the Bible, are evidence of how firmly rooted zealous nationalism is in our culture.'[7]

Hosea stands first among the Twelve Minor Prophets and the book announces indictment and sentence because of broken covenant. Hosea sets the tone for the other eleven prophets. Hosea is an 8th century prophet of the northern kingdom of Israel. The geographical foreground to the book is the rise of the Assyrian superpower and the huge threat of that superpower to this small kingdom of Israel. Broken covenant is the prophet's indictment against the leaders and elite of Israel. Given that covenant is a social vision rooted in social justice, Hosea is concerned with the breakdown and disintegration of his society. At the heart of covenant breakdown is the practice and dependency on violence, internal and in relation to the superpower. The imagery of indictment used by the prophet is of a lawsuit, a call to court, followed by the indictment and then the sentence (see Hosea 4:1-3). The consequences of broken covenant or buying into the mystique of violence is portrayed in terms of undoing the creation. Genesis 1 is being put into reverse, at least that is how the editors of the Hebrew Bible would have perceived it. God is being turned into a violent deity, human violence is a religious act and nature itself suffers violence as a result. Hosea exposes the mystique of violence for what it is, dangerous and destructive, undoing creation and turning ordered life into chaos.

---

7 Jewett, Robert and Lawrence, John Skelton, *Captain America and the Crusade Against Evil: The Dilemma of Zealous Nationalism* (Grand Rapids: Eerdmans, 2003) p 261

Key to Hosea's critique is 'the relationship between the violent mystique and social disintegration'.[8]

You have ploughed wickedness,
you have reaped unjustice,
you have eaten the fruit of lies.

Because you have trusted in your power
and in the multitude of your warriors,
therefore the tumult of war shall rise against your people
and all your fortresses shall be destroyed (Hosea 10:13-14).

Hosea is speaking into a situation of crusades, purges, assassinations and conquests by the nationalistic zealots of the Northern kingdom. Their trust is in chariots and warriors and military arrangements and have ended up in brutal and destructive wars. The massacre of Beth-Arbel was a notorious event of that time (v 14b). Violence has reduced their state to moral decay and social disintegration. Trusting in chariots and warriors does that.

Moving deeper into the heart of that problem of sacred violence, Hosea realises that the violence is underpinned by zealous myths and these need to be repudiated. The most through-going zealot of the time was Jehu who carried out a massive and violent political purge. This purge was fully supported by Elisha, the father of prophesy in Israel. But even leading religious lights like Elisha can turn faith into zealous idolatry and Hosea does not hesitate to critique the religious edicts and personalities of the time.

Hosea recognised that the mystique of violence at the heart of social culture leads to the popularisation of crime and brutality. People become brutalised and do acts of violence which might otherwise be out of character, certainly bypass conscience. In Hosea 4:1-3 the crimes of violence are named. Ecological decay, destructive personal behaviour, breakdown of society and moral decay are all inter-related with the mystique of violence.

The mystique of violence for Hosea causes a perversion of justice. 'By encouraging brutality and crimes against others, it gradually drives society into corrupt practices'.[9] The institutions

8 Ibid, p 261 What follows is closely based on Jewett and Lawrence's insightful exploration of Hosea's critique of the mystique of violence.
9 Ibid, p 266

of law and order become corrupt. Hosea indicts the legal and religious leaders of his day (Hosea 5:1). The imagery is of a snare. People become snared or trapped in the cruel treatment of others. Violence is condoned through moral ambiguity or distortion. No matter how much the violence tries to justify itself or legitimise its actions, it becomes itself a great act of injustice against society.

For Hosea it also undermines respect for law and order (Hosea 10:3-4). Right at the top justice is partial. Justice and equality before the law for all is discarded.

Hosea has no doubt. Violence is corrosive and destructive. The leaders of his day had fallen in love with it and created a mystique of violence which no one will dare to critique or question. Except Hosea, whose critiques of the mystique of violence calls even Elisha into question and indicts his community for the greatest injustice of all and cause of social disintegration, violence dressed up with moral trappings or religious mystique.

Non-violence since Isaiah and Jeremiah
A great Christian delusion is to think that the Jewish faith is warlike and violent and Jesus and his followers were / are peaceful. The Jews rejected Jesus, and put crudely, God has been for the Christians and against the Jews ever since. It is a serious and dangerous delusion based on a mis-reading of the Bible. The stories of holy war in the Hebrew Bible have been acknowledged, though in the distorted reading of Christian supersessionism and anti-Judaism, the violence of the Christian Testament is ignored. The warrior God image in the Hebrew Bible was a prohib - ition against Israel using chariots and horses. The monarchy in Israel ignored that and justified the horses and chariots with appeals to a violent God. The dispute is at its greatest here in the text. As Yoder points out, by the time we reach the last books in the Hebrew Bible, I and II Chronicles, a model of non-violent saturation has become obvious. Exile, of course shattered the monarchy and thereafter there is restoration without political sovereignty.[10]

---

10 Yoder, John Howard, *The War of the Lamb: The Ethics of Non-violence and Peacemaking*, edited by Stassen, Nation and Hamsher (Grand Rapids: Brazos Press, 2009) p 72

The exilic experience not only revolutionised their vision of God, it turned ethics upside down. Chronicles was moving away from victorious salvation ('send her victorious' is a violent image associated with monarchy) and post-monarchy non-violence was becoming more the norm. After all the non-violent creation myth had been imagined in the exile. Through exile and the other side Israel was redefining national community without monarchy or national sovereignty. The driving visionaries were the prophets, though Chronicles is a priestly writing. The critique, often satirical runs through Judges, Samuel and Kings. Isaiah is calling for 'formal renunciation of politics and diplomacy as usual, of alliances with Egypt, and of modernised military technology.'[11] Isaiah of Jerusalem (chapters 1-39) needs to be read in its geopolitical context, where his radical vision of non-violent foreign policy (he knew the court system and politics from the inside) is clear. But did Kings listen?

By the 6th century the Babylonian superpower had crushed and conquered. The catastrophe of the exile happened and Jeremiah appeared on the cusp of the shattering exile experience. He did not end up in Babylon but from his own exile he wrote letters. It is a complicated book and there is much dispute within the text. In the crisis of deportation and loss Jeremiah is calling for the people to renounce kingship, militancy and city. Living as diaspora people is a more appropriate way for faithful people to live. His letter to the exiles calls on them to 'seek the welfare of the city ... and pray to the Lord on its behalf, for in its welfare you will find your welfare' (Jeremiah 29:7). This was a call to give up monarchy and armies, horses and chariots. It was also a call to give up violence and it is significant that the sacred canon did not include the violence of the Maccabees and later Jewish rabbis did not see that violent uprising as being blessed by God. Broadly based on this tradition the rabbinical writings provided moral guidance for the Jewish community by calling 'for a fundamentally non-violent lifestyle, even under persecution'.[12] Judaism, therefore, has a lengthy history of non-violence, something which cannot be said of Christianity. It is in this

11 Ibid, p 72
12 Ibid, pp 73-74

prophetic and rabbinical tradition that Jesus stood as a 1st century Jew. The movement that gathered around him has also to be read in this context of critique of the mystique of violence. Dominating the mystique was the Roman empire with the violence of its militarism and repressive economics.

Luke's subversive Christmas gospel
The gospels are not biographical. They are diverse documents of faith written for faith communities to enable people to reflect on what it means to be followers of Jesus and participants in God's reign in the political, economic and cultural struggles of life in the shadow of empire. Roman imperialism foregrounds the texts and dominates the rural and urban lives of the early Jesus movement. The gospels reflect their struggles. Contemporary Christians need to be constantly reminded

> of the painful struggle of the saints against Caesar in which the Christian faith was born. Christianity's historic origins do not lie in the abstract concern with isolated issues of individual ethics but in the dedication to resist the idolatry of power embodied by the Roman Empire.[13]

Luke's gospel was written for such a community and their struggles are reflected in the key themes. Peace and poverty are two of the themes running through Luke and they are introduced early on in the gospel. They appear in the birth stories, Luke 1 and 2. Matthew and Luke have birth stories which are entirely different from each other and may even be said to be in dispute, if they are read factually. Harmonisation is impossible and unnecessary. Like the resurrection stories at the end of the gospels they are stories told in highly symbolic language, or at least colourful language, quite different from the middle part of each gospel. In Luke 2 there are shepherds, and they were familiar on the hillsides around Bethlehem. Then there are heavenly hosts and angels singing songs in the sky; not at all a familiar experience for human beings! To read a story like this literally is to lack a sense of imagination and wonder. Luke is telling a wond -

13 Horsley, Richard A. and Silberman, Neil Asher, *The Message and the Kingdom: How Jesus and Paul Ignited a Revolution and Transformed the Ancient World* (New York: Grosset/Putman, 1997) p 232

erful story, creatively using vivid, otherworldly language to communicate something subversive to a struggling faith group under imperial domination.

Luke begins chapter 2 with a decree from Caesar Augustus. There may not have been an historical census but Luke is more concerned to place his birth stories firmly in the context of empire. Luke is being subversive from the outset. Caesar's purpose in all things was to establish *Pax Romana*, the peace of Rome. It was essential that there were no disturbances, revolts, rebellions or threats to Roman power, which in turn would keep the economic system flowing in the direction of the Roman elite. *Pax Romana* was enforced peace by a powerful military machine. 'Peace and security' was an imperial slogan and anything that threatened it was brutally dealt with. The Caesars posed as saviours of the world using their military might and an atmosphere of fear to promote law, order and security.

In all of this the Romans claimed divine authority and the authority was inscribed on coins, peace altars and in the local forum and temple. Caesar, long before Jesus was born, was hailed as Son of God, Lord and Saviour and the empire literally proclaimed good news of peace to the world. Those who first heard or read Luke's gospel would have known all this and been very familiar with the Roman vocabulary.

Luke's birth story is a counter-cultural story. The simplicity and poverty of the manger or cattle shed should not be romanticised. Caesar Augustus lives in a palace, has a mighty military machine and imposes Roman peace through violence. God is not with the big battalions but with the little ones, the humanity born in a cow shed, lying in a feeding trough. Roman imperial power has already been named in Luke's *Magnificat* as the 'proud, mighty and rich' (Luke 1:51-53) and as the enemies in vv 71-74 from whom liberation is required. In the cow shed and on the hillside we meet the representatives of the poor and lowly, the nobodies as far as imperial power is concerned. The history makers, certainly those who write history are the Caesars and Herods, but God's preference is for the displaced and those in debt, living in hunger and poor health. For Luke, God is found in the cow shed and not in the imperial palace.

The shepherds who are such a central part of Luke's story are from among the peasantry and poor. They are the ordinary people, probably employed by large landowners and maybe even 'working on large estates supplying sacrificial animals.'[14] If true, then it was the high priests in the Temple who controlled the production of sacrificial animals for the religious ritual. At any rate shepherds were among the economically marginalised, but it is to them that the 'sign' of this birth is given. The birth is not announced to the mighty Caesar or the wealthy priests, but first to marginalised shepherds.

Not only were the shepherds from the peasantry, but from the writings of Josephus it is known that 'other common people looked to shepherds for distinctive leadership'.[15] Shepherds were known to have been leaders of armed resistance against the Romans. They would have been ready to become involved in a resistance movement. This cultural knowledge appears to be echoed in Luke's story of the shepherds (Luke 2:8-20).

The descriptive imagery is subversive at many points of the Roman imperial power. A light shines and Roman coins always had a divine halo around Caesar's head. The angel is accompanied by a 'multitude of the heavenly host'. 'Host' is a weak translation of Luke's word which is military, *stratia*, an army. Luke is portraying heavenly armies in contrast to Roman legions. God's power and Caesar's power are entirely different. The divine is non-violent and the imperial power is oppressively violent.

The announcement of the good news is expressed in familiar Roman imperial terms. Saviour, Messiah and Lord would have been instantly recognisable by recipients of Luke's gospel. Messiah would have been threatening to imperial forces because it was about leadership and in popular parlance, leadership of revolt against Roman forces. Saviour and Lord were not only terms used of the gods of the world, but assumed by Roman emperors. It was their god-given task to 'announce good news'. Almost every word in Luke 2:10 is from the Roman imperial textbook. But Roman imperial violence is not good news and *Pax Romana* is not gospel. The heavenly army announces 'peace on earth' and 'glory to God' and the announce-

14 Horsley, Richard A., *The Liberation of Christians: The Infancy Narratives in Social Context* (New York: Continuum, 1993) p 103
15 Ibid, p 104

ment of of peace is for all people. Luke has already situated his subversive story in 'all the world' (2:1). The word is *Oikoumene*, the whole inhabited earth which is not for Roman imperial purposes of taxation, military and economic control, but for non-violence and more positively, peace, the total wellbeing of earth, animals and humanity. Peace is more than the absence of violence and war, though it includes these. It is total wellbeing, personal, social, political, economic and ecological. Luke's birth story undermines everything the empire stood for and all the *Pax Romana* claimed. It is good news for the economically poor and those oppressed by violence, domination and war. Luke's birth stories reflect the anti-violence strand in the biblical text, a subversive strand against all structural violence. 'Seasons greetings' is way off the planet!

Revelation as counter to Imperial victory

The book of Revelation has been described as 'the most horrific story ever put to paper' and the God it portrays 'so fervent in his destructiveness that the ban seems a model of moderation and restraint'.[16] Read at one level of interpretation there is no question about this and no question about the use of Revelation in the hands of fearful and angry people. Read literally it is a book with frightening political and military implications and there are millions of people claiming Christianity who want to see its violence fulfilled. Even when recognising the apocalyptic genre of the literature we may still feel uncomfortable with its violent imagery and language. And yet it does have a strong critique of its own violence.

Getting inside the psychology of its author is extremely difficult, but John of Patmos appears to be subversive of the violence of empire, even though his violent imagery is extreme. That may be the point. By using the violent imagery and citing the values of imperialism he may be subverting the same empire and ultimately pointing to the active non-violence of the Jesus who is so central to the book. This not an attempt to gloss over or explain away the violence of the book but an attempt to recognise that beyond the literalistic reading and its violent projections, there is something more radical and subtle going on. The clue to an alternative and non-violent reading lies in the use of key ideas.

The Roman empire both celebrated and worshipped the goddess Victory. The Greek name for the Roman goddess of victory was *Nike*, a winged goddess whose brand image dominates our running shoes and other sports equipment. When the Jewish revolt was crushed in 70CE, celebratory coins were mounted showing *Nike* setting up a trophy over a prostrate Jew. Militarily Rome dominated and *Nike* was the all-effective goddess. At the end of the century when Revelation was written graffiti appeared on a rock in Arabia. It bluntly said 'Romans always win'.[17] It was that kind of ideology and practice that Revelation dared to oppose. Rome's domination and victory is opposed by a vision of God's victory centered on Jesus, described in non-violent imagery as Lamb. To the flying goddess *Nike*, John of Patmos opposes a flying angel 'with an eternal gospel to proclaim to those who live on earth' (Revelation 14 v6). Victory through crushing violence and defeat is not Revelation's 'eternal gospel' or good news. The same chapter holds in contrast the Lamb and the beast, one non-violent, the other violent. Yet the chapter ends with disturbing barbarism and shocking violence as using winepress imagery, blood flows 'as high as a horses' bridle, for a distance of about two hundred miles' (Revelation 14 v20). The scene of judgement and revenge is literally a massive blood bath. Without glossing the violent imagery, we are not reading a literal or prescriptive text and the book has been left for too long to the violent extremes in the Christian tradition.

Barbara Rossing reminds us that 'John wrote the book of Revelation in order to lift up the vision of Jesus as a countermessage to the empire's theology of Victory or *Nike*.' Also 'In place of overwhelming military strength, we are given the

---

17 Rossing, Barbara, *The Rapture Exposed: The Message of Hope in the Book of Revelation* (New York: Basic Books, 2004) p 105. Much of what follows draws on Rossing's insights. Rosemary Radford Ruether described her book as 'a powerful indictment of 'rapture theology' with its false Biblical interpretation and war-mongering influence on US foreign policy, especially in the Middle East ... and an authentic vision of Biblical apocalyptic as testimony of God's non-violent love and desire for the poor of the earth'.

image of the Lamb's non-violent power.'[18] Jesus as the 'Lamb that was slain' is one of two key images providing clues to the real purpose of the book. Revelation is the only apocalyptic work that uses this imagery. The book of 4 Ezra uses the image of a roaring lion over against the Roman eagle and its violence. But Lamb is particular to Revelation drawing on the non-violent image of Isaiah 53 and the suffering servant. The Lamb, non-violent imagery is the essence of Revelation's message. In chapter 12:11, the faithful 'have conquered by the blood of the Lamb'. It is an image of violence being overcome not by violence but by suffering love or the power of vulnerable, non-violent love. The Lamb who was slain, or whose blood was shed by the violence of the empire, is the radical symbol of suffering, non-violent love.

The second key idea is 'conquer'. The word is used up to 16 times in Revelation which is more than half its usages in the Christian Testament.[19] 'Conquer' is the Greek word *Nikan*, the same as the Greek goddess of victory and war. But John has God's people conquering, not by war and violence but by other radically different means. John's use of the word is intentional ... 'using such a politically loaded term, sets up the book's programme of challenging Rome's imperial theology of victory or *Nike*'.[20] The beasts of chapters 11 and 13 'make war and conquer and kill'. The in-between chapter 12 has God's people conquer 'by the blood of the Lamb and by the word of their testimony' (12:11). The way of the Lamb is non-violent, vulnerable, suffering love and testimony is witness to that non-violent power, even to the point of giving up life. In Revelation 2:16 and 19:11, John has already declared that Jesus the Lamb makes war not with the sword of battle, but 'by the sword of his mouth'.

The word is Jesus' only weapon – this is a reversal as unexpected as the substitution of a lamb for a lion. These reversals undercut violence by emphasising Jesus' testimony and the word of God.[21]

Those who read Revelation as pointing to a last great cata-

---

18 Ibid, pp 108-109
19 Ibid, p 116
20 Ibid, p 117
21 Ibid, p 121

clysmic war as God's way of realising the kingdom have mis-read, distorted and abused the text. Reading Revelation as a divinely inspired basis for brutality, war, violence and bloodlet-ting, is a serious heresy. It is dangerous, heretical fantasy.

Nowhere in Revelation do God's people 'wage war'. What they do is 'conquer' or 'become victors' (the same word in Greek) – and they do that by the Lamb's own blood and by their courageous testimony, not through Armageddon or war. In contrast to Rome's theology that defined victory as military con-quest, Revelation develops a counter-theology of the non-vio-lent Victory (*Nike*) of Jesus, God's slain Lamb, in which 'evil is overcome by suffering love', not by superior power.[22]

Violent imagery and language occurs in both the Hebrew Bible and Christian Testament. There are undoubtedly texts of dispute also and even if the violent texts could not be read as anything other than prescriptive, there are texts of critique. The Bible critiques its own violence. In a violent world where vio-lence threatens often to to destroy and overwhelm, and where it is too often legitimised by religion and God, what is required is a more ethical reading of the foundational texts. Not everything is the 'word of the Lord' but we can still 'hear what the Spirit is saying to the church'.[23] Only though, if we read critically and ethically.

---

22 Ibid, pp 121-122
23 The New Zealand *Book of Common Prayer* uses 'hear what the Spirit says to the church' instead of the more traditional 'This is the word of the Lord'. The latter is not only inappropriate at the end of some texts, but the response 'Thanks be to God' would be to justify the violence.

CHAPTER NINE

Jesus and active non-violence

Jesus has often been dismissed, domesticated or ignored, especially by the Christian church. This is especially true in relation to his teaching and practice of active non-violence. At this point Jesus has been an embarrassment to Christianity. Christendom preferred to turn him into a warrior king which was more in keeping with its close connections to the states' wars. The pervas - ive culture of violence and the myth of redemptive violence have ensured the domestication of Jesus and the spiritualisation of his teaching. Much of western Christianity has developed an exaggerated emphasis on his death divorced from his teaching. This has usually taken the form of an exaggerated Paulinism, atonement being considered absolutely central to Paul. But this too has frequently missed the extensive ethical dimension to Paul's authentic letters. Atonement theology read into Romans 5 has eclipsed Romans 12 where Paul mirrors the radical ethic of active non-violence of the Sermon on the Mount. In fact Romans was written up to 40 years before Matthew's gospel and the sermon. Not that Matthew copied Paul as the real pioneer of active non-violence. Both Matthew and Paul are more likely reflecting an earlier Jesus tradition, an oral tradition which they each have shaped within the theological and ethical structure of their writings.

The teaching of Jesus is an essential dimension of the faith presented in the gospels and early Christian writings. His death and its meaning make no sense apart from his teaching. Attention to his teaching, especially on active non-violence and a non-violent God might have spared the church from violent doctrines of atonement and a violent image of God. It might also have spared the church from its unholy alliance with state wars and violence, and enabled a more prophetic, critical resistance to the values, commitments and agendas of imperial and domin - ation systems. This chapter will, therefore, explore the radical teaching of Jesus on active non-violence through the Sermon on the Mount and examine Paul's mirror image in Romans 12. But first, it is important to grasp the Matthean framework for this teaching which is, what the gospel calls, the 'kingdom of heaven' and the extensive dependence on the Book of Isaiah.

The Kingdom and its Isaianic roots

Matthew persistently uses 'kingdom of heaven' where 'kingdom of God' is preferred by Mark, Luke, John, Acts and Paul. There is a significant Jewish tradition of never pronouncing the name of God. The divine is beyond naming, a reality too often overlooked by the Christian tradition. Whoever Matthew was (and we don't really know the author either) he was Jewish writing a gospel for Jewish followers of the Jesus movement. 'Kingdom of heaven' is a reverential substitute for 'kingdom of God'. 'Heaven' was a euphemism for 'God'. Unfortunately 'heaven' suggests the future and 'is all too often misinterpreted as the kingdom of the future, of the next world, of the afterlife'.[1] This is not only a misinterpretation but misleading. The Lord's Prayer, very much in kingdom context in Matthew, is concerned with God's will being done on earth, and such earthy concerns as debts and daily bread. Crossan has described the kingdom as 'the great divine cleanup of this world'.[2] When Matthew's Jesus invites participation in the divine kingdom he is inviting commitment and action in this world and not the next. Participants are taught to pray for the 'kingdom of heaven' in this world and to be able to do God's will on earth.

Because the kingdom is this worldly it 'is inextricably and simultaneously 100 per cent political and 100 per cent religious'. Furthermore, 'Kingdom is a political term, 'God' is a religious term, and Jesus would be executed for that 'of' in a world where, for Rome, God already sat on Caesar's throne because Caesar was God.'[3] There is something profoundly radical, therefore, about this 'kingdom of heaven' or 'kingdom of God'. It might accurately be translated the 'empire of God' in radical contrast to the empire of Rome and the God of the Jewish-Christian faith is in opposition to the divinised Caesar. We need also to remember that in the world of the Bible there is no distinction between

---

1 Crossan, John Dominic, *God and Empire: Jesus Against Rome, Then and Now* (San Francisco: Harper, 2007) p 116
2 Ibid, p 116
3 Ibid, p 117

religion and politics, no separation or dualism as in our modern Enlightenment world. Putting our political world into one compartment and our religious world into another (private) compartment would shock and confuse Matthew and every other writer of the Christian Testament and the Hebrew Bible. When Matthew repeatedly used 'kingdom of heaven', he was not encouraging his readers to privatise their faith and keep it apart from the Roman politics of the day. He was proposing radically alternative politics and religion, an inseparable politics and faith which were different to the political theology of the empire.

Not only do we need care in the interpretation of 'heaven', we also need care in our interpretation of 'kingdom'. Matthew would still be shocked and confused by our separation of faith and politics, and be equally shocked by any attempt to turn 'kingdom of heaven' into a theocracy. Jesus was not encouraging Jews to think that Israel would rule over the nations or that any human empire with a King would establish itself as hegemonic or dominant. Neither is there any encouragement here for a Christian empire over other nations. Any human empire or superpower setting itself up over other nations claiming divine power and approval, or that it is implementing God's way of life, is drunk with its own power and self-interest. The Roman empire made the same claim for its hegemony, dominance, militarism and economic oppression, all in the name of the gods, with Caesar as divine representative and saviour of the world.

When Matthew's Jesus taught his friends to pray, 'Your kingdom come' and in the same Sermon on the Mount to 'seek first the kingdom' (Matthew 6:33) it is a call to participate with God in a this world social reality in opposition to Caesar's empire and its oppressive policies. The Beatitudes, which form the beginning of the sermon profile the kingdom values and lived ethics. They include mourning or solidarity with the pain and suffering of the world, showing mercy or compassion, hungering and thirsting for justice, which in a community where water and food were extremely scarce, was an intense longing and action for justice. Peacemaking and a willingness to suffer for the sake of justice for others were also in the Matthean kingdom profile. These are the kingdom values and kingdom ethics. The Beatitudes are the core characteristics of the empire of God in direct and subversive opposition to the empire of Caesar. Participating in the kingdom of God always raises a politico-religious or religio-political question: who rules the world? Caesar or God? At the very least that puts kingdom participants always in a critical relationship to political power and systems. Between the kingdom of God and the kingdom of Caesar there is always a critical question.

The prayer of the kingdom is concerned with earth, with practical, concrete necessities. Debts and bread were core to the serious social deficit in the Galilean world. Poverty and hunger were daily realities as was the struggle with the evil of the empire's military and economic oppression. Liberation from these evils was not only the intense longing of prayer but of very existence itself. The radical non-violence and peacemaking that Jesus teaches in the sermon, including love of enemies, is also set in the context of the kingdom. These too represent kingdom praxis or God's way of life.

Matthew's gospel is also structured on the shape of Torah, the first five books of the Hebrew Bible. The gospel is structured around five blocks of teaching. Torah was not law in a legalistic sense but God's liberating way of life. As the commandments or decalogue, central to Torah and Covenant, were given on Mount Sinai, so the Sermon is given on the Mount. Matthew's assertion is that here is the Mosaic tradition, the Torah, radically reinterpreted for a new and different time. It is also a reminder to the Christian community that the Sermon on the Mount, including the Beatitudes, Lord's Prayer, active non-violence and love of enemies, are all profoundly rooted in the Jewish tradition. But then Jesus was Jewish and Matthew is the most Jewish of the gospels.

This rootedness in the Hebrew Bible is even more recognisable when the pervasive role of the book of Isaiah is noted in Matthew. The frequency with which Isaiah is quoted in Matthew would suggest that both the regional audience of Jesus and Matthew's community of faith were familiar with the prophetic book. The book of Isaiah may well have been the 'best-seller' of the time. The language of the kingdom of God or reign of God would have been heard and understood, not only in opposition to the kingdom or reign of Caesar, but in relation to what it meant in Isaiah. This is true not only in Matthew's gospel but in Luke, the Dead Sea Scrolls and the development of Jewish Targums. All depend heavily on Isaiah and all speak of the reign of God or God's liberation. All of this was doing the rounds at the time of Jesus and after.

Jesus quotes from Isaiah more than anything else. Bruce Chilton has studied all the passages where Jesus announces the kingdom of God and has discovered that Jesus, in each announcement, refers to Isaiah in Aramaic translation. 'Jesus uses words and phrases in 'his' kingdom proclamations from fourteen chapters of Isaiah'.[4] There are also seventeen passages in Isaiah that proclaim the good news of God's deliverance and in his teaching on the kingdom Jesus has quoted from them. What Isaiah visioned for his own time and situation, Jesus proclaims as breaking into the imperial world of the 1st century. 'Jesus chose Isaiah to teach and preach from; he was deeply engaged in Isaiah, and this affirmed that Isaiah teaches the truth – the most important truth of God's reign'.[5] It may well be that the kingdom or reign of God was Isaiah's idea, which Jesus took up and proclaimed in another context. Stassen has identified seven characteristics of the kingdom and God's liberating activity in the seventeen passages from Isaiah. When looking at them it is not difficult to see how Isaiah and Jesus were on the same wavelength.

1 God's presence as Spirit or Light, in nine passages (God's dynamic presence is implied in all seventeen)

2 Deliverance or salvation occurs in all seventeen

3 Peace in fourteen

4 Healing in seven

5 Joy in twelve

6 Return from exile occurs in nine (Jesus interprets this as repentance and return to God)

7 Righteousness or social justice occurs in sixteen passages [6]

---

4 Stassen, Glenn H., *Living the Sermon on the Mount: A Practical Hope for Grace and Deliverance* (San Francisco: Jossey-Bass, 2006) p 23 Stassen has drawn extensively from Chilton's work.

5 Ibid, p 24

6 Ibid, p 25 Stassen goes on to spell out in some detail all seven characteristics of the kingdom in Isaiah and the teaching and practice of Jesus.

Isaiah, therefore, profiles the kingdom or reign of God and the Jesus of the gospels taught and embodied all of these characteristics. His teaching on active non-violence has to be read in this Isaianic kingdom context. The book of Isaiah is a composite piece of literature and covers three imperial powers, Assyria, Babylon and Persia. At the time of Jesus and Matthew's gospel the dominant power is Rome. The kingdom of God, including active non-violence, is subversive of and a radical alternative to all four empires and every domination system, past and present. And the active non-violence of the kingdom, in Isaiah and Jesus, is in dispute with and the counter-testimony to, not only the way of empires and superpowers, but to all of those texts of violence in the Bible itself. It stands over against all our use of violence to achieve or defend our hegemonic causes and domination systems.

Do not Resist Violently
Living the values of God's reign and practising the kingdom ethic will ensure that the empire will strike back. Big powers do not take kindly to subversive or critical threat. Matthew has Jesus recognise the reaction of the *status quo* to a social alternative. 'Blessed are those who are persecuted for righteousness sake' (5:10). In contemporary terms this is not about secular ant - agonism against Christian assertions of personal morality. Nor is it opposition to aggressive Christian evangelism, still less to the Christian right to be homophobic. Righteousness reeks in a overly religious society of self-righteousness. The word is synonymous with justice, and in the biblical, prophetic tradition justice is social justice. The Beatitude has been translated as: 'Joyful are those who suffer because of restorative justice, for theirs is the reign of God.'[7] Writing in the context of the violent and evil Nazi regime, Deitrich Bonhoeffer defined it as the joy of those 'who suffer because of delivering justice'. The divine commendation is for those who suffer in their work for justice.[8] Bonhoeffer's work of active solidarity with the suffering Jews was a justice work and certainly got him into serious trouble which led to his hanging in a Nazi prison.

---

7 Ibid, p 59
8 Ibid, p 59

The just way of life envisioned in 5:3-9 challenges the *status quo*, its commandments, power structures, and beneficiaries. God's reign or justice/righteousness seeks different societal relationships and an equitable distribution of and access to resources.[9]

The seriousness of suffering at the hands of the *status quo* is recognised with the beatitude being the only one to be elaborated, especially through two active words. To 'revile' can mean physical violence, while 'utter all kinds of evil' is verbal violence in order to destroy one's integrity through slander or defamation.[10] Bonhoeffer rightly entitled his book *The Cost of Discipleship*. The only martyrdom Jesus appears to talk about is that experienced in the work of justice for others. The elaborated beatitude also appears to exclude accommodation and retaliation as means of achieving. Kingdom people may live at odds with their dominant culture, including the injustice of its violence and counter-violence, but the only cause of martyrdom is compassionate action for restorative and social justice.

The heart of Jesus' teaching on active non-violent resistance is in Matthew 5:38-42. These and the teaching on enemies which follow are the deepest causes of embarrassment to the Christian church. Glen Stassen has helpfully identified a triadic structure to much of the teaching of Jesus in the sermon on the Mount. The triadic approach has to do with the breaking out of a violent cycle of domination and violence. In Matthew 5:38-43 Jesus is teaching his followers how to take actively non-violent peace-making initiatives. The triad is represented in the following way

- Traditional righteousness – retaliation for injury v 38
- Vicious Cycle – revenge
- Transforming initiative – respond in new and surprising ways vv 40-42

It begins with the familiar 'eye for an eye and tooth for a tooth', the traditional expression of legal justice. Retaliation is allowed but in carefully measured terms. Retaliation means the same penalty as the damage caused by the attack or violence. It was

9 Carter, Warren, *Matthew and the Margins: A Socio-Political and Religious Reading* (Maryknoll: Orbis Books, 2000) p 136
10 Ibid, p 137

good practice as far as it went, putting limits on the penalty paid. But the old Hebrew myth of Cain and Abel understood human nature. Whoever kills Cain may well suffer sevenfold vengeance and the non-violent God places a protective mark on him. But as the myth develops, Lamech kills and fears that 'If Cain is avenged sevenfold, truly Lamech seventy-sevenfold' (Genesis 4:24). Vicious cycles of vengeance were commonplace in Ireland's decade of change and violence, 1912-1922, and frequently repeated themselves in the most recent phase. Palestinian suicide bombers and Israeli military attacks are all part of Lamech's vicious cycle of vengeance. The vicious cycle increases the violence and the lasting hatred. Revenge goes beyond even like for like and in the cycle becomes disproportionate. But even tit for tat escalates into a vicious cycle which becomes extremely difficult to break.

The English translation of the response of Jesus is completely misleading. 'But I say to you, Do not resist an evildoer' (Matthew 5:38). But the word 'evil' should be translated as 'by evil means'.[11] Jesus was not teaching passivity, pacifism or non-resistance. He himself did not practice non-resistance to evil. The word 'resist' has also been badly translated. 'Do not resist evil' from the Greek of the gospel really means 'do not engage in revengeful or violent retaliation' or 'not to retaliate revengefully by evil means'.[12]

Walter Wink has also analysed the Greek word in the Matthean text, *Anthistenai*, and points up its use as a military term. It means to 'set against' especially in battle, to withstand. In Ephesians 6:13, using military metaphors it means 'to draw up battle ranks against the enemy and the related word translated as 'stand firm' means to 'close ranks and continue to fight'. In the Greek translation of the Hebrew Bible, *Anthistemi*, is used 44 times out of 71, as 'armed resistance in military encounters'.[13]

Given the imperial foreground to Matthew's gospel, as with the rest of the Christian Testament, the big issue was resisting

11 Stassen, op cit, p 89

12 Ibid, p 91 Stassen is drawing on the careful translation work on the Beatitudes and Sermon on the Mount by Clarence Jordan.

13 Wink, Walter, *Engaging the Powers: Discernment and Resistance in a World of Domination*, (Minneapolis: Fortress Press, 1992) p185

the empire by force. That would have meant violence of a brutal nature. This is not what Jesus is advocating, certainly not to join a vicious cycle of violence and revenge. Yet the word 'resist' does mean to 'resist violently, to revolt or rebel, to engage in an insurrection'.[14] There were those in Galilee and Judea who were prepared to do just that and died. But Jesus was advocating a third way which was neither flight nor fight. The reading of the text is not 'Do not resist' but 'Do not resist violently' or 'Do not retaliate revengefully by evil means', ie violent means.

Jesus was going beyond the law of equal retribution, the traditional approach. He was also going well beyond passive collusion with oppressive evil or silence. Evil cannot go unchallenged or unchecked, but how that is done is not by using the same methods of the unjust oppressor. Evil is not opposed by becoming evil. Violence is not opposed by violence. 'Retrib-ution, in which violence and damage meet and match violence and damage, is set aside. The cycle of violence is broken. .... Resistance, yes; violence, no. Jesus' third way is active non-violent resistance.'[15]

It has been suggested that the teaching of Jesus does not apply to the oppressive imperial realities, but to the dynamics of life in local villages and communities. Undoubtedly the divide and rule tactics of the empire did cause localised tensions, conflict and acts of violence, but this interpretative move avoids the unavoidable. Roman military and economic might dominated everything. The history of revolts and risings also suggests that when Jesus taught active non-violent resistance, he had the political, economic and military realities of his real-life situation in mind. There was no getting away from the empire. The third of his transforming initiatives directly address the Roman milit-ary reality. Jesus was opposed to the empire's contribution to the vicious cycle of violence and he was also opposed and critical of the revengeful retaliation of those groups of people in Galilee, who, often in the name of their God, justified hitting back at the Romans through violent activity, revolts and risings. It is precisely this teaching of Jesus that Irish churches have ignored in the violent history of Ireland. It has been edited out

14 Ibid, p 185
15 Carter, op cit, p 151

in much of Western history as well.

Teaching active non-violent resistance, Jesus goes on in Matthew's gospel to highlight three transforming initiatives which can break the cycle of violent revengeful retaliation and so participate in the reign of God. He is concerned with breaking up the vicious cycle of violence and counter-violence.

Turn the other cheek

This non-violent initiative involves the right cheek, but a blow delivered by the right hand would land on the left cheek. To turn the other cheek was to invite a blow with the back of the hand, not the fist, and in eastern culture the left hand was used for unclean purposes. In Jewish culture there were heavy penalties for a left hand strike. It was 'the usual way of admonishing inferiors'[16] and an insult to a person's honour. 'To turn the other cheek is not simply to put up with the insult; it is to turn the cheek of equal dignity.'[17] One is not accepting inferiority or inequality but non-violently protesting equality. It was also a surprising move which may have led to another slap, but might also be a way of taking the psychological initiative, surprising the other and enabling the realisation of dignity. The transforming initiative lies in the element of surprise and doing the unexpected.

This kind of action actually happened in Jesus' lifetime. The incident involved the newly appointed Pilate who overnight introduced busts of the emperor on military standards and parading them through Jerusalem. Large crowds protested and there was a stand-off for six days. On day six Pilate called the crowds to the local stadium on the pretext of giving an answer. Surrounded by soldiers the crowd was threatened, especially when Pilate ordered swords to be drawn. The Jews flung themselves to the ground and bared their necks to the swords. Pilate was so surprised and astonished that he ordered the offensive standards to be removed from the city.[18] Galileans and Judeans would have known what Jesus meant.

---

16 Wink, op cit, p 176
17 Stassen, op cit, p 92
18 Wink, op cit, p 177

Give your cloak as well

The scene is a court of law where some wealthy elite has taken one of the 95% poor to court and sued them for their outer garment. The books of Exodus and Deuteronomy were very clear about justice being given to the poor and the poor protected from exploitation. Amos, the prophet, was highly critical of 'garments taken in pledge' (Amos 2:7-8). To do so was to 'trample the head of the poor into the dust of the earth'. Perhaps the wealthy elite always corrupt the legal system at the expense of the poor. 'So in Jesus' teaching the greedy lender sues you for the only other piece of clothing you have, your shirt'.[19]

Instantly recognisable in 1st century Galilee is a debtor in the depths of poverty summoned to court to lose his outer garment by legal means. There is intended humour in the imagery. The poor person not only gives his outer garment to the wealthy creditor, he strips off his inner garment and hands it over as well. That left him standing in court before his creditor stark naked. One can imagine a red-faced creditor with outer garment in one hand and inner garment in the other, with a judge not knowing what to do next and a sniggering courtroom audience. A naked peasant then leads a victory procession through the town, but it is the creditor who is shamed and whose inhumanity and injustice are exposed. According to Torah, 'nakedness was taboo, and shame fell less on the naked party than on the person viewing or causing the nakedness'.[20] Greed and injustice was exposed in all its nakedness with the creditor shamed and embarrassed. The surprising and unexpected action of the debtor becomes a transforming initiative breaking the cycle of violence and revenge. An entire economic system has been exposed, stark naked. A domination system has been lampooned and its naked injustice exposed.

Go the second mile

The third transformative initiative involves a soldier from the occupying forces. A Roman soldier had the right to compel a local to carry his pack for one mile. Empire's make their own rules and enforced labour can be one of them. After all the locals

19 Stassen, op cit, pp 92-93
20 Wink, op cit, p 179

are subject people. At least there is a degree of humanity about imperial law in this case, carrying a military pack is limited to one mile only. The Sicarii or dagger men and later the Zealots would have resisted violently, probably driven a dagger or knife into the soldier's ribs. Jesus was aware of the futility of armed insurrection against Roman imperial might and he was opposed to it. Counter-violence was a no-win scenario. The Sicarii and Zealots might keep up their violent resistance for decades, pick off an occasional Roman soldier every now and then, cheer when it happened. But how many young men would lose their lives to superior imperial violence? The cycle of violence would intensify and a war would drag on without winners, or as happened in 70 CE, the Roman military machine crushed, annihilated and destroyed a people and a city. It is in the context of Roman military occupation that Jesus teaches his transforming initiative. After carrying the soldier's pack for one mile, offer to carry on for a second mile. The initiative is no longer with the occupying soldier, he is surprised, unsure as to his next move. The surprise is a form of non-violent resistance, it confronts injustice and it shifts the balance of power, which 'calls our adversary to a new level of consciousness of what he or she is doing'.[21] It is even possible to imagine that on the second mile a depth of conversation might emerge about Roman occupation and Jewish resentment, that might even begin to talk about family matters. Such a conversation might be uncomfortable for the soldier and he might even plead with the Jewish local to give him back his pack after a half mile! Whatever about the confused and surprised soldier, the local has taken his own power back non-violently and recovered his humanity.

In each of the three colourful and humorous examples Jesus is offering non-violent ways of resisting violent oppression. The element of surprise is crucial to throwing the oppressor off-guard and breaking the cycle of vicious violence. Appearing naked in court might not work next month. The legal system will have passed a law against it by then and the debtor imprisoned for indecent exposure. New, surprising strategies will be needed. Non-violent resistance is imaginative work. The resort

---

21 Stassen, op cit, p 93

to violence and counter-violence is a failure of imagination and creativity.

All violence requires a transforming initiative which is creative and imaginative. Originality also seems to be the mark of Jesus' teaching at this point. For three centuries the church took him seriously but after the 4th century Jesus' originality, creativity and imagination were lost. Perhaps Christendom was a triumph of political power and a failure of radical imagination. What would Jesus do (*WWJD*) has become a sugary, pious slogan, but there is need to recover his teaching on active non-violent resistance which means a recovery of imagination.

Each transforming initiative includes an element of surprise, and some subversive correction of the hostility, domination, exclusion, and injustice that characterise our world. Each is one more mustard seed in the breakthrough of the reign of God in our everyday life. Each brings people distanced and excluded by the desire for revenge, insult, hostility, or injustice into the possibility of covenanting together to work in community. Each is a genuine opportunity in real life to participate in the transformation from separateness to togetherness.[22]

Love Your Enemies
Matthew 5:43-48 are perhaps the most startling and radical verses in the entire Bible. If there is a claim of originality or uniqueness to be made for Jesus, this is it. Loving enemies or taking moral responsibility for them is as counter-cultural, cutting edge and ethically radical as it comes. The book of Isaiah may have originated the lively vision of the kingdom of God and much of the sermon on the Mount, including the beatitudes, have roots in the Hebrew Bible. None of this is surprising given the Jewish - ness of Jesus. Much of his originality lies in his reinterpretation of his Jewish faith and ethics in a new context and for a different time. Christians need to live with the reality that what Jesus was about was a Jewish reform movement. Where he is truly original and where he may be said to push beyond his Jewish tradition and the twenty-one other Jewish reform movements of his time, is in this section of the sermon on the Mount. Even the teaching on active non-violent resistance has roots in the

---

22 Ibid, pp 94-95

Hebrew Bible, as has love of neighbour, but love of enemies goes where no one has gone before. Without making an imperialistic truth claim or making it a source of triumphalism, Jesus has pushed relational ethics to the nth level.

The triadic structure of his teaching is again helpful

- Traditional righteousness – retaliation for injury v 43
- Vicious cycle – revenge v 46-47
- Transforming initiatives – respond in new and surprising ways v 44-45

The first is expressed in 'You shall love your neighbour and hate your enemy' (5:43). The source of this traditional righteousness is not the Hebrew Bible.

Love of neighbour was well attested within the Hebrew scriptures and a common expectation of faithful Jews, yet nowhere in the Hebrew scriptures does it specifically advocate hatred of enemies.[23]

The Levitical text is quite clear about love of neighbour and in Mark's gospel Jesus joins the Levitical text, 19:18, with the Shema from Deuteronomy to summarise the Torah in two commandments, love of God and neighbour. But hatred of enemies is not advocated specifically in textual form. It was when the Dead Sea Scrolls were discovered in 1948 that the source of Matthew 5:43 was realised. It came from the writings of the Qumran Community, contemporary with Jesus. 'You have heard it said' referred to Qumran righteousness in which hatred of the enemy was a basic tenet.

The Qumran community were the Essenes who fled to the desert at the time of the violent Maccabean revolt. The Essenes parted company with, what they believed, was a polluted temple and an illegitimate priesthood. The community base was destroyed by the Romans in 68 CE during the Jewish-Roman war. Various scrolls, including the Community Rule, were hidden in pots within caves and these were the discoveries of a shepherd boy in 1948. Hatred of enemies was part of Qumran theology. Community members, according to the Rule, were to 'love all the sons of light ... and hate all the sons of darkness, each ac-

---

23 Nelson-Pallmeyer, Jack, *Jesus Against Christianity: Reclaiming the Missing Jesus*, (Harrisburg: Trinity Press International, 2001) p 285

cording to his fault in the vengeance of God'.[24] The original crowds whom Jesus taught would have heard of the Qumran or Essene teaching and Matthews post-70 CE community would probably have been familiar with the teaching of a community crushed during the war. In a region occupied by Roman military forces and oppressed by imperial economic, and temple economic oppression, hatred of enemies hardly needed a religious text to support it. Jesus was being at his most counter-cultural. 'Jesus counsel to love enemies would have offended many of his contemporaries beyond the Essenes who embraced hatred of enemies as part of their foundational creed.'[25] There already was a strand of enemy hatred within the Hebrew Bible, given voice by Deuteronomy's permanent exclusion order on the hated Ammonites and Moabites (Deut 23:3), Leviticus 26 ordered enemies to be pursued and put to the sword (Leviticus 26:8). Even though these writings emerged from the Babylonian exile and historically ancient Israel was never in a position to carry out genocide on any ethnic group of enemies, literalists then and now have easily found a credo justifying their violence and hatred. The Qumran War Scroll with its expectation of a war of revenge and retribution involving the 'sons of light' (the Community) against the 'sons of darkness' (the Romans) had biblical precedent, at least with a literal interpretation. In the context of the same military and economic oppression by the Romans, Jesus was not calling people to war and hatred, but to love of the enemy. He was running counter to a whole national theology and mythology, where salvation was understood as 'the crushing defeat of enemies either within or at the end of history'.[26] God saving the Queen and sending her victorious is an identical understanding of salvation. But this, and soldier boys fighting for liberty, as in the Irish anthem, are stood on their head and inside out by the radical teaching of Jesus.

To love the enemy is not about being nice, nor is it soft, sentimental gush which lies down under the enemies violence and power. The only love Jesus talked about was tough love, love which sought the enemies highest good and took moral respon-

24 Quoted in ibid, p 285
25 Ibid, p 286
26 Ibid., p 287

sibility for the enemy. It is an enormous ethical challenge, which for Jesus requires prayer as well as blessing the other, or positive action (Matthew 5:44). Prayer is opening oneself to God, God's love and compassion and passion for inclusive social justice. It is also turning towards the other, in this case the enemy in the energy and power of the non-violent, loving, compassionate and just God. Not only is Jesus turning popular and nationalistic notions of salvation inside out, he is also turning nationalistic and violent images of God inside out. To change the metaphor, this is what it means to participate in God's upside down kingdom. Injustices and oppression are to be challenged but 'How the community challenges (loving, creative and active non violence) and to what end (the fullness of God's empire) matter enormously.'[27]

The teaching of Jesus about love of enemies is rooted in his Jewish vision of God. God is not a violent, punishing God, a genocidal God who wants the ultimate, crushing exclusion of enemies. Rather God is a God of totally indiscriminate love, making the sun rise on the evil and the good and who sends the life giving rain on the righteous and unrighteous, or on the just and the unjust. It is an offensive image of God to those who want to live within the narrow bounds of nationalism, ethnic purity or superior religion. Better a God in our narrow exclusive, restrictive image. But we are called to radically love enemies because that is precisely what God does. According to the Matthean Jesus we are to 'Be perfect, therefore, as your heavenly Father is perfect' (Matthew 5:48).

'Perfect' is off-putting, because it suggests to us moral perfection or some kind of ideal perfection. That is frightening and in some despair we can conclude that it is unattainable. Luke's gospel makes more sense. 'Be merciful, just as your Father is merciful' (Luke 6:36). The Lukan Jesus has just described God as 'kind to the ungrateful and the wicked'. For the Lukan Jesus we are to show active kindness towards the enemy. Merciful is also interchangeable with compassion, a word which suggests solid - arity with the other's pain and suffering. The enemy too has a human face and a human story which may well include pain

---

27 Carter, op cit, p 155

and suffering. Matthew's word in Greek is *teleios*. It can mean
perfect, but not moral or idealised perfection, but wholeness
and completeness. The translation might well read, 'Be complete, therefore, as your heavenly Father is complete'. *Teleios*
translates the Hebrew word *tamin* but 'Neither the Greek word
nor the Hebrew is ever applied to God in the Old Testament or
in the Dead Sea Scrolls.'[28] Again, this points to something new
and unique in what Jesus is saying about God. The context is relational and God's completeness in relation to the ungrateful
and the wicked is really about God's inclusiveness. God's love is
all-inclusive, including enemies. Like God we are to be complete
and inclusive in our tough love. Jesus is not calling people to
live up to high, moralistic, Greek ideals of perfection. He was
Jewish and not Greek, and he was calling participants in God's
kingdom to be whole, complete and inclusive in their loving.
The Matthean text might then be translated, 'Be all-embracing,
all-inclusive, therefore, as your heavenly Father is all-embracing, all-inclusive.' There is nothing that the gospels have Jesus
say, more radical, unique and challenging than that, not least
because the teaching is in the context of Roman occupation and
popular but hated enemies.

Paul's mirror image political ethics
Paul wrote a letter to the small faith community at the heart of
empire, in Rome itself. Romans is often acclaimed as Paul's
greatest letter, even as his most systematic expression of theology. Such an overstatement and exaggerated claim is to impose
a scholastic, confessional framework on the latter. It is to interpret Romans from a later law *v* grace dualism and from an early
Christian propensity for supersessionism. This reading of Romans
has been called into question since the 1960s. There is now a
greater awareness that Paul in Romans is essentially relational
and has to do with God's purpose of just reconciliation between
fractious people. There is also a more profound awareness that
Paul in Romans is not anti-Judaism but anti-imperialism. He is
writing to the heart of empire, the engine room or epi-centre of
imperial power maintained by militarism and oppressive econ -
omics. Since his transformative hero is Jesus whom he has en-

---

28 Stassen, op cit, p 105

countered experientially and whose life event has radically changed him, it would be surprising if he did not endorse and reinforce the active non-violent resistance and love of enemies that his hero taught and embodied. This is exactly what he does in Romans 12:14-13:10.

Watch especially how closely that overall complex of 12:14-13:10 echoes the radical language of Jesus' advocating love of enemies and negating violence against them in the sermon on the Mount. That complex is, in fact, a Pauline version of Jesus' message in Matthew 5:39-48 and Luke 6:27-36.[29]

It is significant that the text is in the context of the complex dealing with the relationship of faith to the politics of the state. Romans 13:1-7 is perhaps Paul's most abused and infamous teaching. Oppressive and unjust governments have been happy to use Romans 13 to justify on theological grounds, their abuses of power. The abusive interpretion has been possible by ignoring or editing out the immediately preceding verses which are the mirror-image of Jesus teaching an active non-violent resistance and tough love of enemies. Furthermore by not ignoring historical context, namely a divisive policy of taxation when Romans was written, would have avoided a simplistic reading of Romans 13 as advocating absolute, timeless submission to all state power. Jesus certainly did not teach such submission and acquiescence. Paul himself in an earlier letter, I Thessalonians, was very critical of Roman imperial claims about 'peace and security'. He thought the imperial claim was a great lie. Revelation 13 with its advocacy of resistance to state power and oppressive economics was still almost half a century away from Romans, but the Christian Testament is too critical to ever allow for an exclusive or absolute submission to the state. Borg and Crossan outline four parallels between the Matthean/Lukan and Pauline texts.

- Matthew 5:44 and Luke 6:27-28-Romans 12:14
- Matthew 5:39-Romans 12:17 and 12:21
- Matthew 5:39-Romans 13:1-7
- Matthew 5:44 and Luke 6:27-28-Romans 13:8-10

---

29 Borg, Marcus J and Crossan, John Dominic, *The First Paul: Reclaiming the Radical Visionary Behind the Church's Conservative Icon* (London: SPCK, 2009) p 118

In the third parallel, Matthew and Paul each use the word 'resist'. The Greek, as we have noted earlier, *antihistemi*, means to resist violently. The resistance reflects military violence and that was commonplace across the empire. So too were violent uprisings and revolts, counter-violence. Jesus and Paul are both opposed to violence and counter-violence and are against violent resistance. In relation to Roman tax policy, it is violent resistance Paul is against in Romans 13. Paul uses a second word in Romans 13, *tasso*, which is stronger than military violence. It is extreme violence by a body of armed men, ruthlessly planned, tactical violence. *Tasso* or *taxis* is the Greek word from which the English word tactics is derived. In keeping with Jesus, Paul is against the use of violence and is for active non-violence, which is active non-violent resistance.

In the fourth parallel, Paul 'manages to mention "love" five times in those three verses'.[30] Not only does Paul mirror Jesus' love of enemies, he elaborates on Jesus' teaching. Love is applied to a range of relational encounters and experiences and 'Love does no wrong to a neighbour ... (Romans 13:10). The latter words are a quotation from Psalm 15:3, in fact the same words from the Greek translation. There are advocates of the active non-violent ethic of Jesus and Paul in their own Jewish scriptures. Similar sounding statements were made in the Greco-Roman world, such as 'Don't "badmouth" your neighbours' and 'Be affable towards your neighbours, not austere'.[31] Ethics, within the empire could be positively relational and frequently at that, but 'none of these references speak of "the love" in such specific terms as Paul does here'.[32]

The teaching of Jesus in Matthew and Luke and Paul's mirror-image in Romans, even though written up to forty years before both of the gospels, strongly suggests that active non-violence and radical love of all, including enemies is the inherent ethos of the kingdom of God.

The teaching of Jesus and Paul and this inherent ethos of the

30 Ibid, p 120 The four parallels which Borg and Crossan use as a textual context for Romans 13:1-7 – the state verses are found in pp 118-120
31 Jewett, Robert, *Romans: A Commentary* (Minneapolis: Fortress Press, 2007) p 814 note 99
32 Ibid, p 814

kingdom is far removed from the ambivalence towards and even collusion with war and violence in Irish and Western history. The decade of change and violence, 1912-1922 and the most recent phase of violence in Ireland, 1969-2004, with fallout still continuing, though in a very much smaller scale, expresses the pervasive nature and dominance of the myth of redemptive violence. So much violence in a country of traditionally high religious practice highlights the 'Constantinian mistake' and is a betrayal of the good news of Jesus and Paul. Superficial changes or formal adjustments by Irish churches will still miss the good news, miss the kingdom. Yoder is correct to insist that 'It is possible to overcome the Constantinian mistake only by a basic renewal of the entire Christian movement.' In the light of the teaching of Jesus and Paul and their articulation and practice of the inherent ethos of God's kingdom, the Irish faith community, including its institutional forms, needs a whole new vision of what it means to live the faith in the context of a tragic history of violence and the struggle to envision a new future. Yoder believes that the converse is true: 'It is possible to renew the entire Christian gospel by overcoming the Constantinian mistake.'[33]

---

33 Yoder, John Howard, *The War of the Lamb: The Ethics of Non-violence and Peacemaking*, (Grand Rapids: Brazos Press, 2009) p 51. The book has been edited by Glenn Stassen, Mark Thiessen and Matt Hamsher.

CHAPTER TEN

Re-visioning a different culture

Modern Irish history has been dominated by violence. In relation to geopolitics, the 20th century was the bloodiest in recorded human history. Much scientific and technological advancement was used in the destruction of millions of human lives and the devastation of the physical and natural environment. Twentieth century Ireland reflected the geopolitical brutality and it kept continuity with the previous three centuries of Irish violence. The pervasive violence of modern Irish history has roots in state violence, the oppressive violence of British political and military colonialism. It also has roots in mythically and religiously inspired counter-violence and collaboration with state violence. The physical force traditions rebelled as in 1912 and 1916, or respectively rebelled as in 1798 or collaborated with brutal state forces in the same '98 violence. The religious factor was always present and equally pervasive. Richard Kearney has expressed it in stark language which ought to be faced and not denied.

> I come from a country – Ireland – where people have been killing each other for centuries in the name of God. Who possesses absolute truth? The Catholic King James or Protestant King Billy (fighting over accession to the Crown in the seventeenth century)? The Catholic IRA or Protestant UVF, pursuing their respective terrorist campaigns over the last 30 years, only reaching a cessation of hostilities with the Belfast Good Friday Agreement in 1998? And there are, alas, still so-called 'peace lines' separating Catholic from Protestant communities in Belfast as I speak.[1]

There may well be discomfort with the killing of each other in the name of God, but there is no morality in whitewashing historical experience, sanitising key players or living with the pretence that God was not invoked or involved. We have al-

---

1 Kearney, Richard in *Violence and Christian Spirituality: An Ecumenical Discussion* edited by Emmanuel Clapsis (Geneva: World Council of Churches Publications, 2007) p 47. Kearney's chapter is entitled 'Interreligious Dialogue: Hermeneutics and Fundamentalism.'

ways killed each other in Ireland for religious reasons, at least in part, or the killing and counter-killing has been given religious legitimation. A more secularist Ireland may be deeply embarrassed by the God dimension, but it is naive to rewrite the political and theological history of violence. Secular humanists are more likely to use the God dimension as a big stick to discredit, even rubbish religion, but that is equally naive. It buries its head in the sand and pretends that much of the bloody killing globally in the 20th century was not carried out by secular atheistic regimes. Stalin and Pol Pot were not religious cranks, or even devout believers! The Gulag was not religiously inspired. But much of our war and violence has been. Brutal killing has religious and anti-religious motivation. Belief and non-belief are involved which should help us avoid any naivety. There are complex and varied dynamics at work and the religious and the secular humanistic are among them. To argue that it is neither authentically religious nor authentically humanistic is hardly convincing, though there is realism in acknowledging that any system of values or ideology can become seriously distorted or warped.

When the American bomber set off with its atomic payload for Hiroshima, it was jointly blessed by the Lutheran and Catholic chaplains. This shared religious act in blessing crew, plane and deadly atomic weapon does seem like a strange form of ecumenism, a totally warped form of ecumenism, but the chaplains and everyone involved really believed in the power of prayer and God. Over 65 years on, Catholic and Protestant still cannot officially share the Eucharist together, supposedly part of the pain of ecumenism. That we cannot share together the remembrance of the victim of imperial violence, state execution and military might, and yet ecumenically bless weapons of mass destruction, shock and awe military strategies, is theological nonsense, to put it mildly. To drop such a deadly and destruct - ive weapon to bring peace is the worst religious heresy of the 20th century and of the history of heresy. And that was the theological heresy of Hiroshima, the classical myth of redemptive violence.

The foundational documents of what became Northern Ireland and the Republic of Ireland were the Ulster Covenant

and the Easter Proclamation. Both documents invoked violence
and God as core. The militarisation of politics and the use of violence were justified, believed to be morally right and legitimised
by God. God was invoked to authorise the gun in politics.
Furthermore, God is the God of our fathers and past generations
and when the documents are read together, God is on both
sides. There is the assumption or confidence that God will deliver
the respective causes. How God can be supporting both sides,
no Protestant or Catholic, unionist or nationalist, loyalist or republican, has ever explained, except to delude themselves that
God was for them and not the other. On the other hand the popular strategy of divide and rule may have had its origins in Godself, if the God-claims in the foundational documents of Ireland,
north and south, are to be believed. And there is no doubt that
the claims were believed at the time. Were the authors of the
documents and the thousands who subscribed to them deluded?
The problem with invoking God in such documents and in national constitutions, written or unwritten, means that in all prob-
ability people are deluded. The God on our side theology is a
nationalistic fiction, made up by the deluded or by those who
intentionally use an authoritative and violent God to delude
others into support for a cause.

Pádraig Pearse combined ancient Celtic myth, an atonement
and eucharistic theology of sacrifice, not only to shape the
Proclamation, but also to provide a theological basis for the
Easter Rising. He was the mystical theologian of the 1916 Rising
with the myth and sacrificial interpretation of Christ's death and
the sacrament steeped in violence. It was easy to produce the
theological legitimation for the violence at the time and it has remained a legacy for the rest of 20th century Ireland.

Edward Carson is proclaimed from the lamp-posts in loyalist
areas as 'the founder of the people's army'. He did form the illegal UVF and left a legacy to the present. Nothing of any substance has been written on Carson's religious convictions. Faith
is not as obvious as with Pearse, but Carson was in the Protestant tradition, which at the time was not only anti-Catholic, but
held a strong theology of empire, God's chosen British people.
Whether like Pearse, he overtly appealed to his Protestant religious beliefs or used religion, as in the Covenant, to galvanise

and legitimise violence and the gun in Ulster's political cause, the God-dimension was every bit as delusionary as Pearse's version. Both gods, and let's not describe them as one, were gods of death, who brought death to thousands of young men and left a legacy of death into the present. That is where the worship of a death-giving god always leads. The delusion also proclaims the dying as sacrifice, but supreme sacrifice is part of the same delusion. Significantly we describe war, violence and related dying in religious language. The delusion produces a liturgy of death, a pseudo religious veneer that gives it heroic status, even sacred status.

It can be supported by a very literal reading of violent biblical texts, but again texts are in dispute in the Bible. There were those who deluded themselves then as now that violence achieves, brings peace and is authorised by the deity. The critical and prophetic biblical voices critiqued and rejected the mystique of violence. They saw it as idolatrous religion and it was no part of the praxis of Jesus who spoke of God and lived active non-violence in the context of a brutalising and violent imperial system.

Giving a future to the past
Acknowledging the past in Ireland is difficult. No one wants to go there. Acknowledgement of Bloody Sunday in Derry and some sense of closure has rightly been achieved after 35 years. The majority of victims in Northern Ireland's immediate past are not going to have the same justice.

Whatever about the enormous costs involved in public enquiries, there is not enough truth around. How much truth can a small community bear? How many organisations, groups and individuals are willing to tell the truth and how much truth are they prepared to hear? The questions of truth and justice may not ultimately be dealt with in relation to the recent violence. They were not dealt with either in relation to the violence during the decade of change. There were the disappeared who almost a century later remain among the disappeared, long forgotten except in the family memory of descendants.

The temptation during the forthcoming decade of centenaries will be selectivity and amnesia. It will be easy to focus on the change such as successful resistance to Home Rule by unionists and the achieving of independence by nationalists. But both were achieved at high cost and the legacy of violence was played out in the last third of the 20th century. The violent ideology has not yet gone away. There are those on both sides who have still not got the message from the people of Ireland that physical force and violence have no place in Ireland's present or future. But then huge ambivalence around violence remains and this will make it difficult to critique and deconstruct the mystique of violence which saturates 1912-1922 and 1969-2004. Acknowledging the destructive and deathly role of violence in the formation of two states and in very recent history may well prove too difficult for most. Critical commemoration and remembering may well be kept in the background or out of sight. And yet without the critical dimension the remembering will be less than honest and a disingenuous attempt to re-write pretend history.

The clock cannot be turned back and neither can there be pretence that violence was not itself a domination system that blighted relationships and life. The reality has been that violence and physical force traditions have been an integral part of our historical experience. Of course there was state violence, colonial violence and paramilitary violence, loyalist and republican, and there is more than one story to tell. Indulging in blame and counter-blame, who started it, whose fault it was, is a counterproductive exercise. In this sense the past is the past and it cannot be changed. It requires historical analysis, honest acknowledgement and critical evaluation, if we are going to overcome the pervasive culture of violence and shape a very different kind of Irish future. By all means let's commemorate and remember the dead, all of the Irish dead of two world wars and other conflicts, and the dead of our decades of civil violence, the noncombatants and the combatants. But we will need to abolish the word sacrifice and the concept of blood sacrifice from our voc - abulary and consciousness and remember the dead instead as victims of our shared inhumanity and acquiescence in violence. Shared acknowledgement and shared responsibility for our violent past is morally important as a bridge to a transformed Irish and British narrative. There are no ethics in a blame-game, nor in sanitising or denying the past, but in critical, ethical remembering there is hope of transformation and future. The violence of the past cannot be left unacknowledged or glossed over. It requires deconstruction, rigorous moral evaluation and given it has long since become a mystique of violence, it requires serious theological deconstruction.

Richard Kearney, writing in the context of principles of tolerance, highlights a number of important features. Though he is more focused on religious tolerance as counter to religious fundamentalism, his important contribution can be extended. The 20th century violence in Ireland was characterised not only by religious fundamentalism, Catholic and Protestant, but also political fundamentalism. Certitudes and absolutes have underpinned our use of violence in politics and history. Following Paul Ricoeur, Kearney posits a first principle as:

An ethic of narrative hospitality
This involves 'taking responsibility in imagination and in sympathy for the story of the other, through the life narratives which concern the other.'[2] Without imagination and sympathy, the life narratives of the other are not likely to be heard. The stories of the political stranger, victim and forgotten one need to be heard and it is an ethical act to enter into such stories and even welcome them. It will not be easy but it is a challenge to move through our violent past to a new future.

An ethic of narrative flexibility
If we remember the past it is often only our past and not that of the other. Our past usually takes on the form of fixed dogma to the exclusion of other fixed dogmas. But this is a failure to recognise that there is always more than one narrative and even then none of our many narratives is fixed or final. Narrative flexibility acknowledges the many and that every narrative is open to deeper understandings and fresh interpretations. The ethic of narrative flexibility opens up 'the possibility of revising every story which has been handed down and of carrying out a place for several stories directed towards the same past'.[3]

---

2 Ibid, p 52 The quotation is from Ricoeur
3 Ibid, p 53

Narrative plurality

Strangers and adversaries need to allow for a plurality of narrative perspectives. These are versions of Irish history and stories, all told from different historical and experiential perspectives and even the same event recounted differently. 'Pluralism here does not mean any lack of respect for the singularity of any particular religious event narrated through the various acts of remembering.'[4] The same holds for political and historical events and is the recognition that multiple perspectives are inevitable since no group, organisation or individual has 360 degree vision. To recognise narrative plurality and practice such an ethic is to begin to share symbolically and respectfully in the commemoration of other groups and communities. This would mean nationalists entering into the unionist memory and story of Ulster Covenant in 1912 and unionists entering into the nationalist story of the 1916 Easter Rising, symbolically and respectfully.

Transfiguring of the Past

As a principle of tolerance, Kearney describes this as trying 'to give a future to the past by remembering it in a more attentive way, ethically and poetically'.[5] To dismiss the other's past or story is to remain locked in the past, unwilling to acknowledge the past, however strange or foreign. It is also a way of asserting the hegemony or dominance of a single past, which is really a single interpretation of it. The past needs a future if we are to be liberated from it into a new and shared future. For Kearney, this means retrieving the 'betrayed promises of history ... the unfilled future of the past'. Furthermore, 'This unfilled future of the past is the major benefit that we can expect from the crossing of memories and exchange of narratives.'[6]

Covenant is an inclusive, socio-political, economic vision in biblical terms and in this light the covenant pledge of 1912 for civil and religious liberties has never been fulfilled. Likewise, the Easter Proclamation of 1916 to 'cherish all the children of the nation equally' and the similar pledge to civil and religious liberties to all remains the unfulfilled future of the past. Both

---

4 Ibid, p 53
5 Ibid, p 53
6 Ibid, p 54

Covenant and Proclamation remain betrayed promises of history but at this point in history there is the possibility for creative retrieval. This requires at least the recognition that 'The past is a cemetery of promises which have not been kept' and the need for alternative and attentive means of remembrance.[7]

Pardon

Kearney describes this as something more, a plus which moves beyond 'narrative imagination to forgiveness'. We need to exchange our narratives, enter into each others histories and memories of suffering, but transforming our culture of violence, which is a culture of death and suffering into a culture of active non-violence and hope, requires release from our pasts, a liberation that is forgiveness. Ultimately forgiveness is a spiritual act, not replacing justice but enhancing it. Forgiveness is not present in our sanitising of a selective past nor in amnesia. 'It demands huge patience, an enduring practice of working through mourning and letting go. But it is not forgetful forgiveness.'[8] It remembers and adds the X factor, the liberation of the other and ourselves from the prison of the past. There are many historical precedents that introduced a transformative, liberating dynamic into the past and present.

One thinks of Brandt kneeling at Warsaw, Havel's apology to the Sudeten Germans, Hume's preparedness to speak with the IRA, Sadat's visit to Jerusalem, Hillesum's refusal to hate her hateful persecutors. All miraculous moments where an ethics of tolerance is touched by a poetics of pardon. But I repeat: the one does not replace the other – both justice and pardon are crucially important in the act of remembering past suffering.[9]

Other gestures and actions can be added to the above. Nelson Mandella and Gordon Wilson, to name but two others. The poetics of pardon, refusal of bitterness and bearing no grudge, all introduced a transformative, liberating dynamic into the historical experience of violence and suffering. The gestures and poetics of forgiveness do not take away from the difficulties and complexities of holding justice and forgiveness together,

---

7 Ibid, p 54
8 Ibid, p 54
9 Ibid, p 54

but they create an X factor, a surplus without which a history and culture of violence cannot be transformed.

Paul Ricoeur's essay from which Kearney has drawn the above five features is entitled, 'Reflections on a New Ethos for Europe'. The title is suggestive. If there is to be a new ethos for Ireland then the culture of violence needs to be honestly and critically acknowledged. Ethical remembering of the past will put the five principles into practice. Narrative hospitality, flexibility and plurality will all be necessary. In this way we can give a pardon to the past and in the work of pardon add surplus to the transforming process from a past and culture of violence to a radically alternative ethos.

A transforming faith community

If the resort to violence is a failure of imagination, then the role of religion in legitimising violence is a failure in theological and spiritual imagination. Institutional churches have engaged at times in the politics of condemnation when acts of violence have occurred. But they have frequently bought into the pseudo-religion of war, its liturgical language, and been complicit through silence, ambivalence, selectivity and the failure to articulate and practice an active non-violent alternative to a dominant Irish ethos. The sectarian nature of Irish religion, the complete identification of religion with political power and loyalties and the oppositional nature of Catholic and Protestant theologies, have skewed religious imagination for centuries. The faith was always going to have a role in the culture of violence. Violent theologies of Christ's death re-presented in eucharistic liturgies and Holy Communions and the blood of the Lamb preaching as violent sacrifice, all led to the blood sacrifice theology of violence, the creation of dead heroes and martyrs, and a shared if sectarian victimhood. Our traditional versions of Christianity has much to answer for. We really did believe the religiously violent Covenant of 1912 and the similar Easter Proclamation of 1916. More than half a century later there was no theological critique of the loyalists literal use of Deuteronomy 7 on a wall mural, or of the republican use of the beatitude, the blessedness of those who hunger for justice during the hunger strikes. The religion of violence and the violence of religion had survived from the earlier era. Neither loyalists nor republicans had much time for the church but religious texts, vocabulary and ethos were used in support of killing, death, martydom and paying the ultimate price. Were the physical force traditions using religion in a mirror image of Remembrance Sunday every November, or was the blood sacrifice imagery already there in the Irish and Ulster faith traditions?

The question is, can religion and violent theology be transformed? Can there be a retrieval of theological and spiritual imagination with the capacity to transform the ethos and culture of violence? Given the role of religion in violence in Ireland, can religion have a role in peacebuilding and reconciliation? To respond positively will require a huge leap of theological and spiritual imagination.

A christology of non-violence and peacebuilding
Christianity represents a Christ-centred approach to and relationship with God. It may be acknowledged, and is increasingly these days, that other religions have their own, even unique way to God. But for Christians, Jesus is their way, even unique way. There simply is no Christian faith without Jesus. Take him out of the future and there may still be faith in God, but not Christian faith. Christians have found their greatest clue to God in his life event.

In the context of a pervasive culture of violence legitimised by religion, which Jesus is being represented? The warrior Jesus, whose blood sacrifice required by God, inspires our blood sacrifice in war and civil violence, may not even be Christian himself! The Christ invoked in the 1937 Irish Constitution looks suspic - iously like a 1916 Rising model! The attempt to say who Jesus is is known as christology. Christology has come up with many different models over the centuries. The Irish Constitutional model is only one, but is it Christian? The classical models emerged from the early church councils, presided over and heavily influenced by none other than the emperor. What emerged were largely imperial models, and were they always Christian? The Lord sometimes looked more like the Lord Emperor, which was standing the original confession of Jesus as Lord in the Christian Testament on its head. By calling Jesus Lord the early generation of

Christians were being radically subversive of the emperor and his empire. By the fourth and fifth centuries, the Lord had become like the emperor and the church was blessing and legitimising the states wars, armies and weaponry.

From time to time there are attempts to retrieve a more original and subversive christology from the Christian Testament. But these are frequently minority voices. Their christologies have never become the dominant voice of Western Christendom, and with the latter in its death throes, if not already dead, christologies of non-violence and peacebuilding are still not widely confessed. And yet this was the essential narrative that shaped the identity and praxis of the early Christians. Christianity is essentially christological. For Christians Jesus is the way, the truth and the life (John 14:6) not in any triumphalist, imperial, exclusivist sense, but as their experiential reality. Put another way, 'Jesus is the story that forms the church.'[10] If this is true then the church is to live out its normative and formative story of Christ's active non-violence and peacebuilding. The church may need to be concerned with its own radical transformation before being concerned with the transformation of an Irish ethos of violence. There are a number of Christo - logical models to be retrieved.

Jesus' healings as reconciliation

A core feature of the Christian gospels is the emphasis on Jesus' healings. In fact there are multiple stories of exorcisms and healings, and shaped by a modern scientific worldview, we don't know how to handle such stories, especially exorcisms. Yet healing is a key characteristic of the gospel of Mark. 'Exorcism and other healings were well-remembered practices of Jesus and the Jesus movement.'[11] It was obviously well-remembered, however, the stories were told by different gospel writers, and these exorcisms and healings were not unique to Jesus and his followers. It was also well known that Jesus was not the only person who

10 Swartley, Willard M, *Covenant of Peace: The Missing Peace in New Testament Theology and Ethics* (Grand Rapids: Eerdmans, 2006) p 401 The quotation is from Stanley Hauerwas, *Community of Character* and chapter 2 entitled 'Jesus, The Story of the Kingdom'.

11   Tilley, Terence W, *The Disciples of Jesus: Christology as Reconciling Practice* (New York: Orbis Books, 2008) p 137

healed. The Jesus movement was one of several prophetic movements struggling for healing and wholeness in the shadow of empire. There is no historical data to know how they related to each other. What is clear from the gospels is that the Jesus movement 'clearly identified healing not merely as a medical practice but as an indicator of God's reign'.[12] In liberation, wholeness and completeness, the reign of God was breaking in and was already present. God's alternative empire was subverting the Roman empire.

Mark's gospel, for which exorcisms and healings have a key role, tells a classic story, the exorcism of the Gerasene demoniac (Mark 5:1-10). There is more to this story than meets the eye and a literal reading of it will miss the point. There are two suggestive levels of meaning in the story as told by Mark. The geographical reference to the Decapolis locates the story in a non-Jewish, Greek region. The man who is 'clothed and in his right mind' belongs there and returns there to share good news. The victim, cut off and isolated from his community is seriously and acutely mentally disturbed. 'Mark depicts accurately the behaviour patterns of some people trapped in acute psychotic breakdown ...'[13] Illness such as this are a common feature of occupied and oppressed people. Oppressive occupation creates such illnesses and disrupts and destroys social relationships. 'Clearly the man is sick, has broken off from friends, family and God, and needs reconciliation with God, himself, and his family and friends.'[14] The demoniac is healed, the totality of relationship are restored and reconciliation is achieved as a sign of the reign of God in community. The region lives under the disruption of the Roman empire and the healing runs counter to the destruct-ive domination system, violence is rejected and reconciliation and wholeness realised.

The story can be read at an even more subversive level and the clue is in Mark's vocabulary. Key words are pigs, Legion and the command language. All of this is Roman military language which would have been instantly recognised by those who first heard the story. Pigs not only suggest Gentiles, a non-

12 Ibid, p 140
13 Ibid, pp 141-142
14 Ibid, p 142

Jewish identity, pig was also the name of a Roman regiment. Legion was the technical name for a Roman troop of soldiers and the commands given in the story were well known Roman army commands. The very command to 'get out' and pigs heading for the sea would have been welcomed by any occupied people. The Roman army withdrawal and heading over the sea to Rome was something people desperately longed for. The military occupation was responsible for high levels of acute, psychotic breakdown. The many exorcisms and healings in the gospels, especially Mark, were subversive of Roman imperial presence and violence and were a reconciling practice that restored the ill and possessed to their lives within community. Mark's story also subverts the violence and brutality of the domination system. These two levels of reading, interconnected as they are, are the point of the healing stories in the gospels. The domination system of violence and brutality, destructive of lives and community is rejected, subverted and reconciliation practised. The stories are part of the christology of active non-violence and peacemaking which is the story that forms the church.

Jesus' controversial dinner parties

Jesus spent a lot of time eating and drinking at dinner parties and his behaviour got him into trouble. A number of his fellow Jews, usually members of the traditional religious establishment, labeled him a drunk and a glutton. Jesus, in their eyes, over-imbibed and over-ate. But the Jesus movement as a reform movement within Judaism was engaged in distinctive and radical behaviour. 'Eating and drinking are a key and controversial element in distinguishing the Jesus movement and its leader from other groups in Judaism.'[15] What made the practice controversial were the inclusive guest lists.

Mark introduces controversial eating and drinking early in the gospel. (Mark 2:15-20) At a meal in the house of Levi, a collaborator with Roman imperial power because he is a tax collector, Jesus and his friends are joined by the regional Roman revenue department. The objectors complain, not that they were bad people but they were good people who saw holiness and purity

15 Ibid, p 175

in the ritual of separation from all people and things unclean. Levi's revenue colleagues were not necessarily immoral types either, but they were collaborating with the enemy. They were on the Roman payroll and that was enough to damn anyone and be dehumanised as 'sinners'. The latter in the gospels are not evil or immoral people. They are classified as sinners by the traditional religious because they do not conform to the rules of ritual purity and traditional religious practice.

Another food and drink story follows immediately. A group of traditional religious and ascetics are fasting. Jesus and his friends are having a dinner party and are severely criticised. For the Pharisees eating at home meant only eating with others who were in a state of ritual purity. They would only eat with those who had 'undefiled hands' (Mark 7:2-4). They had to be 'persons in a state of ritual purity (cf Ex 30:19-21)'.[16] Jesus was being accused of eating with those outside the purity boundaries. What is recorded in Luke is a well deserved reputation. 'Look, a glutton and a drunkard, a friend of tax collectors and sinners!' (Luke 7:34)

Such controversial and inclusive hospitality offered by Jesus was an intentional sign of the reign of God. Jesus' dinner parties were a living out of God's reign. It is not Jesus the Christian superseeding the Jewish Pharisees, but Jesus the Jew drawing on a Jewish tradition of inclusive banquet as an indicator and anticipation of God's reign. Inclusivity at the banquet is what God's reign is like and Jesus will not exclude or marginalise those who do not conform to traditional religious and cultural rules. Those whom society writes off as unclean are at the table and that includes the enemy (Psalm 23:5).

In a society where people manage social relations by dividing into them and us, good and bad, justified and unjustified, saved and damned, superior and inferior, the kingdom banquet is radically inclusive and for all. There are no boundaries and that is more than most can cope with, but if the Jesus story forms the church then his controversial dinner parties are an import - ant model for the church and part of the christology of active non-violence and peacebuilding.

---

16 Ibid, p 176

Jesus' Practice of Active Non-Violence

Jesus' teaching on active non-violence has been explored in the last chapter. The sermon on the Mount, including the beatitudes, not resisting evil violently and love of the enemy, all in the context of Roman imperial rule, are the high watermark of christological ethics. Jesus not only taught active non-violence and peacemaking, he practised it. His christological ethics are virtue ethics based on his actions. In the gospels we see how he 'habitually responds to people, especially to those who oppose him or are hostile towards him, and finally to those who kill him'.[17] Key to his praxis were relationships and he did not escape into an inner religious world and avoid relationships of hostility in his own Jewish world, in the Greek regions beyond the ethnic boundaries of his world, or imperial presence. Jesus by what he did had enemies. Opposition and conflict, hostility and fearful hatred were part of his life experience. Mark's gospel is full of conflict scenes. Traditional religious leadership, often collaborating with the Romans as much as they accused the tax-collectors of the same, claimed that his exorcisms were by the power of Satan (Mark 3:22-30). Satan language had its origins centuries earlier as a way of describing Jews who were believed to have betrayed and sold out their tradition. It was also the name used, especially in Revelation, to describe the empire. In contemporary terms, it is how the Taliban describe the American superpower as the 'Great Satan'. Ironically the religious traditionalists are accusing Jesus of selling out his Jewish tradition, a traitor who is colluding with the Romans. Incredible as that sounds, it is not surprising and has been a frequently used tactic in history. His habitual and subversive actions were seriously rocking the boat, provoking an imperial response, disturbing the 'peace' and putting the collaborative power base and status of traditional religious leadership at risk. So he was really working with and for the Romans; give a dog a bad name and all of that!

Nowhere in the gospel stories does Jesus respond with violence to his adversaries nor does he ever use violence to defend himself or his friends. John's gospel has a story of a woman

17 Schubeck, Thomas L, *Love That Does Justice* (New York: Orbis Books, 2007) p 56

caught in the act of adultery (John 8:2-11). It is difficult to imagine this woman committing adultery by herself, but her accusers who drag her from the house and throw her at the feet of rabbi Jesus for sentencing and punishment, thought it was a solo act! There must have been a man involved but perhaps the moralists helped him to escape through the back door. It's a story of violence against women in a patriarchal world. Moralistic men drag her from the house and demand that justice be done and she be stoned to death. Had Jesus told them to get on with it, they would have accused him of being in opposition to Roman authority which forbade Jews to put anyone to death (John 18:31). Did the empire operate double standards? Had rabbi Jesus ordered them to let her go they would have beaten him with the tradition of Moses (or their interpretation of it). But Jesus exposed their moralism and their double standards and hypocrisy. Why are moralistic religious people shouting hardest for the punishment of 'wrongdoers'? Why are they so violent and supportive of violence, and what dark side of themselves are they trying to suppress? Jesus will not use violence nor condone violence by others and he will not be punitive in his relationships. In this story 'Jesus acted non-violently towards the self-righteous accusers while protecting the adulterous woman from a violent act.'[18]

Jesus' habitual practice of active non-violence is seen at its clearest in the story of his trial and death. It is ironic that the very event that has been used to provide war and violence with its language of blood sacrifice, supreme sacrifice, martyrdom and heroism, has been used to totally suppress the active non-violent core of his response to a violent and brutal system. The popular interpretation of Jesus' death with its violent imagery re-presented in eucharistic language and symbols has ignored the historical reality of crucifixion in the Roman world. Matthew, Mark, Luke, John and Paul did not. In his hymn of self-emptying and refusing to grasp for dominating power Paul recognised the death of Jesus as execution by imperial power (Philippians 2:5-11). 'It was a scandalous and degrading type of capital punishment intended for insurrectionists and other

---

18 Ibid, p 57

criminals of low socioeconomic status'.[19] Jesus was executed by
Roman imperial power, a victim of state violence. He is portrayed in the gospels as facing the legal and religious system of
his own tradition without retaliation or threat of it. Surrounded
by Roman military and before the local representative of imperial might, he maintained his non-violent practice. When violently
struck by a guard he was neither violent nor passive. He questioned the justice of the Roman soldier's action (John 18:23).
Faced with state violence Jesus neither acted nor spoke violently,
nor did he call for the physical force traditions of his community
to intervene. The cross was an act of state violence. From the
side of Jesus and the perspective of God it was a demonstration
of merciful love, active non-violence and forgiveness of enemies.
It was not passive, rather he resisted the evil of violence by non-
violent love and reconciliation. It was consistent with his life
where he had refused to use physical force to promote his commitment to liberation and peacebuilding. '... Jesus related to
people, including enemies, in a consistently non-violent manner,
even as he resisted their evil actions.'[20]

   This too is the Jesus story that forms the church, but it is not
the story that has formed religion and its role in an Irish culture
of violence. Jesus' practice of active non-violence has largely
been ignored and his cross and re-presentation of it distorted
beyond recognition. By his state execution and response of active
non-violent love and forgiveness Jesus has abolished the use of
all sacrificial and blood sacrifice language.

---

19 Ibid, p 58
20 Ibid, p 60

CHAPTER ELEVEN

Nurturing communities of resistance in active non-violence and compassion

Never again must violence be used to resolve differences in Irish politics, culture and religion. The gun has no place in present and future politics. The violence has been death-dealing, wasting human lives and distorting bodies, personalities and emotions of those who participated and suffered as combatants and non-combatants. Violence and killing do something to people, they diminish humanity, brutalise lives and destroy community. Even for those who argue that violence achieved goals or defended causes, the cost was enormous, leaving a generational legacy of negativity and hurt. Was it worth it? Can it really be justified? Could the same goals have been reached without the violence and the guns? The culture of violence and the physical force tradition will answer yes to the first two questions. That is not surprising because life lost and dead comrades must always be justified. History is fixed dogma and can never be rewritten. No matter how many bodies lie in cemeteries and that 'The past is a cemetery of promises which have not been kept',[1] there is a debt to be paid to the dead and the violence must remain justified. The respective stories must not be altered, or immense efforts are made to ensure that, 'our story' becomes the normative story of the 'troubles'. Should 'normative' ever be allowed to appear unquestioned even before the final truce or political agreement was reached? Or why should the violence of 1912-1922 be justified while the violence of 1969-2004 be condemned? The republicans and loyalists of the latter believed they were standing on the shoulders of the men of 1912 and 1916. The memory said so and it was infallible. The old soldiers still around in the early '70s thought their earlier cause was morally justified but the killers of the '70s were not. On what moral basis can that be argued?

---

1 Kearney, Richard in *Violence and Christian Spirituality: An Ecumenical Discussion* edited by Emmanuel Clapsis (Geneva: World Council of Churches Publications, 2007) p 54

History repeats itself as the current dissidents are condemned and the Provisional bombs and killings of 1969-2004 are
justified, as though a morality of violence changes. Perhaps the
only moral case to be made is that none of the violence and
counter-violence was justified, that it was a bloodlust let loose,
revealing not heroism but the darkest side of being human.
There was and always is an alternative way with historical
precedents, and the voices have always been present but
drowned out. And there are too many promises of history unfulfilled in Ireland to allow for an uncritical acceptance of the
violence, or for unethical remembering.

That religion has sanctioned the violence in Ireland remains
a blight to be acknowledged and deconstructed. That no Irish
church has produced a theology of active non-violence is a disturbing fact, which should cause every believer to seriously
doubt their faith and the theological system of their church. To
spare us the difficulty of coping with too much history, but acknowledging historical continuity, we have enough 20th century
violence in Ireland to keep us critically busy. That for half of the
century we resorted to brutal and bloody violence was a massive failure in political imagination and that the violence was
justified by religious vocabulary and symbols was an equally
massive failure in theological and spiritual imagination. So can
Ireland put its failure of imagination behind it and get in touch
with the imaginative part of our being human? Can religion dis-
cover enough theological, moral and spiritual imagination to
ensure that never again in Ireland will it sanction violence, guns,
bombs and killing?

In the last chapter, crucial principles of tolerance were highlighted applicable to our historical narratives, political and religious practices. Christologies of active non-violence and peacebuilding were also highlighted as core praxis for those who
claim Christianity. The Jesus story that forms the church puts all
violence and blood sacrifice ideology out of bounds. The teaching and praxis of the Jewish Jesus, rooted as it was in his Jewish
tradition, and better practised in his Jewish history than in
Christian history, should never have allowed the religious spin
of Ulster Covenant and Easter Proclamation to have happened.
Nor would it ever have allowed the slogans, 'For God and

Ulster', 'For God and Ireland' and the British 'For God and Empire' to have been shaped. Jesus the 'image of the invisible God' (Colossians 1:15) would have called the god of each slogan into question and deconstructed it, certainly rejected it as nationalistic idolatory. However, massive the failure of theological and spiritual imagination in the past and however serious the 'Constantinian mistake', the new diminishing body of practising Christians in Ireland can retrieve imagination through christ - ologies of active non-violence and peacebuilding. There are other practices and resources that can contribute to an Irish future without violence and guns.

Liturgy, language, symbols and rituals
The Jesus story that forms the church is not really encountered in theological systems, dogmas and doctrines. These are always secondary to religious experience and worship experience. People have always been shaped in their faith story through liturgy, ritual and symbols, even the most iconoclastic Protestant.[2] Throughout the centuries the most effective way of shaping believers in faith has been through hymns and songs. These communicate faith through poetry and metaphor which reach parts of the human person mere reason and logic cannot reach. Arius, classified as heretic by an early church council, knew that. Charles Wesley, the Anglican-Methodist, shaped a whole Methodist movement in the 18th century and still does through his poetry and rich metaphors. Hymns and songs have also conveyed distorted faith, including images of violent faith and a violent God. Sacraments are dramatised theology, re-presentations of Christ's death or ritual dying to sin and evil. Popular eucharistic theology has re-presented Christ's death in violent, sacrificial terms which have allowed violent, domination systems, like the brutal Roman empire to get off the hook. The violence of an abusive God has replaced the real source of violence in the imperial pol-

2 The ultra Protestant Orange Order is a classic example. It is steeped in ritual, colours and symbols, both religious and political in emphasis. The 12th July Orange processions are colourful, high profile public rituals using multiple symbols and images to remember 1690 as an event with present political significance. Religious ritual, language and symbols are an integral part of it. One does not have to agree with any of it, even as a Protestant, to acknowledge the multi-sensory power of the event.

itical power, sanctioned as it was by religion. The abusive emperor has been replaced by the abusive Father and the violent
ritual and images have legitimised violence and war, and violence against women and children.

Much Christian liturgical language and symbols are death-
centred. Christianity has become obsessed with death, dying
and sacrifice, yet the Bible has many images and metaphors of
life, birth and nurture. Had there not been a culture of dying for
Ireland, easily rooted in a similar culture of faith, and instead
been a life-centred faith and a culture of living for Ireland,
would history have been different?

The religious, pseudo-religions and civic rituals, symbols
and liturgies matter because they shape people in a faith or ideology. Flags, anthems and memorial days (rituals) are central to
civil religion and sometimes what goes on in church is not that
different. The language of hymns, prayers and the symbols and
rituals in which they are set are never politically neutral. They
shape lives and values and habits of living, reflexive actions and
behaviours. Liturgy and life praxis are inextricably linked. So
too are images of God and behavioural patterns. Liturgy, language and symbols matter. Worship rituals are hugely influen-
tial. We should be careful what we pray!

Perhaps no one in the Christian Testament realised this more
than John of Patmos, the writer of the Book of Revelation. John
was exiled on the island of Patmos, off the coast of Asia Minor,
modern Turkey. He may well have been sentenced to hard
labour in the stone quarries there, a political prisoner. He wrote
to seven churches in Asia Minor, living as he and they were in
the shadow of empire. Life was not easy for these small faith
communities, though endless persecution was not as extensive
at the time as once was thought. They did live in a domination
system with the rituals, symbols and signs of empire all around
them. Roman temples and liturgies dominated every town
forum and even the coins in your pocket carried Caesar's image
and inscriptions of divinity. Roman civil religion was everywhere present and emperor worship was required as obedience
and loyalty to Augustus, Nero or Domitian or whoever was in
the ultimate seat of power. Worship of a deified emperor was a
public and ritual act of allegiance and that created a problem for

Christian faith communities. Every one of the seven churches addressed in Revelation faced this problem. 'Pergamum ... was one of the two first venues in the Roman world with a temple to a living Roman emperor.'[3] Given the identification of the imperial system with Satan, 'it is no surprise that his (John's) vision refers to Pergamum as the place where Satan's throne is (Rev 2:13).[4]

In a world where emperor worship was dominant, it is also not surprising that Revelation is a book of worship. It is not a book predicting the end of the world and detailed events in the Middle East with Muslims slaughtered and Jews who do not respond to Jesus also being eliminated, with only Christians being raptured away from appalling violence. That God is the producer and director of all this end-time violence leaves us with a totally un-Christlike God, a violent, vengeful tyrant who makes Hitler and Pol Pot look positively moral. It would also seem that those to be raptured away by God are mostly White American, with a few Anglo-Saxons thrown in, which makes God a blatant racist. But all of this is one of the greatest heresies of the 20th century, a warped theology reflecting the bloodiest and most violent century in recorded history and which wants to justify even greater divine genocide.

The great irony is that those who worship violence and the god of violence, which is what Roman emperor worship was, are precisely those, described in the beastly image, who are being subverted by the liturgical language of Revelation. It is a worship book, a liturgical text, admittedly full of colourful signs, symbols and icons, and also full of the poetry and metaphor of hymns and songs. Ritual, including incense and smoke filled scenes of ultimate mystery abound. Liturgy, worship language, symbols and rituals are the essence of the last book in the Bible.

Reading of letters in the early faith communities was performance. Only a few in the ancient world were literate, so when a small group gathered in a house church at Pergamum they would have heard John's vision read in worship.

---

3 Kraybill, J. Nelson, *Apocalypse and Allegiance: Worship, Politics and Devotion in the Book of Revelation* (Grand Rapids: Brazos Press, 2010) p 56
4 Ibid, p 56

The book begins with liturgical blessing: 'Grace to you and peace (1:4). What follows is a blend of politics and religion that permeates the entire vision: ... Politics and religion converge in acts of worship, and worship shapes allegiance. From start to finish, Revelation gives a resounding call for believers to avoid giving ultimate allegiance to any power other than God and the Lamb.[5]

Worship in Revelation is a political act subversive of all forms of violence and domination systems and abuses of power. There is no modernist and dualistic compartmentalising of faith and politics. Worship in Revelation is described in seven scenes and all of them take place in heaven, but the heavenly liturgies are completely earthed in the realities of empire, violence and oppressive military power and economics. In each of the seven liturgical scenes John 'has reworked themes from Psalms 95-100, a collection of songs celebrating the victory and enthronement of the divine warrior in heaven over all the gods of the earth'.[6] The poetic and mythical language of the Psalms does not portray a literally violent god, but is a theo-mythical and liturgical reflection on the experience of exile and liberation at the hands of the Babylonian and Persian empires. When John wrote of 'fallen Babylon' (Rev 18:2), those present in the liturgical reading of the vision may have cheered and clapped, because everyone with a Jewish background knew it was a dramatised portrayal of the fall of the Roman empire.

When the next worship song began with 'The Kingdom of the world has become the Kingdom of our Lord and of his Messiah, and he will reign forever and ever' (Rev 11:15), long before Handel wrote the *Messiah* and the premiere audience in Dublin stood for the *Hallelujah Chorus*, the little congregation in Pergamum was already on its feet. They knew what the dramatic liturgy was saying and what they were singing. 'The empire of the world has become the empire of our Lord ...' Whatever the coins in the offertory said and the Temple in the forum proclaimed about Caesar as Lord, only God was Lord and sovereign and the oppressive empire would have its day and cease to

be. Only the empire of the non-violent God and the non-violent
Lamb would last, and it was liturgically clear where their ultimate allegiance and loyalty lay.

Much of John's liturgical language, rituals and symbols were
mirror images of Roman imperial worship. There are images of
lightening, rumblings and thunder (Rev 4:5). 'In Roman tradition, lightening was said to come from the planets associated
with the most powerful gods, Jupiter and Saturn, and the god of
war, Mars.'[7] But in the symbolic language of the liturgy John
holds up a different vision of God to the violent Roman war god,
Mars. It was time to sing again in the Pergamum house church!

> Holy, holy, holy,
> the Lord God the Almighty,
> who was and is and is to come.
>
> You are worthy, our Lord and God,
> to receive glory and honour and power,
> for you created all things,
> and by your will they existed and were created (Rev 4:8-11).

Whatever they were singing and saying in the Pergamum
Roman temple, the small Christian house church could use the
same vocabulary and symbols but with a radically different reference point. Christian worship in Pergamum was a political act,
subversive of everything being acclaimed in the forum temple.

The makers of liturgy in the seven churches of Asia Minor
were highly imaginative people. Liturgical language, rituals
and symbols were all borrowed from the liturgical world of
emperor worship, turned upside down and as high liturgical
drama, sung, said and acted out in dramatic subversion of all
the empire and emperor stood for. At the heart of their worship
was the 'Lamb that was slain'.

> Worthy is the Lamb that was slaughtered
> to receive power and wealth and wisdom and might
> and honour and glory and blessing!
> To the one seated on the throne and to the Lamb
> be blessing and honour and glory and might
> forever and ever! (Rev 5 v12-13)

---

7 Ibid., p 203

The Lamb is the innocent victim of imperial violence who resisted with active non-violent love and who makes known the actively non-violent God. The power of God is of a radically different kind to the military might of the empire and as they sang another song in Pergamum, they knew they belonged to a subversively different empire.

Even in the dramatic liturgy when John describes the fall of Babylon in terms of total economic collapse and in language and symbols which sound vindictive and even violent, the context of liturgy and Jewish tradition need to be kept in mind. This is the Jewish poetic tradition of lament voiced, for example, in the trauma and pain of Babylonian exile.

> O daughter Babylon, you devastator!
> Happy shall they be who pay you back
> what you have done to us!
> Happy shall they be who take your little ones
> and dash them against the rock! (Psalm 137:8-9)

We are unsettled by the Hebrew poet's longing for vengeance, though by the rivers of Babylon we may have felt the same. Living under the military and economic oppression of the Roman superpower, the congregation in Pergamum may not have shared our moral amnesia when their liturgy proclaimed in the tradition of Jewish lament:

> ... they will also drink of the wine of God's wrath, poured unmixed into the cup of his anger, and they will be tormented with fire and sulphur in the presence of the holy angels and in the presence of the Lamb. And the smoke of their torment goes up forever and ever. There is no rest day or night for those who worship the beast and its image and for anyone who receives the mark of its name. (Rev 14:10-11)

The hell-fire preachers who beat people with texts like these because they were considered unsaved, or didn't conform to the preacher's version of religion or violent God, or because they were poor, never understood the text. They totally distorted it and projected their own violence onto God and others. Texts of lament are the cries of suffering, oppressed and traumatised people and are ultimately a cry for justice. That we do not or cannot give voice to anger and a cry for justice in liturgy is a sign of our moral amnesia in the face of the world's violence, militarism, economic greed and oppression.

People today whose homes or lives are destroyed by war or injustice may need to cry out to God with vehement language. Worship sometimes must be catharsis, an opportunity to unload deep pain or anger on God, who can make all things new.[8]

To shape liturgies, language, symbols and rituals that can take the language of the world and its domination systems, including violent systems, and turn them upside down to subvert the powers, requires creative imagination. So too does the ability to weave into our liturgical drama the songs and rituals of lament where people can give vehement voice to their pain, hurt and marginalisation. Worship is a political act and a cry for justice through which we shape our lives against all forms of violence, live from a subversive and alternative loyalty and non-violent ethic and renew hope that the 'The empire of the world has become the empire of our Lord and of his Messiah, and he will reign forever and ever' (Rev 11v15).

Nurturing communities of compassion
Violence not only de-humanises the enemy, it de-humanises those who commit acts of violence. No matter how much we try to justify violence, even when claiming the sanction and blessing of God, we de-humanise ourselves through our violent actions. We are also projecting our de-humanised image onto God and creating a god manageable by our less than human selves. To kill or damage another is to brutalise ourselves, seriously damage our moral sensibility which is supposed to make us more human. Whether the violence is carried out in the name of God, the name of the state or the ideological cause, it is self-destructive. Why so much post-traumatic stress disorder, aberrant behaviour, drug and alcohol dependence and personality dis - orders? To kill another is to kill something of ourselves. When a whole community or nation becomes caught up in a spiral of violence and counter-violence, the collective also loses something of its humanity. Life becomes cheap, there is mutual

---

8 Kraybill, op cit, p 123

demonisation, mirror image stereotypes and a failure in compassion as well as a deadening of moral sensibilities. A violent
society also becomes a corrupt society in a variety of ways
because a violent society becomes anarchist, and authority and
boundaries collapse. In such a society killers become heroes, the
dead, celebrated martyrs and role models for another generation. The destructive, de-humanised legacy stretches far into
the future and the violent generation need not be surprised
when children mimic their parents. In some cases they may be
even more sectarian or violent, or potentially violent than their
concerned parents.

Killing and violence continue. The Irish civil war had ended
five years before when Government Minister, Kevin O'Higgins,
was murdered on his way to church in 1927. In the 1930s old
scores were still being settled. The problem is repeating itself in
Northern Ireland. The spirit of violence possesses people and
they cannot let go, such is the depth of de-humanisation. The
acute psychotic behaviour of the violent Legion in Mark 5, (see
chapter 10) the result of living in a community saturated with
oppressive violence, lives on in contemporary Israel/Palestine
and Ireland. But violent people are the products of violent communities, embedded in cultures of violence. There is crass
hypocrisy in our wanting to exclude the 'men of violence', damage them further as if they were not part of us. We create the
culture of violence, contribute to it even by our silence. There is
no 'them and us' in Irish sectarianism, no political or religious
innocence. In the decade of change and violence priests blessed
the combatants and many loyalists in the recent violence were
taught to hate the other in Sunday School.[9] Of course there were

---

9 The present author was never taught Irish history in his State/
Protestant educational system in Northern Ireland. It was not until he
arrived in his first congregational appointment in Dunmanway, West
Cork, and encountered members of the old IRA, memorials and sites of
ambushes, and headstones to Methodist victims of IRA killing, that he
realised with frustration and anger that there were multiple Irish narratives he did not know. Also that his formal education, including his
theological education, had sold him short and deprived him of a context in which to be a citizen of peace and a Christian minister and pract-
icing theologian. In West Cork, education in Irish history and theology
had to begin again.

bigger systems and structures, like education which taught Irish history as ideology or didn't teach it at all. But the gunmen and the bombers went to the same schools as the rest of us, attended the same Masses and Sunday Schools, participated in the same parades, processions, commemorations and memorials, all with public support and very few questions. The violent community was what we made it by our various levels of participation, activism or silence.

A violent community or a violent culture is a punitive community justifying vengeance and vindictiveness, state or otherwise, or being ambivalent towards it. It is also a community with a deficit in compassion. There is a very low reservoir of mercy, moderation or empathy and care, especially towards the perceived enemy. To overcome the culture of violence we need to re-humanise the other and re-humanise ourselves. Nurturing compassion is key to being more truly human. That means more compassionate relationships, compassionate politics, economics and religion. The judgementalism, carping criticism, power plays, blatant sexism and homophobia, gossip and backbiting often shows up the compassion deficit in congregations and parishes. The collapse of moral authority in the major societal institutions, political, banking and ecclesial, suggest a lack of shared humanity, moral integrity and a failure to practice compassion in structured and formal relationships.

The meek will inherit the earth

The destructiveness of violence can take generations to eradicate. The peace process in Ireland does provide the opportunity to deal with the destructiveness, which in part is the legacy. Overcoming violence and transforming a violent culture requires nurture in the truly human quality of compassion. A re-humanised society is a compassionate society. Compassion is a core virtue and in the biblical tradition there are related virtues that also need to be nurtured.

The beatitudes of Jesus are the essence of the sermon on the Mount. They articulate the key virtues and values, and practices of the reign of God, the alternative to every empire and domination system, including the domination system of violence. They represent the very life of God, God's practices and God-

like practices in the world. Jesus was rooted in the Jewish traditions and its piety. For a Jew like himself the highest form of
piety and faithful practice was the imitation of God. Exodus and
Leviticus made it clear that a faith community is called to be
compassionate as God is compassionate and to be holy as God is
holy. (Exodus 34:6, Leviticus 11:44-45) The holiness or wholeness is in large part to be compassionate. This is the God and
piety of the Jewish Jesus and these core themes appear again at
the heart of his teaching. Those who faithfully live God's life are
merciful (Matthew 5:7) and participants in the empire of God
are to 'Be merciful, just as your Father is merciful' (Luke 6:36).
Mercy, compassion, holiness or wholeness are an integral whole
and are the imitation of God.

To imitate God also means to be totally committed to God,
hunger and thirst for justice, social justice in the community and
to be peacemakers. The latter are said to be the most God-like.
The beatitudes are also realistic showing that the imitation of
God is concrete and practical and therefore in the world of domination systems there will be opposition, hostility, abuse and
even violence inflicted. Suffering for justice and peace are ways
of entering into the life of the suffering, vulnerable God.
Dietrich Bonhoffer in the face of horrendous Nazi violence, especially against Jews, and in terms of his active resistance, wrote
of the cost of discipleship. The imitation of God in a world of
empire, militarism, war, violence, greed, political, economic,
social and religious oppression, is costly.

Before exploring in more detail the God-like virtues of compassion and mercy, it is important to note another of Jesus'
beatitudes which, in the English language, sounds weak and
crazy in a violent culture. It is the blessedness of the meek who
will inherit the earth.

Those who subscribe to the myth of redemptive violence,
that might is right, violence achieves and war brings peace, will
dismiss the meek very quickly. Meek has become an unfortu-
nate English word, which suggests words like 'wimp', 'gentle',
'doormat', 'mild', or 'passive'. Such people inherit nothing but
are walked all over. They are weak and spineless people. But
English like all languages has weaknesses and 'meek' is a glar-
ing one. It does not capture the strength of the Hebrew and

Greek words in the original texts.

As with all the beatitudes and the sermon on the Mount, Jesus is drawing on his Jewish religious tradition. He has read his own Jewish Bible and is quoting from Psalm 37:11, 'But the meek shall inherit the land', an affirmation reiterated in verses 22 and 29, though an interchangeable word 'righteous' or 'just' is used. Psalm 37:11 uses the same word as Isaiah 61:1 which is quoted in the first beatitude, the blessedness of the poor in spirit, for theirs is the Kingdom of God (Matthew 5:3). The word has a double meaning which makes it intriguing. Matthew appears to use one meaning which is humble, or those who are not arrogant or self-sufficient, but know their need of God and an altern - ative energy or driving force in their lives. Those who trust in military might or in the power of violence do display an arrogance towards others and the democratic will of the people. Bush and Blair insisted on going into Iraq in the face of the largest ever global public protest. Ulster unionists and Sinn Féin respectively completely disregarded the wishes of the majority of the Irish people in 1912 and 1921. This is not to say that a majority is always right and never wrong. But in these particular historical moments the wanton violence that followed does suggest an arrogance on the part of those whose decisions and actions caused the violent killing. There is also a blind arrogance on the part of so-called dissidents who currently refuse to recognise the democratic will of the vast majority of Irish people. Humility declines all forms of arrogance, including arrogant power-over others and walks humbly with its non-violent, power-with God and in partnership with its societal sisters and brothers.

The other sense of the word is emphasised by Luke, the blessedness of the poor, for yours is the Kingdom of God (Luke 6:20). Luke has the poor and not Matthew's 'poor in spirit'. For Luke the kingdom or empire of God belongs to the socially and economically poor or powerless. Luke's gospel has more to say about poverty and wealth and economics than any of the other gospels. In Psalm 37 it is the powerless and the humiliated who are to trust in God to liberate them from economic oppression. In the occupied Palestine of Jesus inequitable access to land and exploitative social relationships were rife because of Roman presence and imperial and religious land grabbing and economic exploitation. These too are the 'wicked' of Psalm 37 written during another experience of power elites and economic powerlessness. In both the Psalm and Luke's beatitudes, the meek are not to resort to violence to overthrow their unjust oppressors. The violence of poverty is being imposed on them by the oppressive elite or wicked, but 'God, not the meek, will overthrow the elite so that all may use the earth (Psalm 37:10-11 and Luke 6:36).[10]

The Greek word used in Matthew 5 v5 and translated meek is *praeis*. Clarence Jordan highlights the use of the word in relation to Moses (Numbers 12:3) and Jesus (Matthew 11:29). Neither could be said to be weak, harmless, spineless or passive.

> One of them defied the might of Egypt and the other couldn't be cowed by a powerful Roman official ... Both of them seemed absolutely fearless in the face of men, and completely surrendered to the will of God ... People may be called 'tamed' to the extent that they have surrendered their wills to God and learned to do his bidding ... They surrender their will to God so completely that God's will becomes their will ... They become God's 'workhorses' on earth.[11]

In Greek the word *praeis* is used to describe the taming of a wild, violent horse, hence Jordan's wordplay in relation to Moses and Jesus. Egypt's way of violence and Rome's violence, military and economic are not the way of God's empire, not the divine will. Our human propensity for violence needs to be tamed in surrendering our violent wills to God's alternative and participation in God's subversive and non-violent empire. That is not to display weakness but to be formed and shaped by the fearless power of love and social justice.

For enriched emphasis the Hebrew poet interchanges the words: 'The righteous shall inherit the land' (Psalm 37:29). In other words, those who are in right relations with others based on political and economic justice. It is the blessedness of those who formed by God and imitating God wish to ensure social justice, and in non-violent ways for the economically oppressed,

---

10 Carter, Warren, *Matthew and the Margins: A Socio-political and Religious Reading* (New York: Orbis Books, 2000) p 133

11 Quoted in Stassen, Glen H, *Living the Sermon on the Mount: A Practical Hope for Grace and Deliverance* (San Francisco: Jossey-Bass, 2006) p 49

exploited and powerless. They are the real heroes.

The righteous or those who live justly and work for social justice may need to remember the Hebrew poet's important insight.

> The wicked plot against the righteous,
> and gnash their teeth at them;
> but the Lord laughs at the wicked,
> for he sees that their day is coming (Psalm 37:12-13).

'Our day will come' is not a slogan for those who resort to violence, but to those who have surrendered their violent inclinations to the liberating God of justice. Every domination system, empire or system of violence has its day either through self-destruction, rejection by the people, ultimate failure or any original claim to moral or religious justification being exposed for the self-deluding sham that it was. Our day will come really belongs to the poor, powerless, oppressed and victims of empire and systems of violence.

This is further strengthened by noting that 'wherever the Greek word *praeis* occurs in the Bible, it always points to peacefulness or peacemaking'.[12] The Palm Sunday story in Matthew 21:5 quotes from the Hebrew prophet Zechariah 9:9. It is a vision of a King coming 'humble and mounted on an ass', not a horse the symbol of violence and war. The non-violent, peacemaking King will:

> ... cut off the chariot from Ephraim
> and the war horse from Jerusalem;
> and the battle bow shall be cut off,
> and he shall command peace to the nations.
> (Zechariah 9:10)

Military hardware and weapons of violent destruction are disposed of and peace, total societal and environmental wellbeing is established. The meek are not weak or wimp, they practice dependence on the alternative energy and power of God, social justice, non-violence and active peacemaking.

---

12 Stassen, op cit, p 49

The merciful will receive mercy
Those who live against the domination systems of violence, injustice and oppression practice mercy. The beatitude again has its roots in the Hebrew Bible and especially in ancient Israel's experience and affirmation of God.

> The Lord, the Lord,
> a God merciful and gracious,
> slow to anger,
> and abounding in steadfast love and faithfulness ...
> (Exodus 34:6)

There are liberating, life-giving and transformative words in every line of Israel's credo. The beatitude highlights mercy. Empires and domination systems of violence are short on mercy. Killing and exploitation have no room for it, because they think it a soft word, letting people off easy or cheap forgiveness. But there is a strength in the word, violent macho males find it difficult to see or experience, because they are not in touch with an essential part of their being human. Indeed the practice of violence destroys or represses this dimension of their humanity.

In the Exodus text the Hebrew word is *rachum*, which means womb. There is the deep-rooted strength of mother care and ultimate concern expressed in the word. It is the primary feminine quality of deep-felt womb-compassionate love, caring deeply for the other and acting with embrace, acceptance, forgiveness, total identification and being with and alongside. For the Jewish people it was and is the inner quality of God, who God is in relation to humanity. Unless a child is unwanted, there is a deep bond between mother and child formed in the womb. Our first experience of love 'begins in the womb with the perception of a mother's nourishing care poured out from her heart through the throbbing umbilical cord'.[13] *Rachum* is a primary biblical word, found as a verb or noun some 107 times. It is the rich feminine side of God and something which every human person should experience even before birth. The deep compassionate love is the primary inner quality of being authentically human.

13 Grassi, Joseph, *Peace on Earth: Roots and Practices from Luke's Gospel* (Minnesota: Liturgical Press, 2004) p 69

It is mostly males who lead wars and engage in violence. To be fully human every male needs to get in touch with the feminine side of his nature. It is there from birth, shaped by the mother-child womb experience. War and violence destroy this feminine side of nature. So too does a lot of male conditioning such as 'big boys don't cry'. But to be truly human and God-like, is to be in touch with the feminine side of one's being, to nurture and practice the quality of mercy and compassion in relation to others. Where women engage in community violence, and a minority did in Ireland, they bought into the patriarchal world-view destructive of their own feminine humanity. They were also victims of patriarchy, of suffering sexual and physical violence from male activists and colleagues. Whether activist or non-activist, a culture of violence is de-humanising, destroying or blocking the practice of womb-like mercy and compassion in personal and societal relationships.

The beatitude has nothing to do with a feeling or sentiment. Feeling good about another or well disposed towards them is not mercy or compassion. The Greek word in Matthew is *elelmones* and means generosity in doing deeds of liberation for others. This is mercy or compassion in action. In the Hebrew Bible God's compassion or mercy is the motivation for social justice. Isaiah 58:6-7 is a classic example: 'which mentions freeing the oppressed, giving bread to the hungry, providing hospitality to the homeless, and covering the naked'.[14] The teaching of Jesus on forgiveness is in the Lord's Prayer and a Lukan parable (Luke 7:36-48) is about release from economic debts as acts of mercy.

Mercy, therefore, is very concrete and intensely practical. In 1st century Palestine, and regions like Galilee and Judea, it was bogus religion if it was not. Matthew has 'Blessed are the merciful' and then provides numerous concrete examples of how mercy works.

They provide the destitute with necessary economic resources (Matt 5:42, 6:2-4, 25:31-46). Mercy forgives (6:12, 14-15) and extends love to enemies (5:38-48) and other marginals, foreigners and women (15:22). It marks God's empire. Jesus healings (9:27; 17:15; 20:30-31) and exorcisms (15:22) demonstrate

---

14 Stassen, op cit, p 54

mercy (cf 4:23-25 and 9:36), as do his meals with social outcasts (9:13) and his allowing the hungry to eat (12:7) when religious leaders disapprove.[15]

Clearly mercy is not a soft-centred quality but an intensive and practical social practice. There are those in the gospel stories who think it is not desirable and it was in short supply in the Roman empire. But God's empire was already active in the world of violence and economic oppression and it was radically different, as its citizens were radically different. 'The beatitude shapes a way of life in the meantime, a community of practical and active mercy.'[16] And those who practice mercy will receive mercy.

Mercy and compassion have been used interchangeably. *Rachum* or *elelmones*, it is mercy or compassion in action countering the injustices and oppressions including violence in society and acting in liberating ways. There is a third word in the Bible and it is primarily a Lukan word. It is *splangchna*, found 24 times in Luke and much more than any of the other gospels. In one of Luke's songs, the *Benedictus* (Luke 1:68-79) we can imagine a faith community living with a domination system, celebrating in hope that: 'By the tender mercy of our God, the dawn from on high will break upon us, to give light to those who sit in darkness and in the shadow of death, to guide our feet into the way of peace' (78-79). From the way of violence and death to the way of peace comes through the 'tender mercy' of God and the community's practice of the same.

Luke tells a story of a widow from Nain whose only son had died. That meant that she was socially and economically on the scrapheap, widows being absolutely dependent on the next family male. Jesus 'had compassion for her' (Luke 7:13). It means that he was moved in his gut to do something which would restore her to wellbeing. Moved by compassion he acts in compassion and the crowd celebrate it as an act of God's liberation and love.

The same word occurs in the parable of the Good Samaritan, who as a hated foreigner came on a victim of violence and was 'moved with pity' (Luke 10:33). His compassionate response was to do everything he could, not only at financial cost to him-

---

15 Carter, op cit, p 134
16 Ibid, p 134

self, but at serious risk to his life, not only from violent robbers but from the other community who were enemies. But it was the enemy who 'showed him mercy' (Luke 10:37).

The parable of Luke 15:11-32 about two sons and a compassionate father is well known but it has intriguing insights not always carefully explored. The younger son takes his inheritance and sells out his entire cultural and religious tradition by going over to the other side to lead a wild life. Eating with pigs connected him to Gentiles, who may well have been connected to the oppressive empire. When he hits rock bottom, he decides to re-cross the boundary. When the father saw him in the distance he 'was filled with compassion' (Luke 10:20). He might have been vindictive, like the older brother who believes he has made his bed so he should lie on it, pig manure and all. Or misquoting a verse from the Hebrew Bible, much used in some quarters in Northern Ireland, 'a leopard can never change its spots', which then became the pejorative unreconstructed terrorists. No gut movement of compassion there, but with the father in the story there is and he takes the initiative, runs at risk to greet the rebel. 'He brought new clothes for his son, hired an orchestra, with dancers, and prepared a sumptuous meal'.[17] Meanwhile, big brother sulked, griped and complained and moralised that his brother never deserved any acceptance and he received nothing despite his loyalty, moral uprightness and consistent obedience. Wherever we are in the story, the heart of it is the gut-moving compassion, ready to accept vulnerability and restore the disloyal, violent other to true self and authoritative humanity. Compassion is moved to practice restorative justice.

It is imperative that in Ireland we categorically reject violence and leave it behind for good. To overcome and transform our culture of violence to a culture of active non-violence and peacebuilding, it is essential that we nurture alternative values values that are life-giving and not death-giving. The nurture of death, hatred, dying, sacrifice, all for Ulster and Ireland has been destructive of our humanity and society. It will be a generational process, but using every means and strategy, we shall nurture communities of active compassion.

---

17 Grassi, op cit, p 76

Bibliography

Adelman, Paul and Pearce, Robert, *Great Britain and the Irish Question 1800-1922* (London: Hodder and Stoughton, 2001)

Aldous, Richard (ed) *Great Irish Speeches* (London: Quercus, 2007)

Borg, Marcus J and Crossan, John Dominic, *The First Paul: Reclaiming the Radical Visionary Behind the Church's Conservative Icon* (London: SPCK 2009)

Brewer, John D and Higgins, Gareth I, *Anti-Catholicism in Northern Ireland, 1600-1998: The Mote and the Beam* (London: Macmillan Press, 1998)

Brueggemann, Walter, *An Introduction to the Old Testament: The Canon and Christian Imagination* (Louisville: Westminster John Knox Press, 2003)

Brueggemann, Walter, *Divine Presence and Violence: Contextualizing the Book of Joshua* (Eugene, Oregon: Cascade Books, 2009)

Brueggemann, Walter, *Old Testament Theology: An Introduction* (Nashville: Abingdon Press, 2008)

Brueggemann, Walter, *Theology of the Old Testament:Testimony, Dispute, Advocacy* (Minneapolis: Fortress Press, 1997)

Carroll, James, *Constantine's Sword: The Church and the Jews* (New York: First Mariner Books, 2002)

Carter, Warren, *Matthew and the Margins: A Socio-Political and Religious Reading* (Maryknoll: Orbis Books, 2000)

Clapsis, Emmanuel (ed) *Violence and Christian Spirituality: An Ecumenical Discussion* (Geneva: World Council of Churches Publications, 2007)

Crossan, John Dominic, *God and Empire: Jesus Against Rome Then and Now* (San Francisco: Harper, 2007)

Dillon, Myles (ed), *Irish Sagas* (Cork: Mercier Press, 1968)

Elliott, Marianne, *Robert Emmet: The Making of a Legend* (London: Profile Books 2003)

Ellwood, Robert, *Tales of Darkness: The Mythology of Evil* (London: Continuum, 2009)

English, Richard, *Irish Freedom: The History of Nationalism in Ireland* (Dublin: Gill and Macmillan)

Ferriter, Diarmaid, *The Transformation of Ireland 1900-2000* (London: Profile Books, 2004)

Foster, R. F., *Modern Ireland 1600-1972* (London: Penguin Books, 1988)

Gillespie, Raymond, *Seventeenth Century Ireland* (Dublin: Gill and Macmillan, 2006)

Grassi, Joseph, *Peace on Earth: Roots and Practices from Luke's Gospel* (Minnesota: Liturgical Press, 2004)

Haddick-Flynn, Kevin, *Orangeism: The Making of a Tradition* (Dublin: Wolfhound Press, 1999)

Hart, Peter, *The IRA and Its Enemies: Violence and Community in Cork 1916-1923* (Oxford: Clarendon Press, 1998)

Heaney, Marie, *Over Nine Waves: A Book of Irish Legends* (London: Faber and Faber, 1994)

Herzog, William R. II, *Parables as Subversive Speech: Jesus as Pedagogue of the Oppressed* (Louisville: Westminster John Knox Press, 1994)

Horsley, Richard A. and Silberman, Neil Asher, *The Message and the Kingdom: How Jesus and Paul Ignited a Revolution and Transformed the Ancient World* (New York: Grosset/Putman, 1997)

Horsley, Richard A., *The Liberation of Christmas: The Infancy Narratives in Social Context* (New York: Continuum, 1993)

Howard-Brook, Wes and Gwyther, Anthony, *Unveiling Empire: Reading Revelation Then and Now* (New York: Orbis Books, 1999)

Irvine, Maurice, *Northern Ireland: Faith and Faction* (London: Routledge, 1991)

Jackson, Alvin, *Home Rule: An Irish History 1800-2000* (London: Weidenfield and Nicholson 2003)

Jenkins, Philip, *Jesus Wars: How Four Patriarchs, Three Queens and Two Emperors Decided What Christians Would Believe for the Next 1,500 Years* (London: SPCK, 2010)

Jewett, Robert and Lawrence, John Skelton, *Captain America and the Crusade Against Evil: The Dilemma of Zealous Nationalism* (Grand Rapids: Eerdmans, 2003)

Jewett, Robert, *Romans: A Commentary* (Minneapolis: Fortress Press, 2007)

Kinealy, Christine, *A New History of Ireland* (Stroud: Sutton Publishing Company, 2004)

Kirsch, Jonathan, *God Against the Gods: The History of War Between Monotheism and Polytheism* (London: Penguin Compass 2005)

Kraybill, J. Nelson, *Apocalypse and Allegiance: Worship, Politics and Devotion in the Book of Revelation* (Grand Rapids: Brazos Press, 2010)

Lee, Joseph, *The Modernisation of Irish Society, 1848-1918* (Dublin: Gill and Macmillan, 2008 revised edition)

Leeming, David, *The Oxford Companion to World Mythology* (Oxford: Oxford University Press, 2005)

Lennon, Colm, *Sixteenth Century Ireland: The Incomplete Conquest* (Dublin: Gill and Macmillan, 1994)

Lind, Millard C, *Monotheism, Power, Justice* (Indianna: Institute of Mennonite Studies, 1990)

Lundy, Derek, *Men that God Made Mad: A Journey Through Truth, Myth and Terror in Northern Ireland* (London: Jonathan Cape, 2006)

MacKilliop, James, *Dictionary of Celtic Mythology* (Oxford: Oxford University Press, 1998)

MacKillop, James, *Myths and Legends of the Celts* (London: Penguin Books, 2005) Macmillan, 2006

Mansergh, Martin, *The Legacy of History* (Cork: Mercier Press, 2003)

Matthews, Skelly and Gibson, E. Leigh (eds), *Violence in the New Testament* (New York: T&T Clarke, 2005)

McBride, Ian, *Eighteenth Century Ireland* (Dublin: Gill and Macmillan, 2009)

Moran, Sean Farrell, *Patrick Pearse and the Politics of Redemption: The Mind of the Easter Rising* (Washington: The Catholic University of America Press, 1994)

Nelson-Pallmeyer, Jack, *Is Religion Killing Us: Violence in the Bible and the Quran?* (Harrisburg: Trinity Press International, 2003)

Nelson-Pallmeyer, Jack, *Jesus Against Christianity: Reclaiming the Missing Jesus* (Harrisburg: Trinity Press International, 2001)

Ó hÓgáin, Daithí, *The Lore of Ireland: An Encyclopedia of Myth, Legend and Romance* (Suffolk: The Boydel Press, 2006)

O'Doherty, Gabriel and Keogh, Dermot (eds), *1916:The Long Revolution* (Cork:Mercier Press, 2007)

Price, Bill, *Celtic Myths* (Harpenden: Pocket Essentials, 2008)

Rafferty, Oliver, P, *Catholicism in Ulster 1603-1983: An Introspective History,* (Dublin: Gill and Macmillan, 1994)

Rossing, Barbara R., *The Rapture Exposed: The Message of Hope in the Book of Revelation* (New York: Basic Books, 2004)

Schubeck, Thomas L, *Love That Does Justice* (New York: Orbis Books, 2007)

Siebert, Eric A., *A Disturbing Divine Behaviour: Troubling Old Testament Images of God* (Minneapolis: Fortress Press, 2009)

Stassen, Glen H., *Living the Sermon on the Mount: A Practical Hope for Grace and Deliverance* (San Francisco: Jossey-Bass, 2006)

Stewart, A. T. Q., *The Shape of Irish History* (Belfast: The Blackstaff Press 2001)

Swartley, Willard M, *Covenant of Peace: The Missing Peace in New Testament Theology and Ethics* (Grand Rapids: Eerdmans, 2006)

Tanner, Marcus, *Ireland's Holy Wars: The Struggle for a Nation's Soul 1500-2000* (London: Yale None Bene, 2001

Teehan, John, *In the Name of God: The Evolutionary Origins of Religious Ethics and Violence* (Chichester: Wiley-Blackwell, 2010)

Tilley, Terence W, *The Disciples of Jesus: Christology as Reconciling Practice* (New York: Orbis Books, 2008)

Trible, Phyllis, *Texts of Terror: Literary – Feminist Readings of Biblical Narratives* (Philadelphia: Fortress Press, 1984)

Wink, Walter, *Engaging the Powers: Discerning and Resistance in a World of Domination* (Minneapolis: Fortress Press, 1992)

Wink, Walter, *The Powers That Be: Theology for a New Millennium* (New York: Doubleday, 1998)

Yoder, John Howard, *The War of the Lamb: The Ethics of Non-Violence and Peacemaking* (Grand Rapids: Brazos Press, 2009)